Heartprints
of
Africa

A Family's Story of Faith, Love, Adventure, and Turmoil

by
Cinda Adams Brooks
in collaboration with
Linda Adams Witte

*****

This book is part of the author's life journey as she recollects it. Earliest
memories are some of the most elusive but treasured memories; memories
blurred by the passage of time, by the naivety of youth, and by the
mixture of true memories with stories heard. Others may remember past
events differently. Some events have been consolidated and some names
changed to facilitate the telling of the story.

Dedication

Twins are a Blessing Mapacha ni Baraka

Ten minutes apart
Two beats of the heart
Two cries in the night
Thank God; thank God
We are two

Thank you to my twin, Linda, for helping make this book happen and for so much more — for being my sis, best friend, and heart companion for life. We dedicate our story to our family — to our brothers, Steve, Jim, and Chipper, who journeyed, loved, teased, defended, and supported us, and to our parents, John and Martha Adams, who instilled in us a passion for life, a love for people, a grasp of what is really important, and the confidence to chase our dreams. Thank you for the legacy, your love, and support.

Contents

1   Trouble Brews *Shida Inakaribia*
Uganda 2004

A bullet strikes the tree overhead, solidly emphasizing that the battle approaches. Questions whirl through my mind. Will bolting ourselves behind the storage room door make us safe or corral us in the middle of battle and at the mercy of others? Or do we run into the bush, under the relentless equatorial sun, losing vital contact with possible rescuers? The room is ready and our essential possessions packed. The kids look up, poised to move; their eyes full of trust, courage, and a thread of fear. The decisions and consequences whirl through my heart. My answer chokes on the lump in my throat.

Shifting my load to my left shoulder, I clumsily fight my way across the red dirt to the dry riverbed. Already I feel the sweaty cling of my soil-stained T-shirt underneath my pack. I stride hard; a *kanga* (cloth) tied as a skirt entangles my legs. In northern Uganda, a woman mustn't show her thighs. I grumble to myself. I could be topless, bare, and with boobs bouncing — no different from exposed elbows — but heaven forbid I show my legs. Tossing etiquette and cultural respect to the dry savanna wind, I yank the *kanga* off and stuff it under my pack's waist strap. Distant AK-47 rifle fire threatens as I ponder how I got myself into this mess.

Ahead, Stanley limps, a black and yellow soft cooler slung over his shoulder swinging to the rhythm of his awkward stride. "Babe, what am I carrying in this cooler anyway?" he asks in a tone hinting annoyance, as he jerks the cooler behind his hip.

Avoiding eye contact, I toss him a vague answer. "You don't want to know. Just keep going. Hurry."

Stanley favors his left leg as he plods along, leaning on a worn stick given by a sympathetic African friend. At 63, his gray Hemingway beard and pipe gain him much respect from the local tribesmen. My husband, nineteen years my senior, brings wisdom, grounding, and balance to my world. In the midst of the day's chaos, his calm presence undergirds me with a sense of security and stability.

Linda, my identical twin, pushes along behind. Her dusty running shoes cut through the tall, dry grass as it whips at her long, denim skirt. Our hearts, connected before birth, have stretched across continents and allowed others in without ever losing the special twin connection. Our thoughts shared, not always spoken, as we run for safety.

1

Ben, proudly turned ten, grips his mother's hand. A floppy camouflage hat, pulled low over his ears, covers his eyes but not the tears streaking down his dusty red cheeks. "But Buddy, I don't want them to shoot Buddy," he sobs and tugs away from his mother as he whines for his best friend, the neighbors' dog, left behind.

Linda shoulders a frayed and dusty navy backpack she proudly unboxed and propped in the corner of her college dorm room 25 years ago. If the pack could talk, it would tell riveting stories of journeys through the Davis Mountains in Texas, Europe's trains and hostels, Nepal's treks, New Mexico's honeymoon, and Africa's adventures. Now it contains the essential items a 44-year-old mother would hastily gather as she runs from her home, seeking safety for her four children.

Looking ahead at her load-laden family, she realizes her greatest treasures are not the possessions hastily shoved in the packs, but the load bearers themselves.

Her three daughters stride single file, each carrying a pack containing filtered water and their personal essential items, their remaining treasures abandoned. Pieces of their conversation buffet the breeze as they talk of friends left behind. I'm surprised at the spring in their step and the absence of tears; a third generation doing whatever needs to be done as Linda and I were taught by our own parents on this same continent.

As we stride hard into the unknown, I reflect on each of "my kids," each unique but all accustomed to the lures, joys, and struggles of life in Africa. Since I don't have children, my twin's kids are mine. As an aunt, I savor the sweet spot somewhere between a mother's rich experience — without the stress that often plagues that relationship — and that of a best friend.

Jessica, the oldest, fifteen, tall, and lean, leads the way, calm under pressure and fiercely protective of her siblings. As a preschooler, she strapped a doll on her back as the locals do, until she had a little sister to carry. Jessica's gracefulness, despite a heavy load, mirrors the magnificent graceful walk of an African woman balancing a water pot on her head. The first-born has much responsibility and commands respect. Jessica, even as a fledgling teenager, slips smoothly into the role.

Jordan, Linda's second-born, trails close behind, her blonde ponytail beating a strong rhythm across her back. Born thirteen years ago in Mombasa on the Kenyan coast, Jordan joined the family during turbulent times. Emotional, wonderfully unpredictable, and changeable as the weather on the continent where her life began, Jordan is strong-willed and independent, testing the boundaries and norms set by the world around her.

Twelve-year-old Seve shadows Jordan. Her fast walk, interspersed with running, mirrors that of Noel, their Jack Russell Terrier, bounding alongside,

2

bumping at her legs. Long, blonde pigtails angle out from underneath Seve's floppy denim cap with its whimsical sunflower.

My body strains with the physical demands of a run for survival as my mind swirls on an emotional rollercoaster loaded with a myriad of life-impacting decisions. Yet, somehow, there is still room to reflect. How did a day, which began with a sunrise cup of tea on the porch in the magnificent northern Ugandan vastness, deteriorate to a run for our lives?

2 Two Weeks Earlier *Kabla Wiki Mbili*
Uganda 2004

Linda and John "Byron" Witte sit on small, three-legged wooden stools in the breezeway of their Kaabong home in northern Uganda, waiting for the chai to boil on the charcoal cooker. The kids, sleepy-eyed, tousled hair, and still pajamaed, stumble through the screen door for their treasured daily routine.

The chai boils over and spews on the charcoal. Byron pours the steaming, sweet tea, laced with milk and spices, into six metal cups lined along the porch edge. As the morning sun colors the horizon, doves' songs mingle with the laughter and chatter in the consonant-rich Karamojong language from the village beyond the honeysuckle-lined fence. Sitting in his mother's lap, Ben pesters, "Mom, what shall we do today?"

Jordan and Seve, gowns pulled between their long, tanned legs, set their steaming cups aside as they tickle the top of a cone-shaped burrow with a leaf. A cacophony of giggles joins the morning sounds as black pinchers poke up for breakfast.

"You're miles away," grins Byron, handing Linda her cup.

"Years away actually. I was thinking of the doodlebug hunts Cinda and I used to have 40 years ago as we competed to capture the most on the mud floor of the Songwe Baptist church in Tanzania. We played at anything to survive the monotonous drone of a Swahili church before Daddy began his medical clinic."

"Oh for the simplicity of being a bored child!" Byron sighs, concerned about recent events. The Ugandan military distributed automatic AK-47 rifles to warriors of the local Karamojong tribe several years ago to protect their people from the vicious attacks of the infamous Joseph Kony and his Lord's Resistance Army (LRA). The LRA had wreaked havoc and terror for 25 years in southern Sudan and northern Uganda, massacring villages and forcing their boys into service as boy soldiers and porters.

Recent reports had indicated the enormity of the LRA's devastation: raping, selling women into sex slavery, and ripping the fetuses from the bellies of pregnant women. There were tales of them cutting the lips and tongues out of people to keep them terrified, subservient, and silent. The LRA had displaced two million people and abducted 60,000 children, using boys to make up 90 percent of their rebel army.

5

Fear, violence, malnutrition, and heavy hopelessness plague the people of northern Uganda. With Kony's threats shifting out of Uganda into southern Sudan, the weapons intended for defense have become weapons to steal cattle from neighboring Ugandan tribes. The lives of the Karamojong people center on cattle — a man's measure of wealth, respect, and a mark of manhood.

The Dodoth, the Karamojong subtribe the Wittes work with, are in continuing conflict with the Jia, the opposing subtribe, as well as with the neighboring Turkana tribe. Cattle raiding, retaliation, and warfare are a way of life and a proof of courage and manhood. The tradition of scarring their shoulders to represent the number of enemy they have killed — right shoulder scars arrogantly proclaiming the number of males, left shoulder the number of women and children — evidences the social status of conflict. In a land where cattle are wealth and multiple wives gain respect, the AK-47 has replaced spears and sticks, exploding the conflict.

The Ugandan military changed their minds about arming the untrained Karamojong tribal warriors. Efforts to reclaim the guns brought another front to the conflict. Three months ago, Karamojong warriors surrounded the Local Defense Unit (LDU) barracks, a rural outpost of the Ugandan army. The Karamojong tribesmen forced the soldiers to strip and walk out of their barracks where they faced a massacre of 84 soldiers. A survivor pulled the intestines of a slain soldier over his own belly and lay motionless until night, later crawling out from under the sun-ripened entrails to summon help.

There has been unrest in Linda's neighboring village, the usual home brew mixed with singing, dancing, and occasional AK-47 fire, but it has increased. Their people are irate and tensions escalating. Only the previous Sunday, LDU soldiers confronted two unarmed tribesmen walking along the dry riverbed to Kaabong, taunting and demanding to know where they got military caps. During the scuffle, the soldiers shot them. Their families found them naked and covered by buzzing, bloated, green blowflies.

News moves by word of mouth in a land without newspapers, TV, or radio. The neighborhood, an odd word that doesn't quite fit the world of mud huts and thorn fences, buzzes with news, mis-news, gossip, fear, and tension.

Uganda's army recently launched a new disarmament exercise aimed at seizing over 40,000 firearms thought to be in the hands of Karamojong warriors. Many of the fighters vowed to keep their guns for defense from other clans.

With tensions mounting and an anticipatory atmosphere of retaliation, Byron and Linda decide to avoid town and keep the family close to home. This harsh environment, far from the tourists' well-beaten path, is the most marginalized corner of Uganda and one of the most poverty-stricken areas of the world.

6

3 The Journey Begins *Safari Imeanza*
Uganda 2004

Linda's invitation that Stanley and I should visit hints at *shida inakaribika*, colorful Swahili words for trouble brews:

> Cinda, grab this window of opportunity. Shelve the preparations for your upcoming game warden cadet class and come to a land of no stress... well, almost no stress. We must leave in two weeks because it has become too dangerous here. Byron is gone a lot as he covers the Northern Frontier — Northern Kenya, Uganda, and southern Sudan — which leaves me home alone with the kids.
>
> We quit traveling overland to Kampala because of the dangers on the road. Now we feel that trouble is brewing too close to home. It is time to leave. I want you to experience this magnificent place before we go; it tops any place we have ever lived. We will run, rock climb, join Byron in his walking ministry, and do surgery at the hospital. Just come play with me in Africa.
>
> Please just come! The only stress in Kaabong is waiting, with chai in hand, for our hen to leave her nest so we can seize her eggs. Sure, there is trouble on the winds, but we know the hot spots to avoid. You need a rest. Just you come.

"Let's do it, Stanley! It'll be the only chance we get."

"But it sounds as though there may be trouble ahead." He is *always* more cautious than I am.

"Linda wouldn't ask us if it weren't safe. She says it's the prettiest place she's ever lived in East Africa. She's been bugging me to come so she can show us the place ever since they moved there eighteen months ago. Come on, Stan-a-Lee," I wheedle, hopeful my enthusiasm will be infectious. "We could spend a week there, then fly with them to Kampala when they leave. We could stay with Steve and Chipper while Linda's family finds a new home. Then go join them."

"Well... I suppose we could move our plans forward and go now instead of in September, like we intended. You'd need to sort work first, though."

Stanley grins as I envelop him in a bear hug. Our decision is made!

Like numerous other trips, we shop to fill the allotted four 50-pound duffel bags with gifts, make copies of passports, get travelers checks, shut down home, and stash money in socks, pockets, money belts, and underwear.

We journey 22 hours, crossing the Atlantic Ocean, stopping for a few hours in Europe, then across the African continent for a brief layover in Nairobi airport.

I watch as women wearing bright-colored headscarves sweep the runway with hand-held grass brooms. As the distant, but not forgotten, feel of Africa begins to envelop me, memories awaken and a warm sense of coming home settles in my heart as I begin to embrace its dormant rhythm.

A police officer, an AK-47 slung over his shoulder, questions Stanley about his cap. "You tell me. Why are you a game thief? It is not allowable to poach animals in this country."

Stanley struggles to explain that his Operation Game Thief cap doesn't mean he is a poacher. During his 40 years as a Texas game warden, he worked in West Texas and the state headquarters where one of his projects was to oversee the crime stopper program aimed at thwarting poachers.

At our next stop, Entebbe Airport, we taxi past the hangar where the Israelis rescued hostages during Idi Amin's reign over three decades ago, when I was just a high schooler in neighboring Kenya.

I struggle to keep my brain engaged on the negotiations for visas. A cross-world traveler knows the mind-numbing combination of monotony, jet lag, and a body screaming from inactivity.

We retrieve our four bags and discreetly wipe away the chalk marks a customs official placed to flag an inspection. This proves to be an unnecessary precaution as my youngest brother, Chipper, authoritatively strolls into the customs area with his Texas driver's license clipped to his collar. Chipper grabs a bag in each hand as we follow him with the rest through the check station into the dark night where Steve, my oldest brother, waits to load our bags for the hour-long ride to their Kampala home.

Chipper, a renowned rally car racer, adeptly negotiates the crowded dark streets. Riding shotgun, Steve catches us up on the family news, hardly missing a word as he alerts Chipper to potential hazards along the way. As usual, there is a power outage. Car headlights and kerosene lanterns in the windows of kiosks and bars cast glimpses into the noisy, chaotic night with horns blaring and dark-skinned people wearing dark clothing, walking and riding bicycles.

It is 2:15 a.m. local time, 27 hours since we left our home. A brief slumber under a mosquito net, a predawn cup of chai in Chipper's kitchen, stowing away most of our luggage, and we are on our way to the next leg of our journey — a single-engine Cessna flight along the Nile and north to Kaabong, in the heart of Karamoja, northern Uganda.

The Land Cruiser negotiates around snarled traffic and horn-blaring taxis as we make our way to the dirt runway snuggled between sprawling slums. *Boda bodas*, the Ugandan version of motorcycle taxis, weave in and out, on and off the road, carrying their loads of chickens, pigs, bags, baskets, and up to five people. The driver and male passengers sit astride, while women ride sidesaddle with their legs extended outwards for balance, pulling them in to avoid a car, bicycle, kid, or cow.

Chipper's sun-browned arms steer and shift gears to dodge donkey-pulled carts heaped with mangos, and bicycles loaded with cans of kerosene, charcoal, sugarcane, stalks of green bananas, and dried fish. A quick lunge off the roadway as we narrowly miss a bicycle laden with a Nile perch, its tail fins and mouth almost touching the ground. The smells, mingled with the sounds of humanity, drift in through the windows along with the cool morning breeze. In the pastels of early morning, shop owners hang their wares outside their premises made of wood and cardboard. Dirty sheets of plastic spread along the muddy path display a sundry of goods: clothes, soap, pans, fruit, dishes, bottles of home brew, and baskets.

This is a land of contrasts. The dirt walls of the shops blend with the trash and rotting fruit on the muddy footpath alongside the road. Bright-colored cloths hanging for sale outside the stores jar with the drab surroundings. Laughter and smiles contrast with the desperate struggle for survival in the overpopulated, under-resourced world around them.

Bystanders, recognizing Chipper's honed driving skills and showmanship, call out, "Cheepa, Cheepa Hadams," in an excited singsong greeting. Chipper, a beloved rally champion, is a two-time winner of the Pearl of Africa Safari Rally.

At the airstrip, a uniformed pilot weighs our luggage on a portable bathroom scale. Stanley is surprised when he reaches his weight allotment of 30 lbs. "How can a few clothes, passport, flashlight, and peanut M&M's add up so quickly?" he mutters, setting aside his cowboy boots. He doesn't know I secretly added to his cargo. I removed the plastic bag from a wine box and secreted it into his luggage to savor at sunset. Since I'm going to stay with my identical twin, I'm able to leave most of my clothes. We've shared our clothes our entire lives.

I squeeze into the tiny back seat while Stanley climbs into the co-pilot's, strapping into a seatbelt swinging from the ceiling of the four-seat Cessna belonging to the Missionary Aviation Fellowship (MAF). The tiny plane bumps its way along the dirt runway and circles over Kampala's busy, rosy dawn heading to Kaabong — as rural and remote as its name sounds to me.

9

Wearing headphones, Stanley watches Ugandan kids in faded, dirty, torn clothes running below, casting his memories back to a faraway place in his own boyhood on a cotton farm in West Texas. The land is as rugged as it is vast. The shadow of the airplane skitters along the multiple shades of brown below then turns north, following the green band of the Nile River. His excitement for the adventure mounts as the monotony of cross-world air travel from Texas to Uganda takes a turn to the unknown and unexplored.

The roar and vibration of the engine, mingling with the anticipation of reuniting with family, make me uncomfortable and anxious. My mind finds escape in memories as it did years ago as a girl when I would anticipate the end of the journey as we bumped along rugged Tanzanian roads, hot and sweaty in a crowded Land Rover with our family of seven.

Africa was my home for the majority of my first two decades of life. As a child, visits to America were fun and exciting, but it was "going home" for Mother and Daddy.

Africa-bound travelers, volunteers, and missionaries often go with hopes and dreams of making a lasting impact. Instead, they are surprised to find their influence swept away by time, like footprints in the sand. They find they are the ones forever changed. When a *mgeni*, Swahili for guest, takes time to invest himself in the people — to love, understand, walk, talk, eat, laugh, and connect heart to heart — their footprints become lasting heartprints.

Like a thumbprint, a heartprint is unique. Life experiences, victories, struggles, and wounds are their ridges and valleys. Unlike footprints, swept away as a fading memory, they endure and connect across generations and cultures. Africa lures its people back. A call, dampened by the busyness of American life, never disappears. It still whispers and beckons to me in the quiet.

The drone of the plane buffeting in the savanna's warm wind brings back decades' old memories like flipping through a stack of precious pictures: sitting next to Linda, our legs pushed between the roof rack bars as the Land Rover rocked and pitched its way to Daddy's bush clinic, tears streaking our cheeks as they joined our tangled hair stringing in the wind; Steve and Jim fighting between the jerry cans and the wooden crate of medical supplies while Chipper nestled in the hood spare tire like a tree frog. Too much time and distance has separated me from Linda — my soul mate, best friend, and identical twin.

"Afraid I have to make an unscheduled stop." The pilot's voice jolts me back as the plane circles to land. Village kids run alongside, yelling and cheering as the plane slides to a halt in a flurry of red dust. After the roar of the plane engine subsides, we unfold and step into the hot air, red dust, and a throng of kids.

"There's trouble on the ground in Kaabong. We need to wait until we can get radio contact with the Baptist missionaries to be sure it's safe to land," the pilot explains.

"The missionaries are my family," I chip in. "They should be at the airstrip by now, which means they have no radio communication."

"OK." He hesitates. "I'll continue to Kaabong but we can only land if it looks safe."

Leaving the throng of cheering kids in a billow of red dust, we take off, now carrying additional baggage of misgivings and concerns. My mind checks back to events and apprehension I experienced prior to the trip.

The week before departure was chaotic with the balance between packing and work responsibilities. My boss sent me to some professional training in Galveston on critical incident stress for law enforcement officers, a topic of great interest but, in light of the upcoming trip, a bothersome distraction. I rushed home to co-lead a women's life group in my home and pack for a 4:00 a.m. departure to Uganda. As we debriefed the evening's meeting, Georgia, my friend and co-leader, asked, "Bud, what's wrong? Something seems to be bothering you."

"I've a bad feeling about this trip, Georgia. You know I've been back to Africa many times, but this time is different. I just think this time I won't be coming back... "

"What d'you mean?"

My own thoughts puzzled me. "I don't know. It's just a feeling I have that I won't come back. It isn't fear. I have faith when I leave this earth I will be going home. It's more of a foreboding than a fear."

These concerns received an exclamation mark when, on the plane to Germany, Stanley admitted, "I just have a bad feeling about this trip, Babe."

The murder of the two warriors in the riverbed occurred just prior to our departure. Unbeknownst to us while we were en route to Africa, the warriors' friends, bent on retaliation, broke into the army barracks looking for the man who killed them. They didn't find him, but instead killed a ranking officer, taking his gun and radio. The warrior refused the military's offer to exchange the men responsible for the death of their friends for the radio and gun. Tensions were screaming and trouble was brewing like a stick of dynamite with a lit fuse.

4   Settling In *Kuzoea*
Uganda 2004

The vast countryside below reminds Stanley of the more familiar landscape of West Texas. Among the large rock outcroppings, numerous large circles of mud huts nestled inside thorn barrier fences dot the puzzle of browns and green. With only a rare road, a spider web of trails connects the villages. Shepherd boys run between the goats and the sparse brush, raising their sticks as if to swat the plane. The pilot points out the town of Kaabong with its one shop-lined street. Laundry lies on the ground outside the hospital as family members dry their laundry and cook food for their hospitalized relative.

We fly over the mission compound, its two red-roofed houses snuggled next to a village, and continue six miles north to the dirt airstrip. I recognize Sakatan where the Wittes picnic and rock climb. The pilot circles low, spots a Land Rover with four white kids and an AK-47 armed guard on the roof rack, and searches the bushes for any sign of trouble before making the decision to land. The plane decelerates and makes a final spin in the billowing red dust, the pilot intending to return in one week.

Ahhh, Africa! I cannot unfold and untangle from the back seat fast enough to hug the family I have so longed to see. Hugging my twin, hearts stretched for too long and too far, we melt together with the kids in a group hug. We cannot linger because of the risk of being in no man's land where the Jia and Dodoth clash as well as anyone else that gets between them. Stanley stows the luggage in the back of the Land Rover and climbs on top of the roof rack with the kids and the armed guard. An additional armed guard rides inside the Land Rover with the driver.

I sling my leg over the back of Linda's motorcycle, hugging close as she pops it into gear, a trick from long ago — try to catch the rider off guard with a quick takeoff. The wind ushers in the feel and smells of Africa as we bounce along the dirt road. Looking over my shoulder, I see Stanley and the kids riding the roof rack, bringing back memories of the five of us siblings doing the same decades ago. I sigh with satisfaction, thinking it's time to de-stress, enjoy family, dust off nursing skills, and walk to villages to dance, sing, and story, as missionaries call the telling of biblical tales.

The Land Rover makes a sharp left turn past a tiny, crooked, wooden guard shed and enters a vine-covered, fenced mission compound; the last of wheeled transport until its anticipated hired return ride to the dirt airstrip in one week.

*****

In Swahili, *nini cha kufanya* translates to a what-to-do and is used as a noun, like the word dilemma. Resolving the what-to-do begins with putting the teapot on the charcoal. Then we can work on the issues: Ben's birthday party tomorrow and reconnecting after several years of life on separate continents.

Balancing our steaming cups, we make our way to Picnic Rock, a fifteen-foot rock outcropping in the yard. Short-legged Noel, the family's Jack Russell, finds her spot next to Jordan. As Ben shares his peanut M&M's, he dismisses his sisters' suggestion that they don't mix with chai, laughing, "It works for me!"

Jordan leans against my shoulder as she tells me, "Seve and I race to finish our school work so we can come here and spot our shepherd friends with our binoculars."

"We like to join them while they watch their goats and cows," Seve adds. Just as my four siblings and I did decades ago, my nieces and nephew communicate with friends without a common language, as they run, jump, play, imitate each other, and make toys out of mud, sticks, and gourds.

"Mom, pleeease, can we plan my birthday now?" As the youngest, Ben's agenda often takes a forefront in family conversations. "I want us all to go and make sandcastles at the riverbed under the bridge, climb the rocks at Sakatan, then make hamburgers, chocolate army birthday cake, and ice cream," he gabbles breathlessly.

Linda's guts churn with negative thoughts toward the army theme in light of current events, but she decides not to add pessimism to the festivities.

"I want to bake the buns."

"Have we enough ice and skimmed cream for the ice cream maker?"

"Can I grind the meat for the patties?"

The kids enthusiastically volunteer for the preparations. Linda, remembering the cobra found under the stove and Jordan scorching her hair while trying to light the pilot light, resolves to supervise her daughter's volunteering to bake the cake.

As my internal clock adjusts to African pace, my mind and senses are sweetly satisfied as I savor the sounds, smells, and feel of Africa and of family bonds. It isn't what we say or what we do; it's just the sheer pleasure of each other's presence. Every time I answer the luring call to return to Africa, my mind launches into the sweet memories of my own childhood in rural Tanzania. Although decades separate it from the lives of my missionary kid (MK) nieces and nephew here in rural northern Uganda, there are many more similarities than differences.

Jessica interrupts my rambling thoughts. "Mom, what was it like when you and Nuna came to Africa when you were little girls?" Linda's kids love to hear stories of their mother, twin auntie – Nuna, a name of endearment used for me throughout my life — and their uncles in the "old" days in Africa. A look back into my girlhood may also help answer the question "how did I get here?" What experiences and lessons, imprinted long ago on my heart, shaped and equipped me for this incredible time?

5 Dreams of Africa *Ndoto za Afrika*
Texas 1960s

I beat Linda out of bed at dawn on Saturday morning in our small West Texas country home. At four years old, we pulled ourselves up on the windowsill to peek for sunlight, our signal that it was OK to jump into our parents' bed. I scrambled for the coveted position between Mother and Daddy. My oldest brother, Steve, wearing white undershorts and a not-so-gently-used T-shirt, and next brother Jim, wearing only undershorts, pushed each other as they ran down the hall to leap into bed.

Steve, nine years old, sported a brown burr haircut that failed to disguise a double cowlick, squealed as he elbowed seven-year-old, skinny, red-headed, and freckled face Jim to second place just before the leap. Linda rounded the corner wearing her skier-patterned pajamas, her brown, tangled hair mashed high on one side and red sleep marks streaking her face. But who was I to say? As her identical twin, I guess I looked a lot like her as I gloated in the prize spot in my identical pajamas. As always, she pranced in with arms outstretched and announced, "Ta-da! Daddy's ski 'jama girl is here!"

Two-year-old Chipper rubbed his eyes with fisted hands as he shuffled into the room, wearing lime green, one-piece pajamas with built-in feet. Steve reached over the edge of the bed and cupped Chipper's bottom, boosting him to his warm spot between Daddy's feet.

The family routine before the busy day began took an unexpected turn. As a four-year-old, I had no idea this day would begin a course of events that would take me to the other side of the world.

"All right, kids, it's time for a family meeting." Daddy captured our attention with his serious tone of voice. "We're gonna move to Africa to be missionaries. We'll close my medical clinic here in Seminole and move to a hospital compound in Mbeya in Tanzania."

"Where's that, Daddy?" Jim interrupted.

"East Africa."

In my excitement, all I heard was Africa. I jumped to my feet and bounced on the bed as Linda slid into my spot. There she lounged with that satisfied "gotcha" expression on her face.

Our questions about Africa and African animals tumbled over each other.

"I want a warthog, Daddy," I told him excitedly.

"A monkey, a monkey!" added Linda.

Steve pleaded for a lion, but it was a cheetah for Jim and an elephant for Chipper. Our questions came from our view of Africa — *Tarzan* on the black and white TV with the bent coat hanger antenna in the living room. Steve soon lost interest, hooked his T-shirt over the corner bedpost, and began to spin, delighting in knocking both twins and a brother on the head with his feet.

Africa! Our four-year-old imaginations later ran wild as we pretended to swim together in the wheelbarrow. The looped garden hose, adding water to the wheelbarrow pool, became the trunk of an elephant, bellowing and splashing water. How will Daddy capture our animal? Will my monkey sleep with me? What will I name my warthog? Where will Chipper keep his elephant? Our minds whirled.

"Linda," I started hesitantly. "Daddy says we'll live with colored people. Do colored people have patches of colored skin — blue, green, and purple — or d'you think there are people of each color?" (At the time, "colored" was the accepted term when referring to people of African descent.)

She giggled. "I want to see a purple man. Mother says people live in mud huts with many flowers. I can't wait to pick flowers for my own hut — my own! I don't even have to share with my brothers."

"Daddy says we'll go to Africa by boat because he can swim further than he can fly. Will we live on the boat? How will we go to the bathroom on the boat?" My questions kept tumbling out.

Steve dumped the wheelbarrow, dousing our African dreams.

*****

The following year was a whirlwind as Mother and Daddy closed a private medical practice in Seminole, moved to Fort Worth for seminary, bought household supplies, and shopped at clothing stores, garage sales, and wholesale warehouses to clothe a family of seven with five growing kids for four years. Mother's response to a woman's concern for the safety of a family with five young kids in "dangerous" Africa was, "Since it is God's will for us to serve in Africa, it would be more dangerous for my kids to stay in America."

Once at the seminary, Daddy set Linda and me on opposite sides of the sink, our bare feet facing each other, as we watched him shave and get ready for class. He tipped our giggle boxes as he smeared shaving cream and pretended to shave our cheeks. "Squeak, squeak," he pursed his lips, making funny noises for us. Daddy grabbed Linda as she almost laughed herself off the sink.

It was his job to make our ponytails but he made them so tight it made our faces hurt and pulled our eyes to slits. Whining never got us far so Linda always found something funny about even the most miserable circumstances and we giggled our way through good times and bad.

On his way to seminary, Daddy pulled us to kindergarten in my shiny red wagon with "Cinda Ann" painted in white on the side. I rode in the front because it was mine, while Linda sat behind with her legs wrapped around me, her white shoes in my lap. Daddy's shiny black shoes stepped along quickly as he pulled my wagon, bumping over each crack in the sidewalk, Linda's and my identical ponytails swinging in rhythm as we traveled to a neighbor's house. We had fun in kindergarten but couldn't wait for Daddy to return from class. He held the wagon handle as we climbed back in for our trip home.

"My time to drive," Linda pushed me aside, plopping into the front seat; fair is fair, a concept often disputed between us.

She and I spent uncountable hours somersaulting, rolling, and sliding down a mountain of a hill in our front yard. Twenty-five years later, Linda returned to the same neighborhood to attend seminary in preparation for a mission career in Africa. The mountain had shrunk to a gentle four-foot hill.

*****

The time between the completion of seminary training and departure day was tight to close down a house, buy supplies, and pack. Our grandparents came to help build plywood crates and fill them with appliances, furniture, and supplies. As Daddy and Granddaddy packed the freezer into the crate, Steve transformed its box into his African hut; the first of our cardboard African village, complete with our imaginary animals.

It soon lost its draw with the excitement of helping Mema and Mother, watching them climb inside the crates to fill every speck of space. The freezer, refrigerator, couch, and every nook, cranny, and crack were stuffed with soap, cake mixes, Jell-O, candy, tuna fish, mayonnaise, toilet paper, blue toilet bowl cleaner, cornflakes, and taco sauce mixes. We climbed in to help; my job was to fill the bike handlebars with popcorn. Crawling inside the big wooden crates was like crawling inside a Christmas present.

The fun was over when Mother picked up my black monkey with the yellow banana from my cardboard hut and put him into the tub of the washing machine. My friend was gone. Her assurance I would see my toys again did little to reassure me.

Our play was all about Africa. Linda and I loved family picnics and sleeping "somewhere 'sides our bed." When we picnicked under the dining room table or slept in the bathtub, in a box, or under the dining room chairs, we were already camping in Africa.

19

Linda's fifth birthday, she taunted, "I get to sleep on the rolly polly bed with Daddy." Sleeping on the folding bed on the front porch was a much-prized treat. I was sad sleeping alone without my twin but found a warm spot in Mother's bed.

Linda's birthday is June 27, 1960. I was born ten minutes later, but on the other side of midnight. Different birthdays and we were proud of it. The next night I got to sleep with Daddy and Linda whined, "That's just not fair!" I fought hard against sleep because I didn't want Daddy to ever stop talking about Africa.

We celebrated many birthdays with a slumber party, complete with a cake on each day. Mother and Daddy always emphasized our uniqueness instead of our similarities. Apart from our skier-decorated pajamas, we were rarely dressed alike. In our adult years, we celebrate our birthdays together whenever we can, still complete with cake and giggles but we add wine and go to bed earlier. We were born and gifted with our own personal playmate.

We would continue to dream, somersault, and play but now our play moved to a vast playground in East Africa.

6 Setting Sail *Tweka Tanga*
Texas 1960s

We were still five when the big day arrived: March 21, 1966. Mother and Daddy said their tearful goodbyes to their loved ones and all things known. I was sad to leave Mema and Granddaddy but excited to go to the Africa we had dreamed of, and to get my warthog of course.

My grandparents were pillars of the First Baptist Church in Midland and staunch supporters of missions. Mema was the president of the Women's Missionary Union (WMU). As we boarded the plane, she complained, "I have supported African missionaries all my life but I never dreamed you would take my grandkids there."

We once flew in a small plane Daddy piloted. We flew over our house and saw Mother waving at us. We ran out of gas that day and landed in a pasture. I hoped this big plane wouldn't run out of gas. Steve elbowed Jim and whispered, "Look, Mother's crying again."

I sensed tension between Mother and Daddy at our first stop, an hour-and-a-half layover in Dallas. Mother fussed as Daddy caught a taxi into town to buy one last part to convert our tape recorder to 220-volt electricity, wondering if he would return in time. Just as they were about to close the door to the plane, I heard Daddy's familiar whistle. Mother was in a grump.

Steve and Jim sat together in a row with Daddy and fought as they always did, elbowing, kicking, and stabbing each other with plastic knives we were given with the funny little meal. Mother usually told them, "If you're going to fight, do it outside." I guess that doesn't work well in an airplane.

As we got older and the boys' fights got more rigorous, her warning changed to, "If you're going to kill each other, do it outside." As the boys fought, Linda and I rolled our boarding passes into cones to stick into the hole in the armrest, using them as free earphones to get the kind of country music Granddaddy liked.

Arriving in New York, we sat on our stack of luggage by a column near the baggage conveyer and watched the bustle of strange people at JFK airport while Daddy researched transport. The seven of us caught the train to Princeton, New Jersey. The crowds were thick — legs, legs, legs everywhere, legs all moving fast. I clung to Mother so I wouldn't get lost.

Daddy's cousin gave us a tour of the sights of Washington D.C. and New

York City in his Woodie, a wood-paneled station wagon. He and his family lived in a narrow, tall house with stairs. The only stairs I'd seen in a home were the ones to Mema's musty basement. We liked to sit and bump our bums down the steps while trying to sing a song. It made our voices sound funny. Mema made us put on clean panties and go to the basement whenever the TV gave a tornado warning, in case her house blew away. "How embarrassing to be seen wearing dirty underwear," she would tell us.

Climbing the long flights of stairs inside a big statue, Mother explained the importance of the Statue of Liberty to America. Chipper began to cough and gag. Mother yanked him to her side, hit him on the back, and turned him upside down.

"Mother, why are you hitting Chipper?" Steve was shocked.

"Silly Chipper choked on a penny and swallowed it."

"I wonder what'll happen to the penny," I giggled, my thoughts long gone from Mother's description of how our country got the statue or its message of freedom.

I wasn't impressed with the White House. So what was the big deal if someone had a big white house? I had a white house in West Texas, but now I was going to have a mud hut with animals and flowers. While we followed all the legs through the rooms of the big white house, Daddy stepped behind the curtain to watch a helicopter landing in the front yard.

I didn't understand why he was suddenly in trouble with Mother and the security men. He wasn't swinging on the curtains, just hiding behind them. I guess the security didn't like Daddy hiding behind the curtains when the president was flying in, and Mother wasn't happy when security threw a fit about Daddy.

After two days of seeing the sights of New York City and Washington D.C., Daddy's cousin packed eight suitcases, seven sleeping bags, and the seven of us in his Woodie and deposited us on the sidewalk entrance to Pier 72 to board the Queen Mary for the next leg of our journey. Our luggage was to see us through two weeks' camping through England and Holland, and a month in Africa until our crates arrived.

Pier 72 at New York's shipping port was bustling with noise and people with legs, legs, and yet more legs, but this time they were all carrying bags and suitcases. We clung close as we made our way through the throngs and up the narrow walkway to the Queen Mary. I gripped the handrail as I crossed it and saw waves crashing against the ship, below my feet.

Daddy opened the small porthole to our tiny room, letting in the sounds of seagulls and the smells of the sea. The excitement of being on a ship was uncontainable.

"I dib top bunk."

"No, I get it!" Jim and Steve tugged each other as they spilled over the top bunk.

"Mother says there's a pool."

"Mother, can we go swimming now?" Linda and I chattered at the same time. Daddy's commanding, "OK, kids, let's get these on," stopped us midsentence as he tugged a mammoth size orange life jacket over Chipper's head and pitched one to each of us. With Mother and Daddy's help, we finally got them strapped on facing the right direction and stumbled to our deck assignment for a safety drill. As we waited, Chipper asked, "Mother, when are we going to get on the ship?" The bustle and size of it all hadn't sunk in to his two-year-old experience of the world.

Daddy, eight years old in 1938, had seen the Queen Mary from his view on top of the Empire State Building only two years after her maiden voyage. How could he have dreamed he would board her 28 years later with a wife and five children? The Queen Mary would sail its last voyage less than two years after our trip. Mother, in her weekly aerogramme to her own mother, wrote:

> We watched the skyline of New York fade away. How strange to leave my country, my homeland, and the ones I love so dearly. I thought I never would. I have left part of my heart with you in America as I follow God's call to Africa. Then there was ocean. All I could see was water.

Mother's letters only hinted at the torrent of emotions she must have felt as she left America for the first time in her life; launched on a ship and into a life of unknowns.

We had free rein of the ship. It didn't take long to adjust and leap into our new surroundings with stairs to climb, rooms to explore, bunk beds to jump, and decks to run. Steve and Jim fought a lot, chasing each other up and down steps, trying to throw each other overboard, and riding the elevators, punching all the buttons before they get out.

Mother sent the boys with Daddy to explore the engine and mechanical rooms. Chipper stayed close, with one hand gripping Mother's dress and made small, timid forays to play musical chairs with the British kids.

Mealtimes were so funny. Each of us had enough forks, knives, and spoons for the whole family. That gave more sword-fighting knives for Steve and Jim than Mother could confiscate. Waiters wearing white uniforms brought courses of food with appetizers, soup, salad, meat, and vegetables; followed by dessert and finished by cheese, crackers, and tea. Mother added in her letter:

> Life on the ship is strange. I'm not accustomed to such

finery; if we need a fork that is all I set on the table. They have the whole table full of silver and take care of every need before you have time to want something. The food is fabulous. I've tried not to eat everything on the menu, but the steward says in his funny English accent, "Oh, you must try this." I now weigh 120 pounds, which won't be easy to get off. John will be heavy because he cannot say "no" to any of the five courses. I love the English; it's hard to understand their language but I enjoy their accent. They love children and spoil Chipper.

Linda and I loved watching movies and playing on deck. We somersaulted, chased each other, and twirled in the wind. We competed to make the funniest faces by comparing our reflections in the shiny brass rails kept polished by white-gloved workers. We timed our leaps from the stairs with the ship's descent from the wave crests so we could jump high. The chairs on deck were an endless, entertaining obstacle course. We spent hours at the pool on the ship's bottom deck.

Oh, the pool… the smell of chlorine and the warm, moist air. That must be what heaven smells like. Linda followed me, arms outstretched, as we stepped heel to toe along the narrow strip of tiles lining the pool. We were in our own twin world, filled with giggles and fun as we played for hours. We composed a song about the ocean as we peered into the green depths of the pool.

"I wonder how the water got into the bottom of the ship," I pondered.

"Maybe the pool is a hole in its bottom. Let's search deep to try and see a whale or a mermaid."

Suddenly, an English boy shoved us. Linda teetered and regained her balance but I fell into the abyss. I sank into the blue, surrounded by white bubbles. All I could see was blue and shimmering colors above me. I was five and all my swimming had been in the wheelbarrow.

The shimmering, colored lights above drifted further away. I didn't struggle, I was just sad for losing my family. I was afraid I would lose them in the sea of legs in New York City, but now they were leaving me behind, in the sea. Since the pool was just a hole in the bottom of the ship then this was it; left in the depths of the ocean as the family steamed on toward Africa. The sadness and loneliness consumed me.

I felt a pull on my arm, a jerk, and a yank. The shimmering colors above came closer and closer. Steve, having just returned from the engine room, had jumped into the pool, grabbed my arm, and tugged until he got me to the surface. I was disappointed not to see whales or mermaids on my visit to the bottom of the Atlantic Ocean.

We sailed onward to the African adventure ahead with family intact. Next stop was Europe.

*****

England, and Southampton port bustled with people carrying bags, all in a hurry to get somewhere. We sat on top of our own cases and watched while Daddy gathered transport information. A woman, wearing high heels and a fur shawl, clip-clopped down the hallway, leading two giant poodles. A man with rosy cheeks, big beard, and a Sherlock Holmes pipe, pumped his arms and puffed like a steam engine trying to keep up. People of all kinds bustled by: rich and poor, young and old, carrying backpacks and assorted luggage.

We boarded a red, double-decker bus, grasping the rails as it lurched into the congested traffic. Carrying our tiny suitcases and enormous sleeping bags, we bumped past people to climb the twisting staircase to grab the seats in the front.

"Can we go to the Tower of London, Daddy?" Steve pleaded. "I want to see where they hang people."

"I want to see the furry-headed soldiers at Buckingham Palace," Jim chimed in.

At Buckingham Palace, Steve and Jim acted silly and tried to make the guards grin or jump. Their reward was a fuss from Mother. It was cold and rainy in London. I hoped Africa wasn't cold too. The tent and camping supplies, in the eighth suitcase, came in handy when we rented a small car and headed to the countryside, where we camped out in barns, cheap rooms, and even a closed hotel.

Next came Amsterdam. While Daddy bargained for a rental car and Mother gathered maps and tourist information, we sat on our sleeping bags and pile of suitcases as we compared the contents of our pockets: sugar cubes, tea bags, ketchup, mustard, plastic ware, cookies, crackers, mints, and candy collected from the plane.

Our room overlooked the canal where we could watch bikes, bikes, and more bikes, as well as boats, and people wearing funny-looking wooden shoes. A noisy radiator by the window warmed the back of our legs and dried our clothes.

A long walk along the canal brought us to Anne Frank's house. As I studied the black and white photos on the wall above me, I thought how sad it must have been for Anne and her family. Just like me, she didn't want to get separated from family. I learned she was a few years older than I was and kept a diary, writing "Dear Diary" for each of her entries. I wanted to have a secret diary with a lock on it so my brothers couldn't read it.

England and the Netherlands had fountains with coins. I couldn't believe people just threw away their money. My pockets were full of coins I fished out of fountains, phone booths, and airport seat cushions.

Mother made us stay in the car while Daddy drove our rental car onto a ferry in the Netherlands. With Mother's, "OK," once on board, Chipper jumped out and slammed the door on Linda's thumb. Linda screamed as she jerked her hand, trying to pull it out. Daddy leaped out of the car and opened the door. Bawling, she held her bloody thumb, which made me hurt too. With the language barriers, Daddy had a challenge finding an emergency room. The worst part of the ordeal was, since she had stitches, I had to do the nightly panty hand wash. Not fair!

*****

Finally leaving Europe behind, our suitcases and sleeping bags banged our legs as we ran to keep up with Daddy along the long airport hallways as Mother begged, "Hurry kids, we're about to miss our plane to Africa."

The boys fought on the plane as usual. They strategized how they could get the emergency window open. Why BOAC would trust boys by the emergency exit may be a hint as to why that airline no longer exists.

My eyes, nose, and chest burned as I tried to hold my breath to keep from sucking in the thick, smoky air. I think everyone smoked but us. Nine hours later, we landed for the first time on the African continent. Next stop: Nairobi, Kenya.

7 A Cup of Tea *Kikombe cha chai*
Uganda 2004

"Oh, hey, Honey!" Linda excitedly greets Byron. His six-foot-four-inch frame towers over his Karamojong ministers and companions, Losilo and Tubo. His long canvas shorts, shirt, hiking boots, and Aussie hat sport the colors of African red dirt. Carrying a walking stick in one hand, a hand-cranked tape recorder in the other, and a small belt pack with water bottles around his waist, Byron warmly greets us, shaking Stanley's hand and bear-hugging me. Losilo and Tubo politely greet then, unnoticed, drift out of the compound to return to their families in the nearby village.

Today the three ministers walked to Lochom and back, a thirteen-mile journey. Byron sighs as he collapses on the rock and unlaces his boots to examine the day's wear and tear on his feet. The kids take advantage of Linda's attention to Byron's news from Lochum to give Stanley and me a tour around their home.

A vine-covered fence divides two mission houses. The compound enclosure provides the family an oasis, with thick walls and high windows offering protection from stray bullets in a war-torn area. A covered porch connects the house to a tiny, one-room duplex serving as Jessica and Jordan's bedrooms. Metal burglar bars line the windows and heavy deadbolts secure massive doors.

Jessica's room is messy and girly with bright, hand-sewn curtains, family pictures, and girl stuff. Her love for reading shows in the stack of books on the floor.

"So, She-She came too," I wink at her. Her eyes gleam as she proudly strokes the five-by-ten-inch ragged piece of sheepskin in the center of her bed. She-She, this vestige of a full-size sheepskin, has been with her since the time she formed her first words.

"I couldn't leave her behind," she feigns a pout. "She-She's even been to the foot of Mount Kilimanjaro with me."

"Must be the most well-traveled sheepskin in the world," I laugh with her. She-She has been her companion from her crib in Houston to her long string of homes in Kenya: in the highland tea plantations of Limuru, the hot steamy shores of Mombasa, the slums of Jogoo Road in Nairobi, and the shores of Lake Victoria in Kisumu. One of few constants in Jessica's life, this simple piece of familiarity now holds pride of place on her bed in the semi-arid vast savanna of Uganda.

"Nuna, come and see my room next!" Jordan is keen to have her turn to show what she has created. Stepping into her room, I step from Africa's hardness into the soft, tender world of a young girl. Each of the girls chose their own comforter from America and decorated the room in a way that reveals their unique personality. Somehow, in this hard land, a piece of America's sweetness and home is preserved. Seeing the mix and contrast of Africa and America brings memories of my own childhood when Mother did the same for us.

"Still a beach girl, I see." I squeeze her shoulder as she points out her treasures.

"That's my favorite part, my beachcomber corner." She points to the piece of contorted driftwood, draped with a fishing net, shells, and old seawater-aged bottles. "I love looking at each shell and bottle and remembering where I found them."

Like her sister, she has sought her own simple reminders to provide constancy in her ever-moving life. A well-used Bible, with a beaded outline of the African continent on the leather cover, props at an angle between the burglar bars of the window.

A narrow, steep, outside stairway between the house and the girls' rooms leads to the flat roof and the hub of family life between sunset and bedtime. Making the third side of a square, with a huge shady tree in the center, is the family's storage room where the chicken secrets her clutch of eggs.

Under the clothesline, a hen, followed by a tumble of chicks, pecks underneath the sheets flapping in the breeze. A tree in the center of the square is home to weaverbirds, with over 30 nests dangling like purses from its limbs. The birds' cheery chatter mirrors the mood of the human family surrounding them as both carve out homes for their little ones: nurturing, feeding, and protecting in the harsh African bush.

The front door opens into one large room serving as a kitchen, living, and dining room. Spears, clubs, walking sticks, and an umbrella, propped in a bucket by the door, mirror the practicality throughout the house. To the right, three loaves of homemade sourdough bread, hamburger buns, and cinnamon rolls rise on the kitchen counter. A tall, double cylinder water filter sits next to the propane refrigerator beside eight plastic bottles with each family member's name: Byron, Linda, Jessica, Jordan, Seve, Ben, and now Cinda and Stanley.

"Mom and Dad love the radio," Jordan tells me as my eyes come to rest on the solar charged car batteries powering the radio and the computer on a bench under the window.

"You'll have to come and listen tomorrow, Nuna," Jessica chips in.

"They use it at 7:30 every morning to talk to missionaries in Kampala and Nairobi."

I can imagine only too well how the much-anticipated contact with co-workers and friends serves as a tie to the familiar.

Ben proudly shows off his room and his treasures. Amidst a world of sisters, Ben prevails as all boy.

"That's my AK-47 rifle," he points proudly to his homemade rifle made of sticks, lying next to his spear and stick collection in the corner by the window. "And look at the car my African friend made me. It's made out of wires from an old radial tire."

"Does it move?"

"Of course, Nuna!" I hide a smile at his indignance. "It's got moving wheels and the steering wheel is on this long pole so I can drive when I'm standing. See?" Ben wheels his car around, barely missing a toy jet plane made from an oilcan, its wheels the bottoms of bug repellent cans, sitting crookedly in the center of the room. Even at ten, Ben sports his father's strong character traits: organized, independent, protective, courageous, and decisive.

Walking into Seve's room gives a rich glimpse of the world through the eyes of an artist, with her tiny, intricate artwork and captivating photos lining the walls. Her love of nature and people shows in the small bits of rocks and wood displayed along with black and white photos of faces she has taken herself. A jumbled stack of shoes in the corner of the room hint of the owner's personality: pink ballerina shoes, red dirt-stained running shoes, and a pair of black sandals made from the tread of a truck tire.

"I couldn't leave Bear behind," she says, as I pick up the shaggy brown teddy bear with one eye missing, reclining on her bed. She hugs me tight. Her beloved Bear has shared her bed and her life since she was five, reminding me of the childhood story of *The Velveteen Rabbit*. I think if I had another life to live, I would want to live it as Seve's Bear. Oh, to be in the arms of a precious girl and share her intimate thoughts, dreams, joys, fears, and tears.

*****

Goat bells mingle with the sounds of young boy herdsmen's chatter as they enter their thorn *kraal* (enclosure), signaling teatime. The events of life, not a clock, are the time and calendar keepers in this land. Mary, Linda's Karamojong friend and helper, had invited us for tea at her hut in the neighboring *manyatta* (village).

Wageni (guests) may think a cup of tea is as it sounds... a cup of tea. Here, a cup of tea not only begins and ends the day but ushers life's

29

transitions through ceremonies, friendships, decisions, conflicts, and negotiations. It begins negotiations for a bride's price or a circumcision ceremony, soothes a family crisis, develops trust, and nurtures friendship. Some of my early beginnings of heartprinting began with a cup of tea. "Shall we have a spot of tea?" chanted in a singsong British accent, is a long-standing family tradition when faced with a what-to-do.

With a *kanga* wrapped around my shorts, we approach the three-foot opening in the thick, ten-foot thorn barrier which, in turn, leads to the maze of passageways to the inner circle of mud huts with thatched roofs, all to thwart the efforts of the enemy from entering and stealing women and cattle. Huts built with the floor two feet below the ground allow people to sleep under the level of enemy bullets.

Linda, I'm not sure if from courtesy or humor, allows me to enter the *manyatta* entrance first, followed by the kids and Stanley. I awkwardly squat, bend over, and reach to pull the back of my *kanga* lower. As I begin to stand upright again on the other side of the entrance, a village elder stands in front of me to greet, as elders do. The men wear shirts or jackets and often go without clothing from the waist down — usual sights in the kids' world. Stanley clears his throat and mutters, "Okaaaay." Linda giggles behind us.

Mary calls out a warm, but incomprehensible, greeting from inside her dark hut. As my eyes search the unlit interior, I see her silhouette stirring a pot on a fire in the center of the floor. She steps up and out of her hut to ground level and, after greeting us, goes into an animated discussion with Linda in a language unfamiliar to me.

Mary motions Stanley, an extraordinarily old man in her world, to the only stool, a five-by-three-inch piece of wood on a six-inch pedestal.

"You can use it as a stool and a pillow," Ben whispers to him. "It must be pretty uncomfortable though."

Stanley groans quietly, "You got to be kidding."

The rest of us find a seat on the swept dirt outside the hut. As awkward as it may be for me to lower my 44-year-old body down to a seated position, flat on the ground, while still keeping my legs covered, I accomplish it long before Stanley finds his balance on the stool, his knees jutting awkwardly to his ears.

As we share apparently the only four metal cups in the village — another of Ben's facts — Linda, using her hand gestures to make up for gaps in language, continues an animated conversation with Mary as I savor the sights, sounds, and smells. A small, bare-bottomed boy climbs on top of the beehive-shaped, mud chicken coop and leans over to play with Seve's blonde braids. Seve smiles and teases back. Scraggly, bald-headed chickens run between the huts. The setting sun spears gold streaks through the holes

30

in the barrier thorn fence as the last cups of chai are finished and the tealeaves pitched on the ground.

As the sun sets, all return to their homes, the locals to their mud dwellings behind the thick thorn fence and us to our tin-roofed home behind the vine-covered fence where we find Byron putting the finishing touches to a delicious-smelling, spicy goat biryani on the charcoal cooker. Following the daily routine, we climb the steep stairs to the flat roof for dinner and chat until bedtime.

An African evening is like stepping into a beautiful picture. The larger-than-real sun melts into the dusty horizon, blending shades of blues, oranges, reds, and browns. The birds' singing and a cacophony of crickets blend with the sounds of the neighboring *manyatta*. The acrid smell of charcoal contrasts with the sweet scent of the honeysuckle climbing the walls of the house.

As the evening progresses, the village sounds morph, the volume of conversations, laughter, singing, and drumming increase as the local brew begins to take its toll. Stanley and my concerns over the intermittent volleys of AK-47 fire are dismissed as being "just the sounds of Africa."

8 Curtains Open on Africa *Mapazia Yamekuwa Kufunguliwa Katika Afrika*
Tanzania 1960s

Chaos surrounded us as Linda and I, five years old, stepped into our new life in Africa. We tagged close behind our brothers, each carrying our own small overnight bag with two changes of clothes and sleeping bag through a throng of people. Men bumped, pushed, and harassed us as they tried to take our bags to coerce Daddy into using their taxis and pay porter fees. We clung close to Mother as everything around us was strange and tumultuous.

"The missionaries should be here to meet us," she sighed.

"Maybe they didn't receive the aerogramme. We'll just have to find our own way. Bit of a challenge in a strange land with a foreign language!" Daddy said as he wandered off.

From my vantage point, sitting on our bags stacked against a concrete column, I watched for glimpses of Daddy in the sea of black people. I still searched for "colored" people; purple, green, or orange people like Linda and I had dreamed.

In Holland and England, a taxi wouldn't carry a family our size, but Africa is a land with fewer rules, giving greater room to negotiate. Daddy bargained for one to carry our luggage and the seven of us through the heavy rain on a dark midnight in Nairobi. I sat in Steve's lap with my nose pressed against the fogged window, straining to see through the rain.

I looked for the Africa Linda and I had dreamed and talked of. Where were the mud huts with all the animals around them? Instead, shadowy streets teamed with horn-blaring cars and dark shapes of people walking and riding bicycles. We careened our way onto the multi-lane Uhuru Highway with street lamps glowing across the wet road. The taxi slung us from side to side as the driver negotiated the roundabouts. Traffic lights weren't to make their debut until their chaotic introduction in the '70s when drivers and pedestrians, with no instruction on the meaning of the colors, found the changing light show the best free entertainment around.

Journeying through town and industrial areas, we finally turned into the gate of the missionaries' house on Jogoo Road, a house we later lived in ourselves when we returned to Kenya for Mother and Daddy to go to Swahili language school. A house the next generation, Linda's kids, lived in almost 25 years later when they were the age we were when we first set foot in

Africa. Linda's reveries were big for a little girl, dreaming of a monkey and her own hut. How could her dreams ever have stretched to someday returning to this same house to raise her own children?

Our journey had been a whirlwind, an amusement park ride that sped us through different countries and cultures: from America to England, to Holland, to Italy, and now Africa. Our first morning, we loaded up in the Land Rover with a couple of missionaries and descended the winding, treacherous hairpin turns of the Rift Valley. Pushy salesmen, working out of lean-to shanties, displayed their wares: sheepskins, rabbits, rhubarb, oranges, cassava, passion fruit, pineapple, beaded jewelry, copper bracelets, elephant tail bracelets, spears, and wooden carvings. They were black men and women, but still no "colored" people of the kind Linda and I had imagined.

The countryside changed from thick green vegetation and towering eucalyptus trees to the vast savanna of the Rift Valley floor. We passed Mount Longonot, a dormant volcano, and then went on to Narok. Four hours and 100 miles later, we reached our first camping spot. Our first full night in Africa.

The Maasai men had long hair, caked in red clay and cow dung, wore red and white *shukas* (cloths), and carried long spears.

"Look at the women's ears," I nudged Linda, seeing their stretched-out lobes with long, dangling, beaded earrings.

"I like their necklaces though," she whispered. "But the men look scary with their spears."

Without a common language, Daddy helped Jim and Steve buy spears, knives, *rungus* (clubs), and cowbells. From our bumpy seats in the Land Rover, we slid open the windows for a view of animals we had only seen in zoos: impala, eland, baboon, giraffe, and zebra.

"Daddy, Daddy, there's a warthog," I squealed.

"Not yours I'm afraid, Cinda Ann."

I was so disappointed. I couldn't wait to find my warthog. "How come I can't find my monkey here either?" Linda sulked, not finding her monkey among those inundating us at our picnic spot under the acacia tree.

*****

The next leg of the journey to our new home in Mbeya, Tanzania, was a plane trip to Dar es Salaam on the Indian Ocean. We had frozen in rainy England, barely thawed out in Holland, and then found ourselves not wanting to move because it was so hot and humid. I lay sleepless under a mosquito net, tucked tight under my mattress to keep me from getting malaria. In the stifling heat, my chest fought for a breath of thick air. Linda and I lined a belt down the center of our shared twin bed to divide our space so our sweaty bodies wouldn't touch. The sound of the unbalanced fan overhead failed to drown out the noise of the streets and the eerie sounds of Muslim chants from the towers of the nearby mosque.

*****

"Where's the milk?" I wanted to know as we boarded the milk-run airplane the next day to go to Mbeya.

"Silly Twin, Mother and Daddy call it that because it goes so slowly and stops everywhere to deliver cargo," big brother, Steve, laughed. "It has to leave early so it can make all its stops before dark since Dar es Salaam is the only airport with a lighted runway. Isn't that right, Daddy?"

I followed Linda onto the DC-3, stacked my sleeping bag and suitcase next to hers in the space where the first few rows of seats should have been, then made my way down the narrow aisle to the seats in the back of the plane.

At our stops in Iringa, Songea, and Njombe, black men, wearing khaki shorts and shirts, carried jerry cans of gas to refuel our plane. It took five hours to fly the 400 miles to Mbeya. I leaned over Linda in the window seat, trying to be the first to see our new mud huts in the hospital compound as I watched mountains, farms, and groups of thatched roof huts surrounded by tilled plots of land and vast countryside slide past the tiny window. We flew through a pass between mountain peaks, slipped past Mount Loleza, then over the Baptist Hospital before landing at our new mile-high African home.

As we walked down the narrow aluminum steps, Africans dressed in bright-colored cloth, animal skins, and beads greeted us. They sang a familiar tune with funny words — "*Yesu Kwetu ni Rafiki*" — which is "What a Friend We Have in Jesus" in Swahili. There were throngs of black people, but still no sign of "colored" people. Linda insisted there would be purple people and green people. I was convinced they would be multi-colored, like patches on a quilt.

Mother and Daddy had opened the curtain on our life in Africa. I could only wonder anxiously if this strange land would ever feel like *nyumbani* — home.

9 New Life, New Home *Maisha Mpya, Nyumbani Kwetu Mpya*
Tanzania 1960s

Daddy told us we would live on a mission hospital compound, as he and Mother would be working in the hospital. Linda and I were disappointed to find out it wasn't a compound of mud huts like those we'd seen on *Tarzan*.

Our first day in Mbeya, Steve fidgeted and chased geckos running along the window screens of the hospital waiting room. During our Dar es Salaam stop, he got a thorn in his arm while climbing into a sisal bush, reaching for a spiky thorn to make a spear to chase Jim. He shared the waiting room with an African boy his age. Without a language in common, Cigaretti and Steve pointed to items and taught each other the words in their respective languages.

In her weekly letter home, Mother despaired of the start to our new life:

> Our first day was a whirlwind. We toured the whole hospital before I got to see my new home. There's a little bit of furniture to help us get by until our crates come. I'm excited about the hospital but am drawn to begin making a home for my family. Our first night in Mbeya, a twelve-year-old boy came to the hospital. He had fallen from a tree and broken his arm.
>
> Gangrene had set in and he had to have his arm amputated at the shoulder. I held the arm while Dr. Ralph sawed it off. It had been so long since I worked surgery that I just didn't know if I could take it or not. What was I going to do when I held that arm? I got dizzy, but I didn't let anybody know. My first day was such a long one and then to end with this...

Cigaretti re-entered the waiting room, minus an arm, just a short stub wrapped in a bandage. Steve saw what happened when you went into that room with a sore arm and it was now his turn. His panic level flew as Daddy and Uncle Ralph smeared his arm with "monkey blood" — Betadine — to disinfect the area, and draped his hand to remove the thorn. Steve believed he would lose his arm as Cigaretti had.

A fence circled the two-story hospital built into the side of a hill. Our house was the last of a row of four mission houses. Our parents didn't allow us to cross the fence, but other than that we had free run of the twenty-acre compound. Sometimes we snuck across the fence to buy Bazooka bubble gum and *madazi* (fried bread) from the kiosk a short distance from the fence or our new yard worker, Donut, or our friend, Goodie Goodie, would slip across the fence to buy our bubble gum.

The other missionaries became our family, some closer than our blood family, worlds away, now a distant childhood memory kept alive by a voice on reel-to-reel tape, or letters and stories. Although we called the missionaries "aunt" and "uncle," in many ways they were like additional parents. The missionary kids were close friends, more like a cross between a cousin and a sibling. Like many families, there were differences and conflicts, but the bonds were tight.

We had all-out wars between the fifteen MKs, complete with armies and strategy. The blooms of the flame trees were ammunition, and the trees, bushes, and graves behind the hospital were our cover. Ammunition gatherers climbed to the top of the flame trees and cut stalks of blooms, like a bunch of tiny bananas. Each bloom contained a pouch of fluid that could be squeezed as a squirt gun. It stained our clothes, which we wore like a badge of honor.

Our large living room window, facing Mount Loleza, was like having a big picture that changed with the seasons. There were two seasons — rainy and dry. The rainy season was beautiful and green with a puzzle-pattern of cultivated fields transitioning to a quilt of browns as the dry season encroached. At the end of harvest, the nationals set their fields on fire, engulfing the mountain in smoke and flames. Towering jacaranda trees in the front yard dropped their fragrant, purple blooms, creating pools of blossoms mirroring the trees like puddles of purple. Their sweet scent mingled with the potent smell of the towering eucalyptus trees lining the driveway.

With another month before our crates arrived from America, settling into our new home didn't take long. Becoming accustomed to the new culture and surroundings took quite a while. Eventually, we settled into the rhythm of Africa and family life. Our life in Tanzania was full of change, fun, adventure, and family. The world around us was new and different but our home was known, warm, and secure, which smoothed the transition from new, and somewhat scary, to routine.

A heavily-traveled footpath outside the fence meandered to the nearby village on the outskirts of the town. Bars on the edge of the village sold *pombe* (home brew), providing the night sounds of singing and dancing followed by drums droning into the early morning hours. Routine night sounds became scary when Mother and Daddy weren't home.

Being near the equator ensures some constants: the sun rises and sets at seven, all year round. At an altitude of 5,800 feet, evening family life centered near the fireplace with games, conversation, stories, and reading. Linda and I were good readers, even at five, because we competed with each other to be the first to finish reading. We talked of our books and mingled the characters into our own private, make-believe world and language.

Although our life had interruptions and changes, we began to hit a routine. The sounds of family began early. At 5:00 a.m., our dreams merged into reality with the sounds of Mother and Daddy practicing Swahili in their room at the end of the hall. Monotonous repetition of Swahili phrases followed their teacher's voice on a reel-to-reel tape. Daddy would walk up the hill for chapel and medical rounds for the 120-bed hospital while Mother awakened us for breakfast.

She brought to our family the solid breakfasts she grew up with on her West Texas ranch: eggs, meat, and toast. On Monday, the usual breakfast did a poor job of covering the bitter quinine taste of the weekly malaria pill. When Daddy returned, he met with Bwana Benjamin on the front porch for language study while Mother, in her words, "straightened the house and dressed kids." Daddy's letter gave a glimpse of family life:

> Martha homeschools everyone except Chipper in divided morning and afternoon sessions. While teaching, she washes in an automatic machine with no functioning timer, meaning there's no automatic. She's starting some knitting, teaches quilting to the female tuberculosis patients, shops, hems curtains, writes letters, studies Swahili, and prepares for classes each evening. She manages to keep us all fed, clothed, educated, and happy most of the time.
>
> Steve rides bicycles with other missionary kids. He helps keep Chipper out of the twins' classroom and enjoys hospital rounds with me. He assists with teaching the twins at every chance he gets but his teasing can be a deterrent at times.
>
> Jim enjoys time alone with me, working on projects and planning an overnight camp on bicycles. He invariably has a frog, beetle, chameleon, or some weird arthropod to study and spends as much time as he can with his head in a stream or turning over rocks to see what crawls out. Linda reads well for two weeks of school, colors like a third grader, remains lady-like, and is careful to see that Cinda gets no attention which she does not get

exactly equaled. Martha had a big party for the twins' sixth birthday, telling them we just couldn't have two parties but there would be two cakes. Linda insisted on six candles on hers and only five on Cinda's.

Cinda likes to climb trees, bounce on the trampoline, and enjoys dressing up in a raincoat and football helmet or some equally unconventional garb.

Chipper thinks he is just as big as his brothers and sisters and is in the middle of everything. Given the twins had a birthday party, he is planning another tomorrow for himself. He left the house this morning saying he was going to find someone to bake him a cake — and he did. At three years old, he wants to go to school and thinks he does. He sits on the dining room table in the middle of everyone's studies and way.

Sometimes I think he can tell the twins apart and other times he seems to lump them together as one person. This morning I asked him if Cinda was awake. He told me, "One is."

Homeschooling was challenging and fun with my best friend, my twin, or Twinda, as the other kids often called both of us. Full of giggles, challenge, and competition. Every reading assignment was a race and every test a competition. As enjoyable as school was, it competed with many distractions: chameleons catching flies in the windows, African friends calling outside the fence, and mud swallows feeding their young in their mud nest on the window ledge.

While Linda and I worked on shaping and sounding out our one-inch cursive alphabet letters and reading aloud our schoolwork, Mother made lunch and bread, pasteurized milk, filtered water, and did housework. With seven active family members, she made many trips up the embankment to the clothesline.

The rainy season brought the challenge of drying clothes, but Mother savored the beautiful transition around her:

The rains are here. How it can rain! Every day it rains. The last two days there has not been one spot of sunshine. Annual rainfall is 35 inches per year; we have already had that much in the last six months. Rain is life here. There is much anticipation and excitement; the people depend on it for their crops. The mountains are an intricate patchwork of colors with rich emerald green valleys. The air is thick with the heavy, sweet smell of rain and the beautiful sounds of birds singing.

Daddy's entrance and his whistle greeting for Mother signaled the end of school even if we were in the middle of an assignment. "Daddio!" Linda and I hollered, racing to be first for a hug, spinning so he could hug us from behind. We thought that was just how daddies hug, but it was really to keep our muddy, inky, gluey, or otherwise project-y, dirty hands from soiling his white lab coat. Linda and I each climbed onto his feet and wrapped our arms around his legs for a giggly ride across the kitchen for his kiss for Mother.

"Ride please, ride please," Chipper pleaded. "On your shoulders, Daddy." He knew to duck his head to avoid the doorjamb, as Daddy swung Linda and me along on his legs from the kitchen to the dining room to make a big deal over our schoolwork.

After lunch, Daddy read to us: magazines, and books about nature, science, horses, dogs, psychology, and the behavior of animals. He has the mind of a scientist, the creativity of an artist, the problem-solving skills of a genius, the courage like no other creature on earth, and the playfulness of a puppy. The world of nature and conservation came alive with his stories.

Slapping the book closed, Daddy's indisputable D.M.A.M. — Don't Move a Muscle — signaled naptime on the living room floor, sprawling on his back with arms spread. Naptime, a much-protested routine we dreaded the first two decades of life and have coveted ever since. Usually Chipper lay between Daddy's feet with Steve, Jim, and I spread on each side, using Daddy's long arms as a pillow. Somehow, Linda always got her special spot in a hammock between the couch and its cloth backing, created when the couch upholstery was cut to stash toilet paper, shoes, and soap during crating. She secretly hid her Barbie, knitting, and a book so she could play while the rest of us had to nap. Not fair.

Afternoons were for all-out play. The whole hospital compound was ours; we played hard and we played long. The givens were we couldn't cross the fence and must get home for meals, naps, and before the sun set. The other MKs were our playmates but over time they came and went, some to boarding school, their families assigned to new locations, or went on furlough in America. My brothers and sister were the only playmates that didn't leave.

My constant playmate and best friend was Linda. We were each other's biggest competitor and strongest ally. Linda was the organized one; organizing our play and our fights, which I found annoying. If we had a dispute, we lay on the floor, feet to feet, while she counted to three to signal the beginning of the kick fight. After arguing over "do we start kicking on three or do we say three first then start kicking?" we played or fought the best two out of three to resolve our conflicts. Linda had us so organized I rarely remembered what the conflict was about in the first place. "I give" determined the loser of the match.

We handled many of our disputes with a ponytail pull. Each twin secured a grip on the other's ponytail and pulled on the count of three. Or was it *after* the count of three? We argued about that too. Our disputes didn't always resolve smoothly and, at times, Linda threw in the unfair threat, "OK. That's it. I'm not going to be your friend anymore." That was the worst thing that could happen. She got whatever she wanted when she threw in the "won't be your friend" card.

Our house was the focal point, or at least the starting point, for the play on the hill. The water faucet in the patch of dirt between the house and the fence provided endless hours of road and bridge building. Covered in mud, we kneeled among the intricate road system to smooth and sand bridges, making the surfaces as hard as the roads our Land Rovers travel; at least we thought so. Making our own sound effects, we maneuvered an assortment of store-bought miniature replicas and homemade vehicles of wire and tin.

Our dachshund, Frisky, was much loved and the only one who knew our secret twin language. I could reveal it but I promised not to. I don't want to get in another kick fight and I sure don't want the "I'm not your friend anymore" card played, even more so as an adult.

The gravel road circling our house descended steeply and roughly to the lower levels of the hospital compound. The MK gang — an assortment of Adams, Oliphint, Bethea, and Laffoon kids — lined up at the top of the gravel hill on any rolling stock we could find, from bicycles, skateboards, roller skates, or a push scooter, to a wagon. Frisky sat as a passenger in the doomed wagon tied to a bicycle while the neighbor's dogs, Happy and Smokey, stood ready, roped to one of the downhill riders. The wild, reckless ride down the heavily-pitted gravel road left behind carnage. Gravel-embedded, skinned elbows and knees were battle wounds and badges of honor; fodder for stories, bragging, and challenge for the next day's ride.

Channels of open sewage, the septic system for the Baptist Tuberculosis Hospital, provided soft green grass and a cool place to lie on our backs to imagine shapes in the clouds and to dream. The channels drew frogs, a variety of creatures, and kids. Daddy didn't like us playing there because of the health concerns of contact with the sewage, but where else could you catch frogs and jump water-filled ditches? Our solution seemed reasonable — try to jump all the way across the stream and not fall in. When we failed, we ran home to take the hottest bath possible and didn't tell him.

Mother was always busy. I often heard her tell Daddy she had too much to do. As long as our room was clean, we could play, but we loved to help her knead dough for bread, butcher beef, sift flour, and chase the headless chickens for the boiling pot after Mother chopped their heads off. One day

Linda and I asked her if she would come to play with us.

"Sure, we can play postman," she agreed. She folded and ironed clothes from the mounds in the laundry baskets. "Deliver this parcel to Steve's post box please, Cinda," she encouraged. "Postman Linda, please put this in Jim's."

Postman was interspersed with the "telephone game" where Linda and I had the assignment to track down Steve and Jim to tell them to clean their room.

Daddy always found time to teach and play. We dissected water bugs, lizards, and frogs. He knew the names of all the inside parts and taught us how they worked. He asked us questions that I know he knew the answer to, but it made me feel like I was an expert and that I mattered.

The real world around us was an adventure and so was our imaginary world. A banana tree grove served as a fort, a clinic, and a house. We watched the stalks of bananas grow and ripen around us. We made clothing, plates, and bowls from the bark stripped from the trees. Cut eucalyptus branches made intricate tunnels; their crushed leaves made a heady concoction for homemade malaria medication and aspirin.

Our toys were adapted or imagined from the world around us. We made bows, arrows, spears, clubs, slingshots, and dolls from sticks, gourds, and scraps of things we found. Our African friends mixed easily with our MK friends, play that crossed language and cultural barriers, and prepared us well for the future.

After supper, Mother prepared for the next day's homeschool while Daddy helped with baths before his indisputable and authoritarian Boys Bed Time and Girls Bed Time wound things down an hour later. The day ended as it began, with the sounds of Mother's and Daddy's Swahili practice merging with our dreams.

10 Challenges and Sacrifice *Migogoro na Sadaka*
Tanzania 1960s

"Can I make Daddy a cake for his birthday?" I asked Mother. I'd never made one before but she turned the kitchen over to me while she took a nap. I think she had had a hard day. It was usually Linda who liked to do girl things, wear dresses, and play with dolls. I was always running with the boys, no shirt, wearing a slingshot, but I loved being with, and delighting, Daddy. I puzzled over the recipe and yelled down the hallway, "Mother, d'you use brown sugar or regular sugar? Is the big 'T' a teaspoon or a tablespoon? Why do I have to sift the flour and not the sugar?" As I shook the weevils, burlap twine, and bugs out of the sifter, I was puzzled because I didn't have to sift the ants out of the sugar.

Mother gave no response. I decided I would just have to go to her room since she couldn't hear me.

"Mother, why won't you answer my questions?"

"I've changed my name."

"What's your new name?"

"I'm not telling anyone."

"Is it... Nancy?"

"No."

"Is it Jane?"

"No."

Tiring of my guesses, Mother answered my question and I, unable to guess her name, returned to my cake making. I searched the cabinet for the last ingredient listed in the recipe — vanilla. Though I was unsuccessful at guessing Mother's new name, I yelled down the hall anyway, "Mother, what does vanilla look like?"

I detected a tone of annoyance in her response. "It starts with a 'V.'"

I pondered as I rummaged through the cabinet. "Hmm, a 'V.' I know I can find a 'V,' oh there... a 'V.'"

I didn't know what vanilla looked like but I knew I liked the taste so I added a quarter of a cup instead of a teaspoon. I puzzled as the cake baked. I didn't remember a birthday cake ever smelling like that.

Daddy let me cut his chocolate birthday cake and I passed out the slices. There was an awkward silence as our anticipated first taste was bitter beyond bitter. Steve and Jim didn't want to eat their piece, but they had to. They knew not to complain because the house rule was if anyone complained about the food they had to do the dishes.

Vinegar also starts with the letter 'V.' Daddy loved his vinegar chocolate cake and made me feel like I was a princess for making it for him.

*****

Mother and Daddy wrote letters home on a typewriter, using carbon paper to send them to both sets of parents.

> I just inherited myself the job of writing, at least for this week. Though the job is pleasant, it must take a low place under the stack of "must-dos." An explanation as to the lateness and the authorship of this writing is not only in order, but demanded by Martha. She had a nice letter, with carbon copies, written and dated July 16, 1966. My none-too-well-chosen comments impelled her not to mail it and to cede the honors to me. Eleven years of marriage still leaves me with great strides in husbandship.

Mother and Daddy's ways of describing their lives differ starkly. Mother is a storyteller; her letters were entertaining, light, fun, and meandering. Daddy's letters were detailed, factually correct, and often emotionally understated with a dry thread of humor. Often void of raw emotion, their letters left their parents to imagine the feelings of homesickness, the unknowns, and fears of raising a family in the African bush. Mother's voice comes across loud and clear as she wrote:

> I made the mistake of letting John read the last letter I wrote to you. He said it was poorly written and had many misspelled words so I told him to write it himself. That's why your letter is two weeks late. As he tried to get it written, he began to think my letter wasn't so bad after all.
>
> I teach school and run the Adams's "hotel" and am trained to do neither. My hotel problem is I don't have staff. This month, I've used 35 pounds of flour and 30 pounds of sugar, more than I would use in one year in the States.
>
> I've provided lodging and made 25 meals from scratch for guests. Here, that means making things you would buy in America such as bread, mayonnaise, sauces, and cakes without mixes. We have volunteers and employees of the Baptist Foreign Mission Board and missionaries and friends from other missions and aid organizations that

come to shop and to get medical care.

It's a wonderful opportunity to get to know different people, their work, and their background, but the work is hard without my usual conveniences. I would prefer to be a mother, wife, and do the Lord's work after properly doing those two jobs.

Missionaries are big givers and many struggle with the balance of the unending needs of ministry and the needs of family. My respect for them and the sacrifices they make is huge and I honor them although, for some families, the cup may be empty when the parents get home. Mother and Daddy worked hard in their ministry, but their cup was rarely empty and the sipping was oh, so sweet. Mother's letter, describing a visitor, gave a glimpse of her humor and practicality:

It's always interesting when we have Africans in our home; we also call them Locals or Nationals. It makes us appreciate our heritage and see the gulf between the races. An English-speaking preacher stayed with us last week. I showed him the toilet and asked if he knew how to use it. He said, "Yes, I have seen such a thing when I was in Nairobi." Afterwards, he asked me where he could find the *choo*, Swahili for latrine. I just hadn't got the message across. John had to take over where I failed.

Last Saturday, drums woke me at 4 a.m. It turns out *Bwana Mkubwa*, or Chief, from America is coming for a visit. Senator Robert Kennedy and his wife, Ethel, arrived with six planes of reporters and cameramen. The locals wore their best for the occasion, which meant wearing western clothes and babies wearing diapers. I wore my best dress, hose, and heels. Last week I attended an Asian wedding and got my hands painted with henna, a reddish brown dye. The intricate ink lacework hadn't faded even after all the dishes I'd washed, so I wore gloves to cover my painted hands.

Since I can't drive a Land Rover in high heels, I put my housecoat over my dress, took off my gloves, and wore my house shoes. On arrival at the airport, I took off my housecoat, put on my heels and white gloves, and descended as if I had arrived in Daddy's Cadillac. The Kennedys toured the hospital and gave Kennedy half-dollar coins to the kids. I don't think they understand the coin has a portrait of John Kennedy, Robert's brother, who was assassinated as president before we left America. We'll study about it in homeschool, but for now the kids are fascinated with the coins and the excitement.

Ethel was a surprise to me with her old, faded dress and worn shoes. She looked as if she had just done a day's wash for her nine children. Who am I to judge, arriving in my worn-out, multi-colored striped housecoat and house shoes?

The curtains had opened on our life in Africa and Mother's letters gave a treasured look behind those curtains, giving insight into my parents' most heartfelt struggles, challenges, and joys.

11 Flashes From the Past *Kumbukumbu Kutoka Nyuma*
Uganda 2004

Mother and Daddy's legacy continues through the generations. They taught us to connect, respect, and love Africa — its people, customs, and foods — as well as to connect, respect, and love the America we came from. Somehow, we even missed and longed for the country we only dimly remembered.

Mother made a happy home for our family, regardless of the conditions, creating a warm, safe place, as she wove a thread of America into our lives in the middle of remote Tanzania. She is a fierce defender of her family or, as she would say, "her chickens." She is warm and tender and can wrap you up in a hug that gives you the confidence to face anything.

I look at my sis, in her role as a mother, and see these same traits. They both focus on building, teaching, nurturing, and loving their kids as they go through their life journeys. As adults, looking at our childhood, I see that mother's faith and fervent prayer supported us, just as I see Linda doing for her "chickens."

Daddy is rugged, strong, and independent. Danger and risks are more of a green light or a start gun than a caution in his world. His big, rugged hands and strong arms could sling two full jerry cans to the Land Rover roof rack, and he could wrestle all five attacking kids at once on the living room floor. He could pull the rubber off a Land Rover tire rim and repair it on a dusty roadside. His big, rough fingers, with grease under the closely cropped nails, looked foreign and out of place on the keys of the piano as he played scales, helping Linda and me with our piano lessons. Although Daddy is a creative problem solver with an inquisitive mind and a love for nature, he is also opinionated and pushes back against rules, laws, and norms. From Daddy we learned to question or challenge the accepted and to relish the edges, not the center stripe, of life's journey.

He loved to get our family out into the richness of rural Africa and brought laughter, play, adventure, and a hint of danger — sometimes more than a hint. From him we developed the confidence and willingness to take risks and the tendency never to back down from a battle. From Mother we got a tiny thread of caution and the concept that maybe some risks, endeavors, and battles shouldn't be undertaken.

Mother was more open about her faith; Daddy's clearly visible without a word. Their faith and the desire to bring hope to Africa were a driving force that propelled them both toward their goal, bringing along the five of us for a life of adventure.

Their love and compassion for the people crossed language and culture barriers. The way they lived their lives and the values they taught, with messages stronger than words, imprinted unique heartprints that would shape our lives for the future and the generations that follow.

*****

"Yaaawww… I think it's time to call it a night for our first evening in Kaabong," Stanley yawns and stretches.

"I need a flashlight now to retrieve Kuku," Linda tells us. "I usually get the rooster before sunset so I can see him." She retrieves him from the hedge, where he appears to be baffled by the late hour. He flaps his wings and squawks as Linda grabs him by his feet and flips him upside down, making him silent and compliant as she carries him to his woven stick house, built four feet off the ground for protection from snakes.

Stanley and I follow Ben as he leads the way, swinging a kerosene lantern up the rock trail through the garden and the bougainvillea-covered archway to our room. This simple, converted storage room, next to the adjoining missionary house, is to be home for Stanley and me for a week.

"You can use the pail in the shower and fill it from the solar heated tank," Ben points. He pours the water into a pail and hoists it with a rope on a pulley.

"This little lever releases a gentle flow of water for a lukewarm shower."

"Luxury!" I grin.

"Oh, and don't forget to check your bed for scorpions and snakes," he dismisses himself matter-of-factly as he heads down the hill to his own room. I remember Mother warning me to do the same many decades ago.

Our simple little room has everything a person needs, just different. The bedside lamp has a switch but no electricity. Conditioned to a world where a flip of the switch wipes away darkness, I flip the switch for the fifth time that evening and stand foolishly yet again in the darkness. As with the rooms on the lower property, the doors are massive and secured with heavy sliding bolts from the inside or the outside.

The lantern bathes our small room in a mellow gold light as I wait for Stanley to finish his shower. Muttering to himself, he clumsily maneuvers through his bathroom routine while holding a flashlight in one hand. It's a simple bathroom with a sink, commode, and a shower with a rope bucket. No shelf to prop a flashlight or toiletries.

In the glow of the lantern, with the insomnia of jet lag, my mind whirls over treasured memories of previous trips to Africa. We visited the Witte family a few years previously in their Matapato home, near the village of Maili Tisa in Kenya. Their home was an oasis in the shadow of the great Mount Kilimanjaro. I relish the memory of walking with Linda and the kids to Maasai *bomas* (mud homes) to give immunizations and to check on her patients.

Stanley and I went with her once to deliver a baby. Outside the *boma*, a woman was mixing cow dung, dirt, and termite hill soil to make plaster to repair her home. It was comical seeing her stick her elbow out for Stanley to shake instead of extending her mucky hand.

Delivering the baby in the dark, smoke-filled room was an unforgettable experience. A fire in the middle of the floor provided the only bit of light, and a tiny hole in the roof gave minimal ventilation.

My watery eyes had burned in the thick smoke as they fought to adjust to the darkness. I took turns with Jessica, holding a flashlight as Linda kneeled on the edge of the bed, a piece of cowskin slung between upright sticks. The laboring woman had a cloth cinched around her chest. Linda, staying focused on her task, answered my unspoken question. "To make sure the baby descends downwards and comes out where it's supposed to instead of out of her mouth. You didn't know that? It's worked every time for them — you can't argue with a 100 percent success rate!"

Linda later explained she didn't try to educate past this myth because it did no harm; choosing instead to put her efforts into an almost hopeless battle against more harmful cultural practices. Already weakened by a diet restricted to tea for the last month, the mother had eaten heavily salted porridge so she would feel full, throw up, and not eat. They believe this prevents the baby from getting too big to pass through the birth canal and, of course, cesarean section isn't an option. Anemia, parasites, and chronic malaria compound the problem; the mother-to-be having a cloth tied around her chest was the least of Linda's concerns.

"We sure don't need a baby coming out of her mouth," Linda told us.

She kneeled in a pool of birth fluids on the cowskin bed as she worked through a long delivery caused by scar tissue from circumcision. My muscles ached from stooping and my eyes wept from the thick smoke. Each bleat of the baby goats, behind the stick barrier next to my shoulder, startled me out of my numb fatigue, making me think the baby had arrived.

Finally, the head began to crown in the dim light. I held my breath as the baby's head appeared and Linda angled the first shoulder out. The baby didn't take a breath. Linda positioned the slippery newborn in her arms, preparing to give it breaths, but the mother-in-law yanked the child out of her hands. Spitting in the baby's face, she handed him to the grandmother to spit, before handing him back to Linda.

With an "OK," Linda quickly covered the baby's mouth and nose with her mouth and began to give him breaths. Only after he loudly announced his arrival did I take a breath myself. Linda tied the umbilical cord in two places and cut between the ties, just as we had both learned in nursing school: "tie, tie, and cut."

The women held the baby by its feet and passed him clockwise several times around the center pole of the *boma* as other shrill calls pierced the darkness, signaling the baby's birth. Soon, women began crowding into the smoke-filled home as they celebrated with songs and rituals passed down through the ages.

Thank goodness the story ended well. The baby lived and the women thought their actions saved it. The father was so proud to have a son that he gave Linda a female goat. Linda told him, "Good, my parents are coming next week and we will have goat for Christmas dinner."

"Oh no, you can't eat this goat!" the father exclaimed. "A gift represents the relationship between the giver and the one who receives." The goat's reproduction represents the flourishing of the relationship; therefore, they call each other *Mbuzi*, which is Swahili for goat. Similarly, Byron and an *mzee* (old man) call each other *Fimbo* because they gave each other a stick for a gift.

It was a trip full of family and connecting with the Africa around us. The villagers in the *boma* next door invited us to a circumcision ceremony for two twelve-year-old boys. Three *wazee* (old men) greeted us from a log bench as we approached the entrance to the thorn enclosure to the village. I bowed my head in a respectful greeting, as is their culture. Each of the old men spat in my face. As I wiped the drool off, Linda stifled her laugh and warned Stanley and me, "Hold steady, it's OK." She later told me they knew I had no children so that was their blessing so I would be fertile. Thank you for that.

During the ceremony, Stanley hung out with the *wazee* as they went through the rituals of tapping a cow's jugular for blood to drink and starting a fire with sticks. I would have warned him had I seen the *mzee* hand him the mug of home brew. The women, chewing sugar cane, spit the juices into a pot, where it ferments to a potent brew. Stanley learned on his own to use his teeth to strain the brew but I chose to wait to tell him how they made it.

On a game drive during a later trip, we were charged by an elephant and pursued by lions when I pushed the boundaries and drove too close, just as I had seen my father do years before. That evening, as Stanley and I enjoyed dinner and the romantic ambiance of a luxurious tented camp, I noticed a couple kept watching and whispering about us. Well, come on, sure we were sneaking in a few kisses and a squeeze or two but nothing out of line. I later described the couple to Linda. With shock, she exclaimed they were missionary co-workers. Not knowing she had a twin, they had to have assumed Linda was at the camp with a handsome man who wasn't her husband. Take that, Sis, that's a ponytail pull.

After a full week of family fun with warthog fajitas for Christmas dinner, fried grasshoppers for Daddy's birthday, hiking, and game runs, we had traveled two days to Chipper and Steve's home in Uganda to avoid the riots during Kenya's elections. The regime's opposition threatened they would win — if not in the polls, in the streets.

Although I was content to hang out with family in Kampala, I looked for opportunities to show Stanley a little more of the land I love. We found a colorful brochure inviting us to "See the birds and wildlife as you raft along the great White Nile River... Watch the locals washing their laundry on the banks as you drift by... " I signed us up for some sightseeing and our Nile adventure began.

The New Zealand river guide handed us a four-page liability release and joked, "Basically it says we can do anything we want to you, including kill you, and you can't sue us." We joined one of two rafts full of helmeted youths as we pushed out into calm water just below Bujagali Falls where the White Nile leaves Lake Victoria at Jinja. The vastness of the Nile is hard to describe. Its flow of 23,000 to 53,000 cubic feet per second is four to five times that of the Colorado River as it passes through the Grand Canyon.

We drifted as we received our safety instruction. The guide claimed that crocodiles and hippos were only a rare sight, but told us to stay with the raft if we fell out because the ones that were left were famished and liked to hang out in the calmer water along the banks. During Idi Amin's reign in Uganda, while I was at high school in Kenya, the Nile was said to be red where crocodiles thrived on the discarded bodies. It was hard to tell when the New Zealand guides were serious and when they were joking.

All joking was gone as I heard the roar of the first rapids ahead. Hanging onto the bucking raft, I saw Stanley, in the front, swept out by a wall of water.

"Stanley, hang on!" I hollered, as if it would make a difference. As my face finally cleared the spray, I saw him swimming hard as one of the kayaks paddled toward him to give him a ride back to the raft.

"Just a wee class four," the guide explained unsympathetically.

Our raft capsized on a category five rapid, spilling all nine of us, including the guide. A long, slow drift allowed us time to gather ourselves from the intensity of these rapids and gave us a chance to swim around the raft to cool off.

We carried our raft through the banana trees along the bank to circumvent a class six — better known as a waterfall. The guide rolled out some strong-accented instructions to prepare us for the "hell ahead." With the sound of thunder approaching, I braced my legs, pushing my toes into the crevice between the rubber raft floor and sides. As the roar intensified, I saw the water's edge drop from the horizon, leaving only a visible spray. The raft dropped and I felt as if the breath had been knocked from my chest as I saw Stanley disappear in a wall of water as I plunged in behind him.

With every muscle locked down and my feet shoved into the creases of the rubber, there was nothing I could do to fight the tremendous forces yanking me out of the raft. I felt myself sucked to the bottom of the river, tumbled along the sand, and knocked against boulders. I lost my paddle as the magnificent forces slung me, as if on an underwater rollercoaster. For the fourth time in my life, I felt my life was about to come to a watery end. I felt sad for Stanley because I knew it would be hard for him to return home without me.

Stanley and the other paddlers exited the wall of water minus the river guide and me. Stanley hung on and watched for what seemed to him to be forever, before I finally surfaced. Ignoring all the safety warnings about crocodiles and hippos, I swam for shore as hard and fast as I could. We survived the scenic river excursion, but came away with vastly different perspectives — Stanley looking forward to the next raft trip and I vowing never to get in a raft again.

We often relish the memories, laughing at ourselves because they only seem to have added fuel to the drive for greater challenges. There is excitement on the edge of extreme.

Stanley reaches over to turn out the lantern. "Babe, it seems every time I've followed you to Africa you've tried to get me killed."

"Let's just do family this time," I whisper, sleepily.

I love the deep-down familiarity of Africa and savor the closeness, warmth, security, and familiarity of my man spooned next to me. *I hope I didn't miss any scorpions*, I think, after what feels like a long day. Drifting off to sleep to the sounds of drums, laughter, and drunken singing, all seems well.

12 Hints of America *Dalili za Amerika*
Tanzania 1960s

Our crates completed their three-month journey from Seminole, Texas and lay anchored next to bobbing, windblown dhows in Dar es Salaam, Arabic for Harbor of Peace, Tanzania's capital and port on the Indian Ocean. Although the capital later moved to Dodoma, Dar es Salaam is still the center of trade where the modern merges with the old, a spicy mix of ancient Arabic culture and the modern trappings of a busy portal city. Daddy had to work through the logistics and red tape for customs clearance before the crates could begin their truck journey to our home in Mbeya.

Mother described the trip:

> When we got word our crates were at the dock, we planned to fly to the city, but John and Dr. Bethea were in surgery and didn't seem motivated to rush to make the milk-run flight. Against the experienced missionaries' advice, we chose the two-day, 500-mile overland route in the hospital Land Rover. We slept part of the night in the vehicle at Iringa, waiting for the only fuel station to open. A man cranked a long pole back and forth to fill a glass container on a tall pedestal, similar to the fuel stations in America in the '20s.

Daddy's letter home gave a glimpse of the sights and sounds along the way:

> Warned of the risks of night travel on the Iringa-Morogoro stretch through the Selous Game Preserve, we were glad to take a break from the rough dirt roads and wait for morning at Iringa. We paused occasionally to observe elephant, giraffe, topi, baboon, and myriads of tropical birds. We learned much and enjoyed visiting and practicing our elementary Swahili with people we picked up along the way.
>
> Our new travelers weren't used to riding inside a vehicle. They yelled at their friends walking on the road or in the fields, not realizing the sound would not carry through the closed windows. These people haven't

experienced riding in a vehicle or seeing glass windows. The windows in their huts are open holes, either draped by a cloth or shuttered with pieces of wood. Although it is hot and the Land Rover doesn't have air conditioning, we usually keep the windows closed to keep the vehicle pressurized to prevent the dust from billowing in.

At port, I watched as a crane moved each of our crates onto a barge. When it picked up our only barrel, it stashed it out of sight. I think the crane operator got the idea I wasn't happy with what he appeared to have in mind. A labor strike and the threat of a tropical storm delayed, more than the usual sluggish African timeline, the transition of our crates and barrel to the barge. Tonight we pray that the Harbor of Peace will be peaceful for the next day and a half. Our possessions sit lowest of the group, tied outermost of three, and the barge is disturbingly low for storm waves. So it goes with worldly possessions — what a detriment to missions.

Daddy had his fill of the hassles so he found his things, got down in the barge, and started unloading them himself against the loud protests of custom officials. This country worked on bribes and Daddy refused to participate, which created many conflicts. Long arguments, in such a steamy place, made every little step a huge, miserable hassle. Eventually the crates cleared customs and began their truck journey to Mbeya.

Mother drove the hospital Land Rover on the return trip while Daddy drove a 1960, short-wheelbase, four-wheel drive Land Rover he bought in Dar es Salaam. At the game park, we all joined Mother in the hospital vehicle, riding on top of the luggage rack. We saw elephant, hippo, wildebeest, zebra, giraffe, and buffalo. Daddy kept telling Mother to get closer to a herd of elephants. She held her breath and edged toward them.

The Land Rover lurched and the wheels spun in the deep mud. Despite all her efforts with four-wheel drive and a high-lift jack, there we sat, elephants all around us, and Mother had us good and stuck. Daddy fussed at her. She looked afraid, as if she might cry. Daddy asked if she wanted to stay there or walk back with him to get the other vehicle. She chose the car, having seen all the animals he would have to walk past. Three weeks previously, a couple of teachers had stalled near there. As they walked out, the elephants charged and killed one of them.

*****

Having lived out of suitcases for a month and a half, the arrival of our crates brought the scents of America, the warm feeling of the familiar, and my

56

black monkey with the yellow banana stashed in the washing machine. It also brought the sounds of Mother playing hymns on the piano and the click clack of the typewriter she used to write letters to home. Only someone who has lived away from home fully understands comfort scents and sounds.

Linda and I carried our sorely missed dolls everywhere we went. Linda's had long, blonde hair and mine black, until Chipper decided they needed haircuts. Chipper's adjustment to Africa and his clinginess improved when he eventually realized his familiar pajamas, stuffed toys, miniature cars, and his tippy cup were there to stay.

Despite the equatorial heat and lack of decorations in town, Mother intended to make Christmas special:

> We have to make our Christmas; not a single store in Mbeya has decoration for there are no Christian business owners and they don't care enough to decorate for the few Christians living here. Our church put on a program attended by Hindus, Muslims, Pagans, Catholics, and Protestants. The people of other faiths find our Christmas traditions intriguing because they also have special days for their gods' birthdays. We invite many people into our homes so they can see our religious traditions, which gives us a good starting point to tell about the birth of Christ, His life, and the hope He brings to the world.

> The only Christmas event in town was the arrival of Father Christmas at the British Mbeya club. He arrived in a Land Rover, having consumed too much Christmas cheer and wearing a dirty, faded, red Santa suit. When it was Chipper's turn, he crawled up onto Santa's lap looking miserable. Returning with his toy he complained, "Mother, Santa Claus needs to brush his teeth."

In the warmest time of year, the dry season, seven homemade stockings hung over the fireplace and the window displayed painted snow scenes, holly, and sleighs. A Christmas tree centered the great picture window, decorated with strings of popcorn and handmade decorations. The ants quickly ate the popcorn off the tree but that didn't dampen the Christmas spirit. Our house smelled of baking, with homemade divinity, cakes, and cookies. Mother had hoarded sugar and flour for months to be sure there was enough for Christmas.

Christmas Eve, we kids slept in the living room by the tree Daddy cut in the forest. We made cookies for Santa and put them with a glass of milk by the fireplace. Steve and Jim tied a string from their toes to the bells on the tree, copying a picture in an American magazine. I fought hard to stay awake listening for Santa's sleigh. Santa was stealthy. He made away with the cookies and milk without awakening us.

Christmas morning, with its excited chaos, arrived long before the sun. We had homemade gifts and one present from Santa, who shopped in America long ago to be sure there were enough Santa gifts in the crates for four years. Along with our gifts, we opened cards made from folded construction paper or recycled by marking through the names from last year's cards.

Christmas dinner was as traditional as possible in rural Tanzania. Making everything from scratch made the kitchen the bustling center of activity and delicious smells. Turkey was a luxury that didn't make it to our Christmas dinner that year but Uncle Keith gave us a zebra roast. Daddy never hunted but his "eat what is served" rule trumped his repulsion of eating game meat when missionaries shared. Daddy's subtle opinion on hunting surfaced in one of his letters:

> My missionary associates seem unquenchably and relentlessly impelled to slaughter the beauty and wealth of East Africa then gloat over their gory remains or fragments thereof. Their primary stated reason is they must kill for table meat. A filet mignon, fresh as each morning's kill, sells for two shillings, or 30 cents a pound. They must spend thousands of dollars each year adding economic pressure to the limited economy of this developing nation aimed against an already too poorly protected resource.

When the missionaries exchanged gifts, Daddy received a hunting license and Mother an ivory bracelet from a "slaughtered" elephant. Humor was alive and well among the missionary families. Uncle Keith was probably the instigator of that prank; every time he told the story he would laugh out loud. I loved his stories, pranks, snickers, and deep belly laughs.

*****

Hearing drums and bells we ran outside to find three Christmas trees swaying and dancing in our driveway. Three men, each inside a tree tied to their bodies, wore bells on their legs and played drums as they moved around the yard. We danced, stomped our feet, and swayed to the beat with them. As the trees surrounded me, I felt their hands on my body, reaching into my pockets.

Daddy stormed out of the house when he saw they were messing with his kids and were stealing our stuff as they danced. Daddy tore into the trees. Leaves flew and voices bellowed. It was Daddy against three men and the trees were taking a battering.

"Martha, bring the bat!" Daddy yelled.

Mother jumped up and down screaming, "Oh, John, John! Oh, John!" She sent Steve to get Uncle Keith as she ran into the house to find the bat.

The tattered trees wobbled, stumbled, and drooped before Daddy got his hands on the bat. Steve returned with Uncle Keith as the men gathered the tatters of their branches and their possessions. Their cleanup took a while because Daddy insisted they not leave even one leaf on his property.

Uncle Keith delighted in retelling this Christmas story, describing Daddy's reaction when the men asked to borrow his wheelbarrow to haul their leaves away, their request clearly denied.

We celebrated big and small holidays in our home; even the tooth fairy knew the way to Mbeya. Mother said we couldn't start first grade until we lost our first tooth. I was so excited to be the first to lose one, but felt badly for Linda because she didn't want me to start school without her. Linda's tooth was loose and she kept wiggling it, but it wouldn't come out. I heard you could tie a loose tooth to a doorknob and slam the door, but she didn't want me to help her. She threw a fit so Daddy taped my tooth back in until hers came out.

We both put our teeth under our pillow and found a bar of Bit-O-Honey in its place the next morning. Mother crated Bit-O-Honey, Cracker Jacks, and Sugar Daddies for these occasions. They tasted of nail polish that spilled into the candy on its trip in the crates, but it still tasted like America. The following week we got to start the first grade.

One may wonder how I knew about the tooth fairy's stash. One day, when Daddy was at work and Mother had gone shopping, Linda and I snuck into their room to peek into the forbidden closet where the tooth fairy and Santa stashed their goods. The bedroom ceilings were high; I thought they were about twenty feet high. Shelves towered upwards to a set of large closets with hinged doors. We opened the closet door and I climbed up each of the shelves while Linda stood on a chair to support me. With my knees on the top shelf, I leaned out to reach the door of the cabinets topping the closets.

Linda climbed a couple of shelves to push on my rear as I climbed out, around the base of the cabinet, and back into the cubby hole on top of the world to peek at the treasures. Climbing up was a challenge, climbing down almost a disaster. With Linda pushing my rear to keep me from falling, we both got the giggles, which rendered us useless, making us almost pee in our pants.

Linda often led us into trouble; well, I guess we bumped each other into trouble if I am perfectly honest.

13 Celebratory Days *Maadhimisho*
Tanzania 1960s

In a land with two seasons, wet and dry, the inside of our home had four. Mother painted new scenes on the windows and changed the decorations: orange candles in the fall, yellow in the spring, red and green in December, and red, white, and blue in the summer. She gave us reading assignments and projects in homeschool with American holiday themes. Each season brought new, handmade table pieces, costumes, and decorations. For Thanksgiving, we made a turkey centerpiece for the kitchen table using brightly colored tropical bird feathers for turkey tail feathers. Even the most American of holidays still had a twist of Africa. Mother described our first Fourth of July:

> Today is the big day on the hill; we are entertaining 90, coming from a radius of hundreds of miles. John was so kind to volunteer my service in station meeting last week. I wasn't there to say, "Now, John, do you know what it means to make ice cream for 90 people?" There isn't enough milk and cream in all of Mbeya. We will have games, zebra burgers, hot dogs, lemonade, and will be shivering as we eat ice cream. I never understood how American I really am until writing this.
>
> In the middle of party preparations, Bob Laffoon, the new doctor, came running into our house all out of breath, saying, "I've got a woman about to deliver a baby in the car and the starter is jammed. Take me back and let's bring her in your car to the hospital."
>
> We careened along a trail through the banana trees, coffee bean trees, and bush. When we got there, the people had carried her back into the hut. I would have delivered her right there, but Bob thought she should go to the hospital. The stalled car was right in the path, so I had to put the Land Rover into four-wheel drive and go over the banana trees. I had some trouble with this. The only time I have used four-wheel drive was when I got the Land Rover stuck while watching the elephants in the game park. After a crazy, bumpy ride, we got her to the

hospital and delivered her baby.

As we grew up, celebration of American Independence Day transitioned from a fun day with homemade ice cream to a meaningful celebration as the values of freedom contrasted with the world around us. The African holidays, celebrations, and traditions seemed strange, but there were similarities to our American holidays.

Soon after, along came Saba Saba Day. *Saba* means seven in Swahili. Saba Saba Day, the seventh day of the seventh month, celebrates the founding of the Tanganyika African National Union, TANU, on July 7, 1954 which later led to independence in 1961. Tanganyika became Tanzania in 1964 when it merged with the island of Zanzibar. Saba Saba Day was the most celebrated national holiday. We celebrated holidays without realizing the full meanings of the original celebration, just as conflicts fester long after the meaning of the original conflict is lost. Like the other missionaries and the Mbeya community around us, we celebrated Saba Saba Day thinking it was Tanzania's Independence Day. Mother wrote:

> Drums and singing awoke me and frenzied on into the dawn. The crowds were thick and all was so new and strange for us at the celebration. It was a scorching day as the people danced and drank. The ground shook and the dust rose as they danced in rhythm with rattles in their hands and cans with rocks tied to their legs. They wore all kinds of clothes — baboon skins, beads, western clothes, and even nothing.
>
> Chipper fell asleep in my arms, which disturbed the nationals because they thought I should carry him on my back like their women do. There must have been a hundred men, women, and girls who stopped me to offer their help, even offering to give me a cloth.
>
> When we left, people were stumbling or had passed out from drinking *pombe*. One man frightened Cinda when he asked her to marry him. She was afraid we would take him up on his offer. This is unheard of when they are sober.
>
> At station meeting, we discussed Saba Saba Day and found everyone there had his pocket picked during the celebration. John decided that next year he would put tracts explaining the gospel in his pockets.

Saba Saba Day was a scary day for me. The people, especially the men, dressed strangely, looked mean, and acted weird. The local kids didn't celebrate. Our friend, Goodie Goodie, couldn't even explain what the celebration was about. At Halloween, Goodie Goodie was clueless when I asked him what costume he would wear, as the locals didn't celebrate it.

The three MKs from Tukuyu joined us for a Halloween party. The missionary aunts and uncles all pitched in, making homemade orange bread, and green punch, which bubbled and smoked with dry ice.

Uncle Keith draped a black cloth over his head and told fortunes with his hands wrapped around the blue glass ball Mother used as a coffee table decoration. The fortunes all ended with a specific description of the tree and branch we kids could find a chameleon, which helped to move the line along as we scrambled to find it. Since we didn't have apples, we bobbed for mangos. Maybe apples require a freeze because we didn't see any after leaving Texas.

We were proud of the costumes we made, with Mother supervising our efforts. Linda became a girl pirate by cutting a pair of Jim's jeans off at the knees, wearing a striped blouse, long beads, bracelets, and earrings made from gold construction paper. As an Indian princess, I wore a shift dress made of unbleached cloth left over from making our curtains. I put a red feather in my headband, tied my pigtails with red ribbon, and strapped a doll on my back with a red scarf; a rare occasion for Linda to be dressed as the tomboy while I looked so like a girl.

Chipper chose to be a clown with a tall cap made from construction paper, a Kleenex ball on the tip, and lipstick on his nose, cheeks, and lips. Jim was a scarecrow, using yellow paper for straw hair, an old straw hat, patches on his clothes, and a painted red nose, while Steve decided he wanted to go as a doctor with a scrub gown, cap, and mask from the hospital. He carried a long knife because he said he was a "mad doctor." I think perhaps he got the "mad doctor" idea from spending so much time at clinics with Daddy.

14 Family Routine *Siku kwa Siku*
Tanzania 1960s

I gripped the handlebars as Daddy rode the tandem bicycle, allegedly built for two, along the gravel road to the hospital. He sat on the front seat with Linda balanced on the handle bars, Steve on the rear seat, and Chipper perched on the rear handlebars, his legs wrapped around Daddy. Jim and I balanced sideways on the crossbars with our legs pointing to opposites sides of the bike. With six riders, we topped the gravel road and entered through the hospital's glass front doors. It felt like we were going a hundred miles an hour as we sped past the pharmacy, operating room, and down the stretcher ramp to make the sharp turn to the next long hallway.

The smell of methylated spirits and the autoclave mingled with the cheers of the patients as we whizzed by. We hoped we wouldn't run into the head missionary nurse, Aunt Sarah. She was fun when she wasn't around the hospital but was strictly business and grumpy at work. She wouldn't be happy if she knew we were bicycling in the hospital.

As we sped past the operating room door, I remembered one day the five of us and our MK friends sat on the stairs across the hall where we could peek inside the window to watch surgery. Aunt Sarah ruined the fun by pinning a cloth over the window. She didn't have kids; maybe that was why she didn't know how to have fun.

Everyone except Mother was excited when Daddy drove a shiny, black, 1929 Model A into our driveway one day. He bought it from a missionary who had rebuilt it from several wrecked cars. We picked roses from Mother's garden to put in the blue glass flower vases.

"Auuugggaaa." Its horn was the signal to "load-'em-up." We fought for our favorite spots: mine was snuggled behind the shiny, round moon-shaped headlight on the driver's side — the right side — while Linda's was behind the left headlight. Chipper liked to straddle the hood, his legs barely draping over the edge of the hinged engine cover, as he clung to the shiny radiator cap in the front center of the hood. Steve and Jim usually rode on the running boards. Daddy drove with Frisky as a companion on the back seat. Frisky was as much a part of the family as any of my brothers and a lot less annoying.

We regularly cruised the hospital compound honking "auuugggaaa" as we swung by the other missionary houses, slowing so other kids could run alongside and jump onto the running boards and the back luggage rack; then off to the dirt roads in the eucalyptus forest.

We helped Daddy build a homemade sled — a beautiful round disk made of wood, with the underside covered in galvanized tin. It was the closest to snow sledding we could get in Tanzania. Daddy turned the Model A in tight circles in a grassy clearing in the forest, slinging the sled in fast-moving, exhilarating arcs. Linda, my friend Cynthia, and I hung tightly to the rope handles as Daddy spun us toward the edge of the clearing. We leaned inwards, flattening our bodies on the sled as we hit a series of bumps… one, we were still hanging in there… two, still there… three, and we were gone in a flurry of dust, ouches, and giggles.

At the weekly station meeting, I told my missionary aunts and uncles that Daddy slept on the couch because Mother was mad at him for buying the Model A. I sensed I'd said something wrong, but I wasn't sure what. I'd remembered hearing her say, "John, you can't keep up with all you have to do for the hospital and the family. You don't have time for a fixer-up project." (I'm sure Daddy doesn't still sleep on the couch but, if he does, I'm not telling anyone.)

Our family found its busy rhythm of five kids in homeschool, household tasks, and Daddy's busy hospital schedule. Highlights of our life were the many family camping outings and Daddy's bush clinics. Trips to town for shopping, bills, post office, and the driver's license test were long and frustrating for Mother and Daddy, but for us kids it was all an adventure. Mother gave a glimpse of family life:

> We enjoy the closeness of our children and do more together here than we did in the States. Together we learn to play tennis, bake, school, camp, and go to bush clinics. Without the distractions of TV and entertainment, we spend our evenings reading or playing games by the fireplace.
>
> Chipper is maturing and getting tall and thin. He likes me to read books to him. The other day I told him I would read only one book before he went to sleep — I was referring to one of his small books. He brought in a big Childcraft Encyclopedia. A mother can't win. He is learning his numbers by playing cards with anyone he can convince to play with him. He expresses himself well in English interspersed with Swahili. He has outgrown the clothes I brought for him. When we return to America, he will be wearing shirts above his navel and pants above his knees.

Steve is almost as tall as I am and is as strong. The other day I was playing with him and told him I would throw him on the floor and spank him. I tried and tried, but couldn't get him down. He just stood there. John asked him why he didn't do anything. He said, "Oh, I'm afraid I might hurt Mother."

He goes to the market each day during school break and comes home with all kinds of things he has bartered for — he loves a good bargain. He is always proud when he makes what his Daddy considers a good buy. He wanted a walking stick an old man was selling for five shillings (75 cents) but he had only one shilling. John said he could have the stick if he could buy it with that. Later, Steve came back with a big grin and a stick in hand.

Bargaining was a part of the culture, a necessity and a developed skill. Mother hated to, but accepting the asking price would turn business into confusing chaos. After returning to America, I found my bargaining skills didn't go smoothly at the Piggly Wiggly in Seminole. It took time, but I was skilled and experienced. As the rest of the family waited, I finally bargained down the price of a bottle of pickled onions.

Steve and Jim picked up Swahili quicker than Mother did, which gave us more independence. She found it embarrassing having to ask them to translate. Steve kept begging to go to boarding school at the Rift Valley Academy (RVA) in Kenya as the other MKs his age did. He may have been old enough, but Mother said she was certain she wasn't!

I look at Steve, so tall with blonde hair hanging in his eyes, and think, "Oh, you're growing up so fast." At other times he goes running through the house, squealing like a wild pig, and I think, "Won't you ever grow up?"

Saturday, John gave the boys their haircuts. Steve likes his hair long, like a mop. Chipper says to turn him upside down and use him as one, which makes Steve mad. Chipper just wants to get through with the haircut as fast as possible so he can get back to his play.

Jim still looks and acts like Tom Sawyer, with his stringy build, red hair, freckles, and cute crooked grin. He loves to fish; every time we pass a stream, he wants to put a hook into it. He has yet to catch anything but he never tires of trying.

Chipper still looks a lot like Jim but without the red hair and freckles. He is in the middle of everyone's projects and loves to help John with his mechanical work. Yesterday, Chipper and his best friend, Glen, were helping John put a new windshield in the Land Rover. John hit the glass, trying to get it to fit, and it exploded into pieces. Glen jumped up and down saying, "Do it again, Uncle John, do it again!"

Today, on our way back from a picnic at Mbeya Peak, we met a boy who had a homemade musical instrument Jim has been trying to get for a long time — a wooden gourd with metal prongs. Jim offered him one shilling (15 cents), but the boy wanted three. It was wet and cold and the boy wore only a cloth around his shoulders, so I suggested Jim trade his pants for it. The boy walked off with his first pair of pants and the only pair of Levis he will probably ever own. Jim walked back to the car in his white undershorts carrying his belt, billfold, and musical instrument.

Linda lost two bottom teeth this week, three ahead of Cinda. This is bad for Cinda because Linda has received three peppermint sticks from the tooth fairy. The twins are extremely competitive, even when it comes to losing teeth, which makes them excellent students and athletes.

Cinda says you can tell her apart from Linda because she is the youngest, the tallest, and the sweetest. Many think the twins are so much alike but to a Mother they are different and unique. The girls still think they have their names written on the back of their necks. If someone asks, "Which twin are you?" Linda replies, "Says Linda," as she turns and lifts her ponytail so they can read which twin she is. She has a birthmark on the back of her neck, which she thinks spells her name. Cinda does the same thing but doesn't know she hasn't a birthmark.

I loved animals and had five chameleons, giving each a name. To me they were individuals. I liked putting them on different colors and patterns of materials to watch them camouflage. They had bug eyes that swiveled independent of each other and scanned front and back at the same time. I just wished my eyes could do that so I could keep an eye on my brothers. Mother liked them because they were clean, didn't make a noise, and ate flies all day, which was good as Mother couldn't find a fly swatter in town.

Mother caught me at the bathroom sink one day, my long hair dangling forward, covering my face. My hands gripped the sides of the sink as I cheered, "Go, Greeny, you can do it, Greeny. Go!" Greeny's arms and legs stretched wide as he desperately floundered for life.

"What're you doing?" Mother asked.

"Teaching Greeny to swim." I don't know if I taught him or not, but he was swimming for dear life.

As Linda and I stood in front of the bedroom mirror one day, mimicking each other making funny faces and sounds, we discovered I couldn't hear out of my right ear. Our parents said they would get my hearing tested in America as Daddy suspected I might have lost the use of one ear when I had spinal meningitis at six months old.

Linda and I were best friends to each other and got along surprisingly well. We usually worked out our conflicts between ourselves. Mostly they were due to our competitive natures. We each had a best friend; mine was Cynthia and Linda's her sister, Wanda. The four of us were together as much as possible and often spent the night at each other's house. These friendships, forged early in life, are life-long and we took a part of each other with us as we went forward on our respective life journeys. Cynthia would later become my roommate at Baylor Nursing School and serve with Linda as a missionary in Kenya and Zambia.

15 Dancing With the Rhythm of Africa *Kucheza na Ngoma ya Afrika*
Tanzania 1960s

Keeping a family healthy in a world with a large menu of tropical diseases was a momentous challenge. A large filter in the kitchen provided water for drinking and ice. Despite our efforts, diarrhea was just a part of life and it was a big problem without public toilets. We drank chai with the locals because we knew the water was boiled in the process, but Daddy didn't let us drink unfiltered water or even accept ice for a Coca Cola on the rare occasion ice was available. We all, especially Steve and I, had trouble with boils.

Jim was sicker than a dog for several days in a rugged fight with tick fever which climbed to dangerous levels accompanied by bad dreams and mental confusion. Steve and I sat on the edge of the bathtub to watch as Mother plunged him into an ice bath. Already freezing from high fevers, it was like trying to bathe a cat or a monkey. Finally he quit fighting and just cried. So did Mother. I was scared for him so I snuck Frisky into his room to cheer him up, but he wasn't even interested in his dog.

Malaria was a constant threat because of the low altitude, mosquito-infested areas where Daddy had clinics. I usually knew when I was getting malaria because the backs of my knees would ache then my whole body hurt. We called that the Swahili phrase, the *mwili wotes*. When the fever hit, nightmares, sweats, and freeze-outs began. We all had malaria. Mother described the struggle:

> I've lost sixteen pounds since coming here; I now weigh 104, my weight before marriage and five children. If I put on weight, the next bout of malaria takes care of it.
>
> Last Wednesday, John came in from work saying he ached and had fever. He took aspirin and sat against the white wall of the house to let the sun warm him before returning to the hospital. He came home after his X-ray conference, saying he had to stop work because he could no longer think. I gave him another aspirin for 103-degree fever but he became worse, confused, and depressed for three days.
>
> We had trouble finding the right medicine to bring his

fever down without causing psychosis; our drugs are so limited here. As his depressions became worse, I had to drop the medication and put him into the cold shower to lower his temperature. At first Dr. Bob thought he had typhoid fever. The epidemic has taken the lives of many, most recently a young pastor leaving a wife and children. We couldn't see malaria parasites in the blood test, but we don't have anything else to blame for John's illness.

*****

The only times we children were home alone were station meetings on Tuesday evenings when missionaries rotated to different houses to discuss hospital and mission business. The sounds of drums, drinking men, and owls seemed all the more loud and spooky when Mother and Daddy were gone. Jim and Steve capitalized on this heightened fear by finding new and creative ways to scare the Twindas.

Kids weren't invited to station meeting and we didn't have any babysitters so we were on our own and there was usually trouble. Steve was the worst instigator, with Jim quick to jump in to torment us, and Chipper often joined in, mimicking his big brothers. Steve loved to grab Linda's and my long ponytails, one in each hand, as he yanked to bang our heads together.

If I'm honest, I would have to say it wasn't all one-sided; we knew how to push our brothers' buttons too. One of the tactics we leaned heavily on was the threat to tattle, which got them in trouble. Steve was quick to remind us of Mother and Daddy's rule: "If there is any trouble tonight or if anyone tattles, we won't try to figure out who did it, everyone will get a spanking."

Although Mother and Daddy rarely followed through with the spanking, it wasn't an entirely empty threat. Their discipline was consistent and we knew the consequences ahead of time, leaving no room for guesswork. Punishment, worse than a spanking, was time out in my room. It hurt my feelings, I felt lonely, and I hated missing what everyone was doing.

*****

Kufanya biashara (doing business) crawled in the small, lazy town of Mbeya with its two main cross streets lined with *dukas* (small shops). The African's internal clock ran not much faster than the town clock that didn't run at all. Service was slow and frustrating with no customer service niceties — at least it seemed that way to those used to an American way of life. We got our fruits and vegetables at market, a large open area surrounded by small *dukas* with bright-colored *kangas* hanging outside along with buckets, pans, and wares.

Women, most with babies on their backs, displayed pyramids of passion fruit, bunches of mangos, stacks of oranges, stalks of bananas, cassavas, potatoes, onions, tomatoes, small balls of tobacco, dried minnows, dishes, and piles of yellow Sunlight soap used for bath and laundry on their colored *kangas* and bright plastic sheets. The market was a quilt of bright colors, a mixture of pleasant and rotting scents, and a cacophony of sounds. The women beckoned to us to try to get Mother to buy from them. Girls our age didn't get to play like we did because they had babies on their backs and took care of brothers and sisters while their mothers sold produce.

We carried the baskets for Mother as she bargained, but she let us bargain too. There wasn't a store to buy everything; we went to the market for fruits and vegetables, the butcher for meat, and D'Souza's store for everything else.

Outside the butchery, we gawked at the fly-covered window with pigs, goats, and cows hanging upside down, their heads still on. Flies covered the meat and tried to crawl into my eyes and nose. The butcher cut any slab of meat Mother wanted with a quick slice of a machete. The first to buy got the slab of choice; all cuts were the same price. Luckily, our choice cuts were not the same as the Tanzanian's; we liked steak and they loved organs, tongue, and stomach. Yuck.

Our luck ran out when we were guests in a Tanzanian's home. They respected Mother and Daddy so they gave us the best of their food: the tongue, stomach, and organs. Yuck again. Daddy taught us to eat whatever people served because it showed respect and gratitude. Often I had to breathe fast to keep from vomiting but, as soon as I saw that look on Daddy's face, I closed my eyes and swallowed hard. Oh, come on; have you felt the texture of the huge taste buds on a cow's tongue?

Our family ate a lot and we often had guests so Daddy frequently butchered a calf at home. It was a long project with all hands on deck. Mother and Daddy cut, chopped, and sawed meat while we hand-ground it with a grinder clamped to the kitchen cabinet. Every time we butchered a calf, Mother said she would never do it again.

One day we traveled down a muddy road after the dry season broke in a wet fury. There was a pause in the rain and steam rose from the ground as our Land Rover slid and bumped along. Daddy slid to a stop to avoid hitting a woman bending over a small hole in the middle of the road where winged termites spiraled out like twisting smoke. From the foggy windows of the Land Rover, we watched the old woman show Daddy how to pull the wings off and eat the termites.

Soon after, we saw patients in hospital gowns gathering winged termites near the graveyard. We joined them, plucking the wings and eating the crunchy termites. During supper, we learned that Daddy had only pretended to eat the termites on that rainy day. We've since cooked them in a frying pan.

The menu in Africa was a smorgasbord of unusual foods: tongue sandwiches, zebra hamburgers, warthog fajitas, eland, topi, impala, ostrich, slimy *sukuma wiki* (boiled greens), wildebeest, and buffalo. Fried grasshoppers were salty and crunchy like overcooked popcorn. They had to be swallowed headfirst so the small spines wouldn't stick in your throat. The hardest to swallow were the soups because anything was thrown in — beef stomach, chicken feet, and cow eyeballs.

The Masaai cocktail is hard to top. A warrior shoots an arrow to puncture the jugular of a cow and collects the stream of blood in a charcoal-smoked gourd, rinsed with urine. He plugs the jugular with a wad of grass and cow dung so the cow can be tapped another day like a Masaai soda fountain. Swallow this blood, mixed with warm fresh raw milk, and try to keep a smile on your face as the blood slides down your throat in threads and clots. Yuck. Although Daddy taught us to drink whatever people served, he preferred we find an out on this one because of the risk of disease.

At first the rhythm of family life beat out of sync with the unfamiliar rhythm of Africa but, after time and some stumbling, we began to sync like two new dance partners that give up a little of their own uniqueness and control in order to meld into a smoother, more beautiful dance together. A dance that would continue down through three generations, maybe more.

16 Sand Castles and Memories *Majumba Mchanga na Kumbukumbu*
Uganda 2004

I awaken to the excitement and anticipation of our first morning in Kaabong. Cross-world travelers know jet lag's dragging, restless wait for dawn and the smothering, droopy drag of late afternoon until the body has a chance to reset its internal clock. Oh, to be able to turn the hands or "press and hold" to reset a body clock. Kuku, the rooster, didn't sleep in; he stands on top of the thatched roof of his stick house with much to proclaim.

Stanley and I beat the sun to our place beside the charcoal cooker on the porch. The milky tea wafts its mingled smells of cinnamon, cardamom, and charcoal as the steam mingles with the fresh scents of morning. I feel relaxed, satisfied, and mellow as I savor the sounds of the African dawn with dove calling, goat bells, and local kids chattering.

"Nuna, don't forget we have things to do for my birthday," Ben reminds me. He crouches like a miniature African man, with his red *shuka* and *fimbo*, on his big rock next to the porch.

"Last year," he tells us, stumbling in excitement, "my ninth birthday started with us all having chai with me in my bed. Mom always makes a treasure hunt for us."

"Where was the first clue?"

"On the tray beside my cup. I followed clues into the storage room, on top of the roof, in Kuku's house, and on top of Picnic Rock. Each stop had a little present and the next clue."

He rolls his eyes comically as I interrupt his story with laughter. Mother did treasure hunts for us as kids, even into our early adult years.

"It led to Aunt Jean's Land Rover with the horns on the front and—" he attempts to continue.

"Woah!" Stanley interrupts, "What d'you mean by a Land Rover with horns on the front? What's that all about?"

"Jean is an American veterinarian working this area of Uganda," Linda jumps in. "She has monstrous Acholi cow horns attached to the front grill of her Land Rover. The locals respect her because she helps with their cows and goats. The horns help to identify her and prevent her from ambush as she travels through no man's land. We fondly call her 'Crazy Jean.'"

"So… the treasure hunt led along the road toward the bridge where we

75

build sandcastles," Ben tries again. "At the river bed, there was this huge rock, this one I'm sitting on. This was my present. Everyone helped to shovel it loose and lift it into the back of Crazy Jean's Land Rover. The best birthday present ever!"

"Well, you got a rock for your birthday, but I got a hen for mine and look… I now have chicks." Jessica chimes, leaning playfully against Ben.

"Aaahhh," Ben grins and leans back as he perches happily, sipping his chai, as he plans our day. First a trek to build sandcastles in the dry riverbed, then return for the birthday lunch, followed by a hike in the other direction to climb, play, and slide at Sakatan rocks.

"Shall we go for a run first?" Linda asks me, pitching the last dredges of chai leaves into the dirt. Seve, Linda, and I double-knot our shoelaces and stride out on the dirt road with Ben and Jordan following on bicycles. Linda matches my pace as we run, reconnect, and get lost in the beauty around us, and the joy inside us.

"I like riding behind you two because it's so funny, Mom," Ben giggles behind us. "You and Nuna run just alike."

Back on Ben's agenda, he leads the way for his birthday treat, along the meandering sandy road past Mary's village. Although it was only yesterday, it seems days ago we sat outside her hut for chai, soon after our arrival. Jessica carries a backpack with sand candle making equipment. Next to her, Jordan has a climbing rope, dragging a loop along in the dirt, while Noel bounds and weaves between their feet. We wear caps for protection from the equatorial sun, a habit Daddy deeply engrained in us. The females among us wear *kangas* over our shorts to prevent the cultural clash of showing our thighs.

Nearing Rapanyo, Tubo's *manyatta*, I am amazed at the way it blends into the countryside. Like Mary's, a thick, impenetrable thorn wall surrounds the thatched roof mud huts interconnected by a maze of thorn passageways. Women hand-grind sorghum on a smooth rock under the shade of a tree outside the thorn enclosure. As we greet, my eyes feast on the blackest of black skin, contrasting sharply with their bright red, blue, and green clothing. Their faces and necks, intricately adorned with patterned scars, are marks of beauty in this culture.

Magnificent smiles sport ivory-white, healthy teeth; each with one front tooth removed so they can sip fluids through a reed if their jaws lock closed with tetanus. Flies are a constant companion, resting on the eyes, noses, and mouths of babies strapped with a cloth to their mother's back.

"See those twins," Linda points. "The Maasai in Matapato, near Mt. Kilimanjaro, view twins as a bad omen and often kill the younger one. You would be history, Sis, if you were born Maasai. On the other hand, these people see twins as a blessing. The frequency of twins among the Karamojong people and their goats is surprisingly high."

"I think this is one thing these people have right — twins are a blessing," I agree. One of the advantages of living in many cultures is one can embrace the best and reject the weaknesses in each.

We are the subject of much laughter and admiration. I don't know the language but I know we are being watched and compared as they talk to Linda. They appreciate us for being twins and for having reached an unusually old age. I savor the feel of Africa — relationship and real conversation, not just politeness; and rich laughter that fills and satisfies my soul.

The men and boys have gone with their cows and goats for the day. Tubo, one of Byron's ministers, has gone with him on a long walk to story at a distant village. A mangy, brown dog lies in the dust, scratching his ears, leaving the flies on his eyes unperturbed.

With Tubo's village behind us, we turn onto the larger dirt road leading to the bridge at the riverbed. The vastness of this country reminds me of the scenes in Western movies where the horizon seems endless, broken only by large rock outcroppings.

"Look, there's Crazy Paul's place," Linda interrupts my reflections as we approach the church.

"Where? I can't see anything."

"See there, in the clearing in the brush. That stack of plastic and cardboard under the bush is his bed. The *jiko* (charcoal cooker) with the four sitting rocks is his living room. The strips of plastic, cardboard, plastic jugs, and cans hanging from the bush serve as decoration."

"How did he get his nickname, Crazy Paul?"

"He's been called that ever since we knew him," Ben chimes in.

"Not sure," my twin replies. "But one Sunday we prayed for peace, a rare occurrence in this land, and one of the men added, 'God, we pray for peace and pray for our safety as we go and raid.' Crazy Paul cupped his hands to his ears as if to hear better and asked, 'What is it that I hear? Is it the sound of Turkana cows crying? How can we pray for peace when we are the ones that have stolen the Turkana's cows?'"

"So he's not genuinely crazy?"

"No, he's brilliant; he can think circles around everyone else," she grins. "He's probably one of the most intelligent men around, but Idi Amin drove him crazy when he imprisoned and tortured him."

"Ouch."

"You know Africans are accepting and tolerant of mental illness."

We stroll past the church, a simple structure with a tin roof, no walls,

77

and a simple cross hanging crookedly on the front. The church is bare inside except for two rows of narrow, wooden benches. Men sit on one side with women and children on the other.

The birthday boy is keen to impart his knowledge. "Crazy Paul often puts sticks, rocks, plastic sacks, or string in the offering plate."

"It's all he has to give," Linda agrees. "The plate rarely contains money because there isn't much of it around; people trade and barter."

"It's all such a far cry from our lives back in Texas. I guess as kids we were too young to notice these things in Tanzania."

"Women give the copper bracelets off their arms as an offering. When a tribe raids another tribe, taking their cattle and women, they will often strip the women of their jewelry to de-humanize them. Giving their jewelry as an offering is a big deal."

"Paul usually carries a Bible, but I don't think he can read," Ben adds, but birthday anticipation overtakes him and he races to the bridge with his siblings and disappears out of sight into the riverbed.

Linda and I descend the steep path to find them digging in the sand under the shade of the bridge. The plan is to make sand candles first then they can play while the wax is setting. Jessica balances an aluminum pan on a camp stove to melt wax for the candles while the other kids dig holes and tie candlewicks to sticks in preparation for the hot wax.

"It's a blast when the rains come, Nuna," Jessica tells me. "The dry riverbed turns into a watery playground so we can walk to the bridge then float almost all the way back to the house."

"Buddy, our neighbors' dog, runs along by the river, barking and biting at the water," Ben adds. "He jumps in and tries to grab our clothes between his teeth and drag us to the shore."

"Maybe poor Buddy thinks you're drowning?" I ask, but his attention has leaped to the activities of his siblings.

The knots, learned years ago on family rock climbing trips, come back to me as Linda ties the climbing rope to the bridge rail. Jordan and Seve pull the end of the rope up the riverbank and place their feet on the knot for a wild, giggling, squealing swing. The kids' laughter beckons kids from the bushes to join in the play.

When they return to the shade under the bridge to build sandcastles, Linda and I make half-hearted attempts to involve ourselves with their construction, but our focus is on catching up. Our hearts are forever connected, but our journeys are far apart.

Jessica and Ben work on an oversize castle complete with turrets, drawbridge, and a moat dug deep enough to draw muddy water. Sand flies as Jordan buries Seve, leaving only her head exposed. Her blonde pigtails stick out from under her denim cap and her infectious giggles waft our way. Noel joins in, vigorously digging for whatever dogs dig for. The kids watch her closely since the time she observed them from the bridge and fell, frightened by a snake, breaking both front legs. Linda added vet to her many hats that include mom, nurse, doctor, farmer, teacher, wife, and missionary.

"All the places we have lived and visited in Africa, I can't remember seeing people with so little," I frown. "Did we see this in Tanzania and Kenya and just not notice because we were kids?"

"What we saw then is all we knew; we didn't have anything to compare it to. These people live on goat, sorghum, and *ugali* (corn meal). We usually lived where people grew crops; these people are cattle and goat herders. The land here just doesn't support crops, nor are they a part of their culture."

"So how do they get water?"

"They dig holes in the dry riverbed to collect it to survive; it would be unheard of to pour it onto plants. I remember in high school traveling to Turkana in northern Kenya where Mother and Daddy did clinics and famine relief. Now that was desolate!"

"You're right. I remember now. The tribal raids killed most of the men and livestock, leaving the women to survive with nothing. We are so lucky."

The missionaries taught the survivors of the devastated tribe to build portable rabbit cages so they could still move to where water was available. They gave the chief the stud rabbit and the families the female rabbits so the chief could remain in control. The missionaries distributed hoes and seeds along with the temporary lifesaving handouts of corn, beans, and rice. Mother taught health, nutrition, and hygiene while Daddy provided immunizations and medical care. Linda and I usually helped in the clinic while our brothers helped with food distribution.

Our childhood was full of laughter, fun, family, and adventure. I wasn't aware of struggles or fears; we had full confidence in Mother and Daddy to handle anything that came our way. The only haunting fear was of separation from family.

17 At Play in Africa *Kucheza Katika Afrika*
Tanzania 1960s

My legs burned to keep up with Daddy's long strides as the grassy plain transitioned sharply into dark, thick jungle. Colobus monkeys, with their lengthy black manes, long tails, and white faces, jumped from tree to tree, screaming and watching like white-bearded old men. Sharp blades of sunlight sliced through the thick darkness of the forest with its layers of growth and vines; orchids nestled like jewels in the crevices of the trees. The sounds of the jungle surrounded us: monkeys, birds, crickets, and frogs. We swung from long, dangling vines. Even Mother swung from one tree to another, pretending she was Jane from the *Tarzan* movie.

We climbed and climbed, the fun eventually transitioning to putting one foot in front of the other as I began to wonder if we would ever get to the top. Finally, the jungle dropped its green curtain to an exquisite turquoise lake sparkling like a jewel in the crater below. Word of mouth and a crooked wooden sign with "Crater" and a black arrow marked the turnoff to Lake Ngozi — one of our favorite places — the second largest crater-lake in Africa.

Our Land Rover, with Chipper nestled into the spare tire and the rest of us scattered around the roof rack, bumped to a stop in a flurry of dust. Ahead, four roadblocks, constructed with big logs and rocks, blocked the road. We put our Land Rover into four-wheel drive and careened across the fields. The kids ran after us yelling "*Mzungu, Mzungu*" (white people) and tried to climb onto the back of the Land Rover. It suddenly jolted, throwing Chipper out of his nest followed by the rest of us being flung from the roof rack, over the hood, and onto the ground. While watching the running kids in the rear view mirror, Daddy failed to see an aardvark hole.

Mother's cries of "John, John, John!" eventually subsided.

Steve jumped up, dusted himself off and said, "Daddy, don't kill all de kids!" A phrase that has stuck with our family ever since.

*****

Camping trips were as integral a part of the family routine as eating. We camped for fun and necessity as Mother and Daddy visited churches and held clinics. The camping gear was always ready to go, but food preparations took some planning because Mother had to prepare from scratch. She made homemade cinnamon rolls and loaf bread and prepared sloppy joes or spaghetti. We helped convey the supplies to the Land Rover, but it was Daddy's job to pack. On long camping trips, he packed the back of the Land Rover above the metal bench seats running lengthwise along the rear windows and finished the load off with sleeping bags.

We kids either rode the roof rack or lay flat on top of the soft padding in the back. Chipper usually got the coveted position in the front seat between Mother and Daddy. I loved that seat, not only because the spot between my parents was the best place in the world, but it also provided fun challenges.

"Which gear next, Daddy?" I asked excitedly when it was my turn. My legs straddled the floor gearshift as he called out, "Third please, Cinda," and pushed the clutch to the floor. There was a little diagram on the knob to use like a map to find the requested gear. Using both hands, I wrestled the gearshift into place.

His reward of "Good job, baby gal" made me feel like such a good helper. We loved helping Daddy drive and I wondered how he got by when we kids weren't there. When he needed four-wheel drive, he had to stop and put his head down by my knees to reach the short knob on the floorboard.

Stopping to camp, we looked for all the qualities of a good campsite: avoiding unlevel ground, rocks, animal trails, elephant dung signaling an elephant highway, safari ant trails, and the potential for a flash flood. We had a large, one-room canvas tent with aluminum poles marked with small colored stripes on the ends to help with the construction puzzle. Daddy rigged a strand of electric light bulbs, powered by the car battery, to give light for cooking, card games, and Forty-Two domino game if other missionaries were along. The only electric bulb for hundreds of miles drew people, moths, and buzzing insects of all sizes and types.

The sights and sounds of an African day contrast sharply with those of night as if in a completely different world. The day offers the sweet sounds of tropical bird melodies, cattle, goats, and donkeys. Mocking baboons scream, throw fruit, and bare their teeth. The African dawn and dusk are the richest times of day in sound and color.

Africa at night is a mixture of tantalizing sounds mingled with haunting tunes; subtle notes interspersed with nerve-wracking chaos. Crickets, frogs, and unknown insects create a loud backdrop of sounds punctuated by the cough and deep resonating roar of a lion — felt in your chest, not just heard — like the percussion of a bass drum. Add the nerve-jangling sounds of hyenas' laughter. Whoever described that as laughter hasn't slept in a thin canvas tent in Africa. The sounds of a tree hyrax wind up in intensity like a clock, then hang on, as it lets loose with a spine-tingling descending scream. Whip-poor-wills, goatsuckers, and owls add their haunting musical tunes to the night sounds.

Only in the early morning hours before dawn does the night become silent, a silence so loud it awakens you from sleep. An African night without moonlight is one of the darkest of dark nights on earth. The stars are a dense, multi-layered canopy overhead, uninterrupted by artificial light or even a car headlight for hundreds of miles. The full moon seems to be bigger and brighter than anywhere else I've been, bathing the landscape in a warm light and giving life to the sounds otherwise hidden in darkness.

With the rosy dawn, the noises battle once more. The harsh, haunting sounds of night give way to the sweet melodies of the myriad of birdlife announcing the morning. A Yellow-vented Bulbul sings a welcome to the morning with a repeating warble sounding like it sings, "Did you sleep comfortably?"

*****

Although we were closest to our MK friends, we had friends who were Muslim, Pagan, Christian, Hindu, Pakistani, African, Swiss, German, Afrikaans, British, Scandinavian, American, and Indian. It was about making connections and finding commonalities instead of focusing on differences. From each of these friends and groups we took with us jewels learned, and a tolerance and interest for views and perspectives far beyond our small beginnings.

We loved to visit friends who had farms: the Scandinavians raised sheep, Afrikaans grew crops, and our British friends, the Egans, had a large coffee farm. We traveled a long way down dusty, red dirt roads to visit the Egans. The dry savanna landscape abruptly changed to a bougainvillea-lined road as it entered rows and rows of green trees with red berries, stretching as far as I could see. The coffee farm looked more like a country club with a swimming pool, big white house, and beautiful green grass to run barefooted.

Oh, the swimming pool… full of fun, splashing, chasing, jumping, and diving. Chipper, Linda, and I stayed in the shallow end with forays, wearing a mask and snorkel while holding onto the side of the pool, to peer underwater at the others swimming. Steve and Jim kept dropping jawbreakers in our snorkels; I wished Mrs. Egan hadn't given them those candies.

While Mother and Daddy toured the coffee plantation, we ran barefoot along the long water ditches, feeling the slippery coffee beans under our feet as we sailed homemade boats through the drifting coffee husks traveling down the long, winding streams. Mother described the industry from an adult's perspective:

> The Egans invited us to their farm, at the base of Mount
> Mbeya, to see a coffee estate at the height of harvest,

followed by British high tea. They are harvesting a 200-ton bumper crop, handpicked by 400 women of the Wasafwa tribe. These women carry straw baskets on their back as they pick the bright red coffee beans, or carry cans on their heads if they have a baby strapped to their back. At the end of the day, the women line up for the final tally to collect their four shillings (60 cents).

The farm taps and diverts a mountain stream for many purposes; it powers the machinery for the coffee bean separation from the berries, carries the hulls back to fertilize the coffee trees, hydraulically separates the beans of various qualities, fills the swimming pool, and irrigates the whole plantation.

The bright red berries flow into a mill of rotating wheels, washed with water, and emerge as separated red hulls and white beans. The lighter hulls flow downhill, past the vegetable garden, and back to fertilize the field where the berries originated. The white beans flow down another concrete trough where workers use the flowing water to stir, mix, and divide the beans into three grades according to density.

A three-day fermenting process in six-foot concrete vats digests the pulp from the beans. Workers spread the beans on acres of drying racks as they walk back and forth, stirring the drying beans. They sack and store them when dry in small warehouses by the big house until shipping. Mr. Egan arranges his own truck transportation because the nationalized marketing and shipping procedure is so time-consuming that the quality of his beans deteriorates before they reach market. He pays a premium price for his independent transportation, but gets his beans there in prime condition to command a premium price himself.

On the way home, we stopped many times for Daddy to run into the bush. He was the only one that learned the hard way that the British orange juice, Squash, is a concentrate requiring dilution.

18 Underwater Wonders *Maajabu ya Maji*
Tanzania 1960s

I was surprised when Mother said we were going on our first real vacation because we'd been on lots of camping trips. She said a vacation was just for fun, not for work. It all seemed fun to me except when it got hot, sweaty, and crowded in the Land Rover.

The road to Dar es Salaam in January 1968 was under construction, rough and muddy with unprecedented rains as we launched on our ten-day beach vacation. The dirt roads regularly took a beating because of the heavy traffic trucking copper from Zambia to Dar es Salaam. The pounding worsened when, in response to Rhodesia's declaration of independence from the UK to delay black majority rule, the UN imposed an oil embargo, which inadvertently cut off oil to landlocked Zambia. Barrels of oil were flown into Zambia and trucked overland along the Tanzanian roads.

Twelve miles out of Mbeya, we came upon a big oil truck that had slid on the wet pavement and plummeted over the cliff. "Kids, stay in the car," Daddy warned as he slammed the Land Rover door. "And behave," Mother added as she grabbed a flashlight and disappeared into the darkness.

Straining my eyes to see silhouettes through the steamy windows and wall of rain, I whined as Steve and Jim's fight caught me with an elbow. Mother and Daddy were gone a long time and I began to worry they may have also fallen over the cliff. Finally I saw shapes appear. They carefully laid a heavy object on the pavement behind us. Mother climbed in and slammed the door. She was soaked to the bone.

"Kids, we'll wait here a while. One man didn't make it and your daddy is trying to find rides to the hospital for the others."

Looking out of the back window, I saw that the dark shape on the ground was a dead man, his wet, black skin shining in the rain. The eerie feeling faded into giggles as Mother wrapped herself in a sheet and stripped off her muddy clothes. Daddy finally returned and stood in the rain as he took off his soaking wet clothes and climbed in, wearing a sheet. The pavement soon disappeared in our rear view mirror.

Forty miles east of Mbeya, near Chimala, we came upon long lines of trucks with trailers, cars, buses, bulldozers, and graders stuck, nearly buried, or waiting in line to get into the muddy mess. With the rains, the road had become impassable and declared closed by the authorities, stranding the entire trucking industry and all transport. Mother described:

> There were 250 to 300 trucks lined up or stuck and many had been there for days. We decided to chance it because John will never back down and we really wanted this vacation. Two road graders blocked the road. When one moved to allow a truck carrying rocks through, John jumped through the gap. He accelerated to keep momentum as we slid and bumped between the trucks. Then we came to the bog.
>
> What a mess! One truck, and the tractor that tried to pull it out, were stuck right in our away. Another truck, turned on its side, blocked the rest of the road. Some vehicles had sunk up to their windows in the mud. A construction crew built a road to go around the mess but it just widened the bog. John decided to go off into the bog, knowing we would get stuck and have to use the jack to get out.

"Go, Daddy, go!" we cheered as the Land Rover hit the bog, careening at wild angles, then slid and bumped, all the while Mother crying, "John, John... Oh, John!" Some road workers cheered, others pointed and shook their heads, and others shook their fists and yelled as we slopped away through the boggy mess, leaving a muddy plume behind us.

Each time we lost momentum and got bogged down, Daddy jacked up the Land Rover so we could fill in under the tires with rocks and branches to get traction to continue. On one occasion, we stuck near an overturned gasoline tanker where people were smoking cigarettes as they waded through the mud to scoop up its leaking contents in cans. Daddy began to yell and a conflict ensued because he wanted to keep us from getting caught in a fire, but they thought he was trying to keep them from getting the gasoline. We had to fold in the side mirrors and tie up the side step so we could slip, slide, weave, and squeeze past the stuck trucks to finally hit firmer ground three hours later.

We camped a little bit beyond the bog, having traveled 110 miles in seven and a half hours. We were exhausted when we arrived in Dar es Salaam the next night. It was sweltering beside the beautiful Indian Ocean. We swam in the sea in the mornings before 10:30 a.m. and the afternoons after 3:00 p.m. — Daddy's rules because of the intensity of the sun. The tidal pools were full of fascinating creatures: shells, baby octopuses, eels, sea urchins, fish, sea cucumbers, and starfish. Steve taught Linda and me to swim in a concrete square pool that filled up with saltwater at high tide. I was so proud I could now swim.

Daddy went skindiving, forgetting his own sun rules, and came back as red as the lobster Mother bought from a fisherman at the beach. He was sick in bed for a few days and the skin on his back and legs began to peel like a snake. I was scared his eyes would peel like a snake too.

*****

I wore a mask and snorkel on my forehead and Daddy's orange rubber scuba diving gloves on my hands as I descended a wobbly wooden ladder down a craggy cliff behind Mother and my brothers. Linda followed close behind, also wearing a mask on her head, complaining that she should get to wear Daddy's gloves first since she was the oldest. "Duh!" Steve responded to my question as to why this beach was called Ladder Beach. He could be so annoying at times.

Linda looked like a duck with her tail in the air as she bent over to peer through her mask into the shallow low tide pools. Looking through the mask, I entered into a completely new watery world bursting with color and constant movement. I kept thinking I needed to hold my breath when my face was in the water but I could just breathe away. The pools teemed with creatures of every kind: some funny, some goofy, and a few scary. It sounded comical when I laughed in the snorkel. Even with my face in the water, I could hear someone call when they saw something elsewhere I needed to see. Stepping into another pool opened up a completely new underwater world to explore.

Sea cucumbers looked scary but turned out to be harmless; when I squeezed one, sticky, stringy innards squirted out. Mother fussed at Steve and Jim for having a sea cucumber fight; they had stringy stuff tangled in their hair. Every nook and cranny of this underwater world had a spiny sea urchin of some type; some had short spines and others had long black ones with florescent shapes that looked like eyes and a mouth. They reminded me of the Tar-Baby in the Uncle Remus story Daddy read to us.

The underwater world was mesmerizing, with fish that looked and swayed like seaweed. We watched, from a respectful distance, the long, spiny, poisonous lionfish and stepped carefully to avoid stepping on a lethal stonefish, sea urchin, or stingray. The water world has such beauty but so many things sting or stick. Barefooted, Linda stepped on a sea urchin and a spine broke off in her heel. She stood there in pain and panic realizing she still needed to walk through the throngs of black spines to get to the safety of the beach. Mother said it would eventually work its way out.

We captured a blowfish, which was small and inconspicuous but, when scared, blew up into a large, spiny ball. We passed it back and forth, delighting to see it rotate slowly through the water. It wobbled to stay upright, like the men who drank too much *pombe*. The spiny ball had tiny fins that gave it little propulsion or direction.

The fun ended when Chipper decided to stick his finger in the large, swollen, purple mouth. The coral-eating fish clamped down on Chipper's finger and wouldn't let go. Linda jerked the fish, trying to get it to release his finger as Chipper's blood colored the water around us. His legs dropped out from under him and he crumbled into the water. Steve grabbed him and towed him to the beach as Mother splashed toward us.

Mother lifted Chipper in her arms. "Chipper, Chipper... are you OK, Chipper? Talk to me, Chipper." There was no response from Chipper's limp body. The fish is poisonous to eat. Mother was worried the bite may also be poisonous. She left Steve in charge and ran, carrying Chipper, along the beach and up the ladder to get help.

The four of us stood silently and waited. I was terrified, seeing the fear in Mother's face and her focused intensity as she ran, Chipper's head limply bobbing over one arm and his lifeless legs swinging over the other. I had a sickening feeling he was going to die. We watched with unspoken horror as Mother hauled him up the rickety wooden ladder and disappeared over the top of the cliff.

Time and the sounds of the ocean froze in place as we stood in ankle-deep water. Steve attempted a tackle on Jim only to be disappointed as Jim shrugged and turned away. No one spoke. The ocean no longer lured.

19 Birthday Fun *Siku ya Kuzaliwa*
Uganda 2004

Running back from the riverbed, Ben reminds us we still have a lot more to do for his birthday. We gather up the rope swing, the beautiful sand candles, and Noel to continue working our way through the birthday itinerary with a trek back for homemade hamburgers. Homemade means buns made from scratch, hand-ground meat, sliced and fried potatoes for chips, and mayonnaise made from oil and eggs. Seve perches on top of the hand-cranked ice cream maker while the other kids crank.

Next on Ben's list is a two-mile trek northeast to Sakatan rocks. As with many places in Africa, there is a web of human, cow, and goat trails to follow, but no roads. Ben leads, wearing new army pants and a camouflage army hat.

"Remember how the Masaai in Kenya hung cowbells they made from gourds and turtle shells round the necks of their cows?" Ben asks as we walk. "I used to lie in bed and listen to the Morani warriors calling to each other during the night, 'Eeeyooo.'"

"Those guys all knew their cows by their sound," Linda tells me.

"I don't remember much about Matapato but I really remember lying in bed and hearing the roar and cough of lions outside our gate," Seve laughs. "I was afraid they could jump over it."

Most of these sounds the kids associate with the comforts of home; known and secure, as the sounds of a TV would be to a kid in America.

"You used to ride on my shoulders, Ben, when your mother took us on a tour of *bomas* to check on her medical patients and give child vaccinations. D'you remember?" Stanley nudges Ben, who knows he's about to be teased. "Whenever you saw a donkey, you would mock, 'Hee Haw, Hee Haw… ' It was all you said the entire walk."

"So, Mom, you had dogs, a kitten, an owl, and chameleons for pets," Ben whines to move on, "so how come we only get to have a dog?"

"Oh, Ben, that's not all we had. When Cinda and I were in the fifth grade, we lived in the same house in Kisumu that you lived in a few years ago, right on the shore of Lake Victoria in Kenya. That's when Rascal came into my life. She lived with me all the way through my high school years."

"Rascal? Another dog?"

"If only," I laugh. "Rascal was a Copper Tail Monkey and she just about adopted your mom. They were inseparable when we were growing up."

Ben giggles, "Like you were triplets."

"She was beautiful, though. Rascal, I mean, not Cinda," Linda teases. "She had yellow-tipped, dark gray soft fur, a shiny copper-colored tail twice the length of her body, and a black face trimmed by a mask of white with a triangular-shaped, white, flat nose."

"Don't forget her captivating shiny brown eyes. Your mom spent so much of her time sitting in the mango tree, Ben, reading a book while Rascal sat on her shoulder or played, leaped, and explored. That monkey could store a packet of round jawbreakers in pockets inside her cheeks, doubling the size of her face. She retrieved the treats by rolling the back of her hand along her cheek."

"The day Rascal died was one of the saddest days of my growing-up years," Linda admits. "I was a senior. I had her from the fifth through the twelfth grade. I remember Daddy held me in his lap while I cried."

"What other pets did you have, Nuna?" asks Jessica.

"Well, we tried to raise rabbits for meat, but that didn't work well with the dogs and eating pet rabbits didn't go down well with us kids. We had pigeons too. Your granddaddy tried to use them to carry messages to his medical assistants. That creative idea came to a pretty abrupt halt when our dogs ate the pigeons!"

"Cinda had snakes as well," Linda shudders. "She was jealous of my friendship with Rascal, so she got a bush baby for a pet too."

"Can we get one, Mom?" Ben is wide-eyed.

"Even I don't recommend a bush baby, Ben," I have to tell him. "It had a bushy tail, gigantic brown eyes, and bat-like ears but, boy, it was smelly and noisy. I finally let him go free, as I got tired of him climbing the burglar bars inside my room and making spine-tingling screeches. Who could sleep through that? Snakes are a lot quieter."

"Your Uncle Chipper had a baby chick, though, that rode on his tricycle handlebars," Linda tells the kids. "When he tapped its back, it chirped cooperatively, acting as his tricycle horn. He was sure it knew his name whenever it said, 'Cheep Cheep.'"

Daddy made the world of nature and science come alive for us kids. He helped us catch mice, shrews, tadpoles, snakes, and frogs, which we kept as pets. I caught a shrew once in a live mousetrap he bought me, but when I let Chipper hold Nosey it bit him. Daddy had to quarantine the shrew to watch for signs of rabies. I was terrified Chipper might die.

When driving at night, Daddy would stop so we could sneak up and try to catch goatsuckers, a type of nightjar, frozen in the headlights. I'm not sure what we would have done had we caught one.

We aspired to learn taxidermy too but Mother just ended up with a freezer full of dead birds, snakes, and animals.

As we reach the dry creek bed, Ben stalks his sisters with his homemade mud rifle as they compete to see who can leap the widest part. We follow its meandering route toward the colossal rock outcropping, a natural playground. The familiar, musty smell of rock hyrax and bats triggers childhood memories as we climb. We share a slab of rock where green lizards bob their heads and puff out their red throats as we pause to enjoy the unfolding view. The immensity of this country makes me feel small. We savor our conquest as we take in the view of our house, the village, and many miles around.

The local women and children find refuge in these rocks when the Jia or the army raid and, at times, torch their villages and crops. Shiny, smooth scoops worn in the rock serve as bowls for the women to grind their sorghum. Byron's attempt to convince the villagers to live in the rocks for defense failed because of their belief that the rock spirits will only share their space when people are taking refuge.

The people here have almost nothing, but the Jia burned the little they had. The Dodoth, the tribe Linda and Byron work with, is in constant battle with the Jia, the other sub-tribe. They raid each other's villages and steal their livestock and women. It is all about cows, which represent manhood, respect, and pay dowries for wives. The people now use the AK-47 rifles, given to the tribes to defend themselves against the LRA, to raid, which means men, women, and children are shot. The feuding has continued so long no one remembers which side committed the first offense.

"I'll never forget the day the Jia burned our people's village and fields," Linda shudders. "I went to the hospital, knowing there would be many patients with gunshot wounds. I was puzzled to find the men's ward empty. I found the gunshot victims in the women and children's ward because the men weren't home during the raid."

"You tried to help," Jessica reminds her.

"But, Jess, sometimes I just wish I could do more. Byron and I worked with the villagers nearby, Cinda, to gather food for those who lost their homes in the neighboring villages. Since their houses are made of sticks and mud, there were only charred remains left. People poked through the ashes to try to save anything of value, perhaps a metal teacup. All that was left of the sorghum fields were a few charred stalks. It was so horribly sad… " Her voice falters. "Look into the face of a child with tear streaks through the ash smears on his face and see how well you sleep at night."

Reflecting on Linda's story of the Karamojong church members praying to God to give them peace and safety as they made their plans to go raid, makes me understand the unending cycle of poverty, hunger, hate, and retaliation. Raid and be raided is just a way of life here.

20 Stormy Times *Mara ya Dhoruba*
Uganda 2004

Battles had moved close to home when Steve, our oldest brother, brought his Ugandan friend, Peter, to stay in Kaabong some time ago, both seeking help with their addictions. Peter had open sores all over his body from injecting drugs. He was hanging to life by a thread and his doctor in Kampala had advised amputating his arms. Steve and Peter were under the care of Dr. Mark for two weeks to detox and build up their health.

Linda discovered Peter had been in the army and had taken part in the torching of her people's villages. She was careful not to let the locals know he had been a part of the army's tank attack which had killed some of their people too.

Suffocating with anger and resentment, she listened to his story under duress. President Obote's army had taken Peter from his family as a young boy to be a soldier. His mother thought he had died until she saw him riding on an army tank with Obote's triumphant re-entry after overthrowing Dictator Idi Amin.

It was during their visit that Noel fell off the bridge and broke her front legs. One day Linda was struggling to give Noel her pain shot when she heard Steve say, "You can give it to Peter or me, either one of us would be happy to have it."

Hearing Dr. Mark's voice on the radio as she made chai one morning, Linda knew from his tone that something was dreadfully wrong. First on the scene of an ambush, he saw a body in the road next to the hospital's overturned, torched ambulance. For his own safety, he drove onward toward Kampala. Later that morning, when the Catholic missionaries stopped by for tea, her heart sank when they mentioned they were worried because they hadn't heard from their beloved priest, Father Mantovani, since he traveled to Kampala yesterday in the hospital ambulance.

Byron wasn't due back until late afternoon. She had her kids and a man detoxing in her home who was meant to keep a low profile. Her family worked hard to maintain a neutral position between the Ugandan army and the two Karamojong clashing sub-tribes. Feeling they needed to alert the LDU — part of the Ugandan army — Linda and Steve put Peter in the back seat, forbidding him to get out, and drove to the barracks. Peter immediately recognized the commander he had worked with several years ago when the army torched the villages where the Wittes lived.

The commander said they closed the road yesterday because of troubles. The army fired the big cannon to call in the men of the LDU to begin the search for Father Mantovani. They found his body near the torched ambulance. The soldiers shot and killed a young boy wearing Father Mantovani's shoes. Linda wasn't sure what happened but several lost their lives that day. That is the way retaliation works in this land.

The beloved Father Mario Mantovani, a renowned linguist, ended his 50 years of helping the Karamojong people in an ambush in no man's land. He had been Byron and Dr. Mark's language teacher and loved by missionaries and community.

Since Linda wouldn't allow Steve or Peter to jump into the investigation and the fight, Steve gave the army money for petrol and she arranged for the two to fly out before the trouble escalated. Their exit was a big step to relieving her own tension.

*****

Conflict in no man's land has been ongoing for many years but guns have intensified the danger. Before Byron embarks on the grueling 470-mile overland route to Kampala, he checks the position of Kony's LRA and the status of the two fighting sub-tribes before venturing into no man's land — an area missionaries previously living in the Witte's house narrowly escaped, ending up with three rounds fired into their Land Rover and one blown tire. The escalation of violence prompted Byron's decision to avoid the road trip and rely on missionary air transport, which meant minimizing reliance on supplies from Kampala.

From our perch on Sakatan, we see the tiny village of Kaabong and the hospital where Linda works with missionary Dr. Mark. All of the girls are involved with their mother's medical work at the hospital and in neighboring villages. In Matapato, at the foot of Mt. Kilimanjaro, Jessica helped Linda provide medical care to the Maasai tribe, suturing a buffalo gore wound, delivering babies in their *bomas*, giving immunizations, weighing babies, and counting medicine.

Looking over the vast plain below us, I think of today's activities. The kids, having no TV or electronics, are fit and physical in their play. In the harsh environment of Africa, perhaps one day their survival may be dependent on their physical abilities.

21 Doctor Adams *Daktari Adams*
Tanzania 1960s

Mother raced along the sandy shore with Chipper motionless in her arms. "Talk to me, Chipper! Say something!" Frantically, she ran to three beach houses for help but no one was home. Chipper returned to consciousness as she knocked on the fourth door. To us kids waiting anxiously, it seemed days later when she finally returned to the top of the ladder, Chipper's pale grinning face beside her.

Never daunted by family calamities, Daddy was keen to visit the old Arab island of Zanzibar next, which meant going to Dar es Salaam's government offices and the health department to get visas and medical clearance. Words cannot capture the misery as we five kids sat, shoulder to shoulder, on a bench in a long row of hot and sweaty humanity. We needed yellow fever immunizations and a stamp in our health card. It was without air conditioning, fans, or even a breeze. The air was heavy, humid, and hot. I could hardly breathe. The throng sharing our room sweated a lot and didn't wear deodorant. The walls of misery closed in on me with babies crying, stench, illness, and misery with sick, coughing, and feverish people.

Daddy argued with the officials to try to get us out of having the shots. He was concerned about the cleanliness of the needles and didn't think we needed the immunization. He told us to sit in the line to get our yellow health cards stamped then slip out and avoid the line where they gave the injections. So there we were, five white kids in a sea of black people, and we were supposed to slip out without anyone noticing. We followed Steve's lead and approached the tall wooden counter together to get our cards stamped. Once done, we stumbled over each other, following Steve as he turned sharply and exited the building instead of standing in the injection line.

All that, and we still didn't get to go to Zanzibar because of visa red tape. Instead, we got red itchy bumps on our bums and thighs from bed bugs or fleas from the wooden health department benches.

Unfortunately, all vacations have to end. On our return trip, stuck and overturned vehicles looked like the carnage of a battlefield. We passed long lines of cars that were waiting for something to change as we launched once again into the bog.

*****

Home once more, my eyes focused on Daddy's shiny black shoes, his rough hands swallowing mine as I scurried to match his long-legged walk up the hill to the hospital. Linda, holding Daddy's other hand, wore a nurse's uniform we shared, bartered, or fought to wear: a nurse's white cap, blue cape, and black bag with plastic pill bottles, stethoscope, thermometer, and syringe. Regardless of whose turn it was, we both couldn't be any prouder because we were Daddy's little nurses.

Walking along the hallways as Daddy conducted medical rounds, Linda asked, "Daddy why can't we do this while riding the tandem bicycle? It would be quicker and a whole lot more fun."

"Daddy's assistants can't keep up with us and Aunt Sarah might see us, isn't that right, Daddy?"

He was clearly deep in thought about other things. The smells shifted as we walked through the hallways, the air warm and steamy as we passed the boiler, laundry, and autoclave. Passing the pharmacy, the smells of methylated spirits tweaked my nose, reminding me of Daddy's clinic box. The smells of African food and cooked grains wafting our way as we passed the kitchen didn't make me feel hungry. They smelled like the food Mother cooked each morning for Frisky.

"*Jambo, Daktari*, (hello, Doctor)," patients and staff greeted Daddy. Everyone liked Daddy, but then... how could they not?

On the equator there is a greater diversity of animal and plant life than anywhere else on the globe; this also applies to the diversity of diseases. The Baptist Tuberculosis Hospital treated the whole menu of tropical diseases and injuries through its operating room, 34,000 patients through its clinic, and 2,000 a year through its 120 inpatient beds. In addition to those treated at the hospital, Daddy treated 80 to 100 patients on his bush clinic days. About 65 percent of the inpatients had tuberculosis (TB), which required them to stay in the wards for two to three months. The hospital fee was two shillings per day (30 cents), which covered lodging, food, medication, treatment, and surgery.

The metal chart clanged as Daddy removed it from the end of the bed to confer with the circle of white lab coats. He wore a stark white lab coat, black dress pants, white shirt, black shoes, and a black stethoscope around his neck.

While Daddy talked to his assistants in Swahili, Linda and I retreated and sat next to each other on a nearby empty bed.

"I wish Daddy would hurry up," she whined. "I can't wait to see the babies in the nursery. I hope Nurse Esther is there so we can hold them."

"It's not fair that the patients here wear gowns in the daytime," I grumbled. "Mother never lets us wear pajamas all day."

The patients wore masks, coughed, and spat into little cardboard boxes like the ones we'd seen in a movie on the Queen Mary. People walked out of a Chinese restaurant carrying food in little boxes like that.

"I saw a woman bring one of those boxes to Daddy for him to check her poop for worms," Linda giggled. "Yuck! There is just something not right about using a carry-out box for poop."

Boredom set in and we began to jump back and forth between two empty beds to compete to see who could jump farther. Daddy pointed his finger at us, not breaking his Swahili conversation, and we dropped our tails to the bed.

If we couldn't jump on the beds, what were we to do? We turned toward each other to slap hands and play "Patty cake, patty cake, baker's man." The Swahili droned on and on. Tiring of "Patty cake," Linda turned and sat close beside me, our shoulders touching. We swung our legs as hard as we could to see who could swing theirs the fastest and highest. My heels hit the underside of the bed and swung straight-kneed as high as I could get them because I liked to win. Luckily, Daddy was so focused he didn't notice when the empty metal chart fell off the foot of the bed and clattered on the concrete floor. Linda and I got the twin giggles — unstoppable, contagious, be-careful-or-you-might-pee kind of giggles.

In the nursery at last, Linda and I swept our hands along the life-size sheep and jumped to reach the big, fluffy clouds painted on the wall. We loved the paintings, not just because they were colorful and bright, but also because Mema painted them. The nursery was our second favorite place in the hospital, next to the long hallway — so perfect for bicycling and running races. Sitting side by side with our legs straight, Esther carefully snuggled a blanket-wrapped baby into our arms. I never saw village babies wearing diapers so I wondered why these did. People in America sent us cloth diapers but the hospital used them for packs in surgery and the women used them for scarves.

There was always a fire going in the hospital incinerator. Chipper and Glen thought they were quite the scientists as they experimented with throwing different things in to see how they burned. One day they doused the fire in the incinerator. Daddy had read to us about Smokey the Bear in *Ranger Rick* magazine at naptime and Glen and Chipper thought they were Smokey the Bear. Daddy was *not* happy with his bears.

Jumping up and holding onto the ledge of the screened morgue window, we peered into the darkness. Our muscles quivered as we hung on the ledge, watching to see if the body on the concrete table would move. Women sat on the grassy hill above us, weeping and wailing. They waggled their tongues back and forth to make a funny noise when they grieved or danced. I couldn't make the noise and Mother got tired of me trying at home. The sounds were spooky and it made me sad, especially when a baby died.

Daddy sat in front of a man, thumping his stomach, which was swollen like a watermelon, using the middle finger of one hand to thump the back of the middle finger of his other hand.

"Why are you thumping that man?" Linda asked.

"Juma here has a sick liver. I'm listening for fluid; he needs to have it drained from his belly. Can you hold this bowl for me and catch the fluid when it comes out of the needle?"

Next, Daddy examined a woman with monstrous, deformed legs. He said she had elephantiasis, which fit since her legs looked like elephant legs.

"It's a disease caused by worm parasites," he explained. She spoke Swahili so Daddy translated. "She has eleven children and lives far away at a lake."

"I think her legs look like hippo legs, not elephant legs," Linda remarked, "because they're lumpy and shiny."

"Maybe they can change the name of the disease to hippotitis, not elephantitis? Can I touch her legs, Daddy?"

He spoke to her in Swahili and she agreed. I wondered if she hurt as I reached to touch her monster, lumpy legs. Losing my nerve, I recoiled, but didn't forget my manners, as I said my sorries in stumbling Swahili — "*Poli sana, Mama, poli sana.*"

In the children's ward, Daddy sat on the bed next to a six-year-old boy. Linda and I knelt beside him as we watched Daddy slowly unwind the bandages from his leg. The boy's eyes were wide with fear-tinged anticipation as the last wrap dropped away. For the first time, he saw a normal foot instead of his twisted, calloused clubfoot. He wiggled his toes and silently reached to touch his new foot. His wide eyes looked up at Daddy.

"*Nataka kutembea,*" he whispered. I want to walk. He had always walked with his leg twisted around a stick.

"*Hapana. Bado.*" No. Not yet. Daddy wouldn't let him because his foot needed more time to heal. The boy giggled as Daddy teased him, touching his nose before he could grab Daddy's hand.

Shadowing Daddy, we moved through the wards, bandaging wounds and checking on patients burning and delirious from the ravages of malarial fevers, and children with the swollen bellies and red hair of malnutrition. In the TB ward, he studied X-rays, charts, and listened to chests with his stethoscope. He spoke softly, asked many questions, and listened to his patients. He used his eyes and ears more than diagnostic tests. With his thumb, he pulled the skin down from a man's eye to check the color for anemia, thumped his chest with his fingers, and prodded his abdomen.

He acted out questions he couldn't put into Swahili words. Squatting low to the ground, as if using the *choo* (the hole in the ground serving as a toilet), he asked the man about diarrhea. From squatting, Daddy struggled painfully to a standing position to ask about arthritis then swayed, holding his head, to ask about light-headedness, and wheezed heavily to mimic asthma. He pointed to the east, then overhead, and to the west, pointing to piles of pills named for the days of the week to give instructions for taking medications. It was fun to listen to him speak in Swahili and watch his gestures like an actor in a play.

Linda and I sat on the floor, playing with a girl a little younger than we were. She squealed with delight as Linda let her hear her own heartbeat through Daddy's stethoscope while he carved shoes out of white foam to fit the girl's leprosy-ravaged feet.

We loved to help. We practiced on each other and our dolls; listened with a stethoscope, checked eyes, gave imaginary injections, and thumped chests just as Daddy did. He not only told us about someone's illness, he told us about their kids and their life. He taught us to see past the strange diseases, scarred faces, and foreign language to see the real person.

22 Not Just a Mother *Sio Mama Tu*
Tanzania 1960s

Mother had many jobs: teaching school, being Mom, keeping the home front going, helping Daddy in the clinic and the hospital, and her own hefty ministries. The TB patients stayed several months at the hospital so she taught them to quilt, giving them a useful skill and her a way to connect with them as it gave her common ground to learn about their families and their lives.

She stumbled into many cultural obstacles as she taught at the hospital, clinic, and churches:

> Thursday I went to a nearby village to give smallpox vaccinations and to teach hygiene and nutrition. I was sure we vaccinated 250 people, but when we counted the needles, we had used only 100. This was my first time to work with John in his clinic. I finally got to see the things he has described to me. Some I just had to see before I could really believe. I now understand why he doesn't have to use instruments to do dental work. He just takes his thumb and flips their teeth out. Babies and young children have cavernous cavities.
>
> These people are starving for protein, but they won't eat eggs. I told them they should eat them and feed them to their children too, not give them away. I showed a picture of a little boy brought to the hospital almost dead of starvation and lack of protein. They were impressed with the picture because they are never shown pictures, but did not get my message because they see this all the time — they live it. I'm not sure why eating eggs is taboo. I don't think even they know.
>
> After we gave our last few vaccinations by flashlight, the women made tea and guess what I got — a special gift of twelve eggs. And I thought I was making progress in my teaching...

We went with Mother, one of our missionary aunts, Aunt Hannah, and her kids to a church near the Zambian border. We arrived to find a scattering of people; even the pastor was missing. A kid rang the tire rim bell with a hoe and the congregation began to appear out of the bushes. The preacher introduced us by saying that, for what we had spent on gas to come here, we could have done other things such as buy a *kanga*, or even a cow. Instead, we had come all the way to speak to them. Mother's account of it recalled her humor at the service:

> The congregation expected us to sing for them so they just watched as Hannah and I sang horribly off-key and mispronounced our Swahili words. We began to giggle like two young teenagers. We couldn't sing because we couldn't stop giggling. Hannah's Swahili talk lasted less than a minute, then she asked me to pray. I meant to finish my short prayer with, "I am finished," but again mixed up my Swahili and actually said, "I am dead." Hannah tried to correct me, which made us giggle all the more.

The world around us moved at a snail's pace but the missionaries' lives were hectic with raising a family and juggling ministry. The busy schedule picked up to high speed once a year during the Tanzanian Crusades. On top of school, family routine, and medical work, were the responsibilities of housing, transporting people, feeding visiting ministers, giving devotions, and preaching.

"How am I going to feed houseguests on top of everything I need to do?" Mother fretted.

"Just take things as they come."

I don't think Daddy's reply was what she wanted to hear. She had been baking bread all week, making ice cream for desserts, and putting meat dishes into the freezer.

The women were worn out and walking about in a daze once the crusades were over. Kenya and Uganda reported 1,400 conversions to Christianity, and Tanzania went over the 2,000 mark.

Mother was active in the WMU in Seminole Texas and in Tanzania too — same organization, literally a world apart:

> I planned the food and arranged for the women who traveled far to sleep on the church floor. Since Keith Oliphint helped the church build a smokeless stove out of bricks, I arrived late, thinking the cooking would already be going in the new stove. Instead, I found three big fires in the middle of the church floor. The women said the new stove "defeated" them.
>
> With only one door, the smoke was thick and the room

so dark I could hardly see. Tears streamed down my cheeks and my nose ran like crazy. I was determined to stay and help, but I was mostly in the way. I gasped every time a woman put her hand into the fire to pick up a live coal and move it or pick up one of the heavy pots right off the fire. They never used a pad.

Sixty-five women sat on the ground outside the church to eat. After the meeting, I took nine of them over the rough road to Muvwa. I am so short, I have to stretch my full length to reach the Land Rover pedals, and it takes a lot of maneuvering to manage the gears and clutch for the four-wheel drive. I was exhausted.

*****

It was big news when the hospital got a real ambulance; they no longer had to transport critical patients by Land Rover. The ambulance served many duties beyond its usual hospital tasks: school bus, church bus, and a spare vehicle for missionaries. We stood in the back of the ambulance and challenged each other to balance without touching the sides. If you touched, you had to sit down until we had seen who could balance the longest. Uncle Keith was our driver and he let us thrill the village kids by blowing the siren and running the red and blue lights.

We rode the ambulance to the July 7, 1968 Saba Saba Day celebration and, since it fell on a Sunday, we got to ride it to the Sunday night church service too. The fun came to a sudden stop when we felt the ambulance lurch and bounce off the road, throwing us against the front. We squeezed to look through the front windshield and saw a wrecked, open-bed truck in the middle of the road.

The truck, with its intoxicated driver, carrying the schoolboys' choir had overturned while returning from their performance at the Saba Saba celebration. The upside-down vehicle pinned the boys underneath. Cries of pain and fear, along with a growing flow of blood, seeped out. Daddy and our uncles worked quickly, using Land Rover jacks to lift the truck and release the pinned boys. It was a sad day on the hill with many young lives lost. Christened in blood, riding in the ambulance was never the same.

Thankfully, not everything we did was so frightening. A lot of the medication the hospital used was liquid, and the bottles needed were hard to come by. Daddy kept some but had to charge to encourage patients to bring their own. Linda and I set up a little booth outside the hospital and sold bottles for less than people would have to pay inside. We got our bottles from around the house but couldn't keep enough merchandise to stay in business. When Mother caught us emptying a Prell shampoo bottle, brought in our crates, our business went down the tube.

Although there were some similarities in hospital work in America and rural Tanzania, Mbeya's remoteness added challenges in communication, purchasing supplies, and conflicts with family time, as Mother described:

> These last weeks at the hospital have been extremely difficult. We really miss our main medical assistant and our missionary nurse, who is flat on her back with an injury. John has had the hospital to himself. He needs to do surgery, but he must see clinic patients by 10 a.m. or he can't get through in time for afternoon X-ray studies.
>
> Last Tuesday he planned to treat me to a birthday dinner at the hotel in the evening. I had all the children bathed and dressed in Sunday best. I even put on hose for the occasion. When John hadn't returned in time, I walked up to the hospital to find him doing an appendectomy. He didn't have an assistant and the nurse was so scared she couldn't hold the instruments still.
>
> Last June we ordered sponges. When they didn't come, we placed orders with every company that handled them. It has been three months and still our hospital doesn't have any so John was trying to do surgery without. As I watched him quietly work under the worst conditions, I thought of *my* days in surgery — when you handed a doctor the wrong instrument, he would throw it across the room. Maybe they should just come out here for a while.
>
> Wearing my best Sunday dress and hose, I helped John operate on a little boy, the son of a man from England working for the government to start sheep farming in Tanzania. After settling the boy and his family at my house, my family finally climbed into the Land Rover to discover John had an African and his son in the front seat. John said the boy came to the hospital for treatment of severe burns. Since there was no gauze, he was taking him to the government hospital. After waiting to get the boy admitted, we arrived at the hotel, only to find the dining room closed. I get frustrated as I see John try to balance his work and his family but I'm so glad he cares.

All roads out of Mbeya were closed at the time and the bridges down. There was no way in or out so the whole town was without gas and food —

no flour, sugar, or canned goods. We always had plenty of vegetables and fruit because they were grown locally. Mother learned her lesson last Christmas when she couldn't do any baking because the town was out of sugar. When plenty of the basic necessities were in stock, she bought ten or twenty cases because it took fifteen pounds of flour just for the bread she made in a week. There was no longer any diesel for the big boiler at the hospital, so surgery came to a screeching halt. Food was cooked, and laundry done, in boiling pots outside. There was no way to get medicine or supplies. Oh, the challenges of living and working in Africa.

23 Storytelling *Hadithi za Mungu*
Uganda 2004

Dawn of our second full day in Kaabong begins smoothly with the usual routine; the rooster crows on top of his thatched, stick house as we gather around the charcoal fire for a steaming cup of chai. Today we are heading out for a full-day trek to the village of Nakaramoi to experience Byron's Bible story mission.

Linda, her four kids, Stanley, Tubo, and I walk out of the gate, circling clockwise around the compound, and follow the footpath past Sakatan, the rock outcropping where we played yesterday. The trail through the scrawny sorghum is narrow and well-trodden by human and goat traffic. Tubo, with his knobby bowed legs, strides ahead with a surprisingly long, graceful rhythm. He wears his only set of clothes — faded blue shirt, shorts, and worn rubber shoes made from tire retreads. In this country, you can identify people from a distance by the color of their clothes since they wear the only garments they own.

The girls lead. Their animated chatter with an occasional giggle wafts our way on the gentle breeze. Ben's long stride has no trouble keeping up with his sisters' but he lingers back to listen to our conversation.

I'm not sure how long it's been since I just walked. Not for exercise but for transport. We move into a purposeful, easy stride. The distances are so great the horizon looks flat, with no visible signs of civilization except footpaths — no power or phone lines, roads, vehicles, buildings, or fences. Seeing only a few people along the way, I am startled when I hear a voice in the bushes.

"*Toyei*," a Karamojong greeting that translates to, "Are you alive?" as we would say, "Good morning."

Linda's response translates, "Yes, I'm alive." Somehow, these greetings seem to fit in a land where life's focus is on survival. Three shepherd boys and their goats move into view; two wear oversize, holey shirts and rubber tire shoes. The third wears a jacket, and shoes made from a thin piece of goatskin with a thin thong between his toes. All three are naked from the waist down and carry sticks to herd their goats.

The path takes us between giant rock outcroppings to the edge of a dry riverbed with steep sides, hinting of the fury when rains hit. As we begin to descend into the riverbed, three young men with AK-47 rifles slung over their shoulders call out to Tubo and a heated discussion follows.

As we wait from a distance, Byron and Losilo stride into view. With prayer and preparations to make, they got off to a later start but easily caught up, their bodies accustomed to long-distance walking. Tubo, Losilo, and Byron each walk three to thirteen miles to the different villages five or six days a week.

With an uncomfortable tension in the air, we wait for Tubo to fill us in on the dispute. His face troubled, he gestures to Byron and Losilo for a private conversation, then returns to the warriors to resume an animated debate, punctuated with dramatic hand gestures.

"These guys don't want us to cross the river," Byron fills us in. "Three years ago, when white men crossed, looking for rubies, the river dried up and hasn't flowed since. They believe the men took away the River Spirit. The warriors threatened Tubo if he crosses with 'the white people.'"

"So what are we to do?" Linda hesitates.

"Tubo asked me to go tell those men the first story." Byron looks amazed. "The first story I taught them about the beginning, about God, Satan's fall, and God giving men free will to choose who to follow. I told him he should go tell them."

"So Tubo gets it, Honey!"

"Yes, it's the first time Tubo has seen it. He's not just copying my words, he is seeing the application!"

With Byron's assurance that Tubo can easily catch up, we stride on contentedly toward the village. The local Karamojong tribe is illiterate, relying on oral communication; their stories link their culture and history, and guide their future. Byron uses story as a tool, teaching Locilo and Tubo biblical stories and truths. The trio use dramatic storytelling to pass the message on to surrounding villages. The stories morph into songs adapted from their own songs about harvesting, cows, and their lives. They make the rounds to six villages to give the next, much-anticipated, biblical story that will eventually evolve into a song and dance. A hand-cranked cassette recorder, kept by the village chief, captures the villagers' music.

Africans are storytellers — creative and musical. Song and dance imprint the stories into their culture and lore, making lasting impressions. The power of story crosses barriers of culture and language as it connects with the heart. The Old Testament tales of Abraham, Isaac, and Esau are so fitting in this land where the basics of cattle, goats, and the struggle to survive are the building blocks of life.

The path inclines gently as we approach Nakaramoi, a village identical to all the other *manyattas* I have seen. The villagers have already gathered around the rocks by the only tree outside the kraal. The men sit on narrow, six-inch wooden pedestal stools; some wear only *shukas*, others drape a *shuka* over their western clothing. The villagers are either barefoot or wear shoes made from tire treads; many of the men wear knit caps or felt hats. They keep their *fimbo* with them as they prop their weapons against the tree: an assortment of rifles, bows, and a hand-cranked tape recorder. Warriors down through the ages have been doing the same, putting their weapons to the side to gather.

Some women stand, others sit straight-legged on the ground or on the rocks. Every age is here, from newborns feeding at their mother's breast to wrinkled old women who look as if they could be over 100 years old. This is a hard land and its harshness shows in the weathered look of these people, making it hard to guess their age; they don't even know their own age. The children are dirty and many have the swollen bellies of malnutrition. Flies are a constant companion; resting unbothered on lips, eyes, and noses. Babies and children are everywhere; mothers with babies on their backs, grandmothers with them on their laps, and small girls with them strapped to their backs.

Ben and Seve climb onto a boulder followed by a throng of local kids. I laugh as I see their white faces in a sea of black. Linda greets the women and admires their babies, a commonality crossing cultures. She tends to some health concerns with a little rock-side medical diagnosis while Byron, Losilo, and Tubo visit with the chief and elders.

Stanley sits on a rock next to the oldest man in the village who is sporting a green felt hat with a prominent ostrich feather, and a half-dollar size, bone lip plug. His only clothing is a faded, worn, green jacket, buttoned only at his belly, exposing his dangling privates to the sun. A young, naked boy leans between his knees, stick in hand. A fly-covered, mangy dog suns itself next to him. The *mzee* takes a pinch of snuff from a pouch and thumbs it into his nostril, snorting loudly, as he watches Stanley pinch tobacco out of his leather pouch and press it into the small bowl of his pipe. They now have a connection. The *mzee*, intrigued by Stanley's pocket-size pipe, turns it over in his leathery hands, inspecting it through a thick pair of cataracts. He clears his throat and speaks to Tubo. Respect for elders is apparent as everyone listens when the *mzee* speaks.

Tubo, obviously filling a request to translate, helps Stanley and the *mzee* share a little of their world with each other. They have some things in common like kids and grandkids but, to the *mzee's* dismay, Stanley doesn't have goats or cows and only has one wife. Stanley tells him one wife is trouble enough, he cannot imagine having more. For a man to reach gray-haired age without goats or cows and with only one wife is mind-boggling to this Karamojong elder. Cows and wives are the ticket to success and respect.

In a search for commonalities, the *mzee* asks Stanley where the sun comes up in his country. When Stanley points to the east, the *mzee* exclaims, "Aha!" and excitedly points to the east where the sun comes up in his country. A discussion follows about how the sorghum is growing. The *mzee* is dumbfounded when he hears people in Stanley's country feed sorghum to their livestock. The cultures may seem worlds apart, but there is still common ground to connect if one makes the effort.

Byron smoothly transitions from conversation into the Old Testament story of when Abraham, following God's command, goes to the mountain to make a sacrifice without a sacrificial animal. God tells Abraham his beloved son, Isaac, will be the sacrifice. Astonished, the villagers mumble among themselves. Byron is a dramatic storyteller. He is on his feet, gesturing with his hands and animated in his speech, pausing while he waits for Losilo to translate.

Byron pulls a young boy aside, whispers in his ear then gently lays him on a rock. He raises his voice and speeds his speech to build the tension as he acts out the moment where Abraham raises his knife to sacrifice Isaac. Then he abruptly halts as he dramatizes how God called out to Abraham to stop and provided a substitute for the sacrifice. Byron releases the boy and walks down the hill toward the goats. He pretends to free one from the bushes then gathers it in his arms as he dramatizes the substitute sacrifice. Everyone focuses intently on the story.

A discussion follows about the meaning of the tale. Byron doesn't preach to them about its message of obedience, about Jesus being sacrificed in our place, God's provision for our needs, or of putting God first over your "Isaac," whatever that represents in your life. Instead, he patiently asks questions, listens, and guides them into their discovery of the truths themselves. When God stopped Abraham from killing his son, he provided a ram for sacrifice. "How often have you seen a goat or a ram get its horns caught in a bush?" Byron asks the herdsmen.

"Never."

The consensus is that God Himself provided. These people connect with the Old Testament stories; they are living similar lives.

Byron usually only tells one story, but the people beg for another, so he begins to tell the story of God calling Moses to tell Pharaoh to let His people go. Byron walks over to a bush as he tells them how God talked to Moses through a burning bush that never burned up.

"How can a bush burn and not burn up?" he asks them. "Have you ever seen this? Have you ever heard a bush talk?"

After much mumbling and discussion, the consensus is many have seen bushes on fire but the bush always burns; no one has ever heard a bush talk.

110

One of the elders speaks. "Surely it is God Himself who does such a thing."

"God told Moses to speak to Pharaoh but Moses had many fears. Pharaoh was a big chief, the most important man in the land. Moses was worried because he stuttered when he spoke, and truly afraid the big chief would kill him."

The villagers roar with laughter as Byron acts out his fear and stuttering, followed by Losilo's attempts to stutter in translation. Byron describes the plagues Moses brought on Egypt to show Pharaoh God's power and to convince him to let His people go. As he describes the plague of grasshoppers devastating their crops, I think how well these people can relate to such stories. They know what it is like to survive on a thread and have crops wiped out with grasshoppers, fire, or drought.

When Byron tells them how Pharaoh's magicians were able to copy some of the plagues, he asks them, "Where do you think their power came from?"

The consensus is "from God."

"Where do your *imurans* (witch doctors) get their power?"

"From God."

"If the *imurans* get their power from God, then wouldn't they know these stories about God?"

"Yes!"

"Have your *imurans* told you these stories?"

"No."

"If they don't know these stories about God, then they must not know God."

Exclamation and discussion rumble through the crowd. This is something they have never thought of. One of the matriarchs in the village exclaims, "Then we should learn these stories."

This may seem like a minor realization, but it is big for this village. The elders hold tightly to the old ways as they pass down tradition and beliefs to the younger generations. When an elder makes a statement like this, it opens many doors to the rest of the villagers.

It is incredible to see people hear about God for the first time and to see the Holy Spirit breaking through the darkness, bringing hope to their lives.

24 A Struggle to Belong *Mapambano ya Kushirikiana*
Uganda 2004

The trek home brings us back through vast fields of head-high sunflowers. Their large, face-like blooms make me feel as if they are staring at me as I walk through a crowd of people. Maybe there has just been too much closeness today. I find myself annoyed by the lack of personal space as the locals touch my skin and play with my hair.

Then the begging... I am so acutely aware of how little these people have and how much I have, but I find my annoyance quickly overrides guilt because of the constancy of begging. Many times today, women asked me for my shirt. I do like to try to bridge the cultural gap but I draw the line there. I'm going home with the shirt on my back.

In the thick of the sunflower field, we hear the piercing cry of a baby. It isn't that the cry is loud; it is a weak, desperate cry that pierces the heart. Following the sound to a small clearing, we find an emaciated woman sitting at the base of a tree, trying to breastfeed a baby. Without Tubo to translate, Linda doesn't have enough language in common to get the story. This is either not the woman's baby or she is the mother and unable to produce milk. I feel desperately helpless in my inability to help.

"Often when a mother dies of HIV, leaving her baby without milk, the grandmother will allow the baby to nurse her flabby, flat breasts," Linda explains. "Occasionally the baby's cries will trigger milk production in the old grandmother."

"Does it work?"

"Sadly it's rare but it's a desperate measure against the usual — the baby dies. It's so hard being surrounded by profound poverty and hunger and knowing I can't meet all their needs," Linda sighs as we walk toward home. "When I help, it sets up jealousy because I can't help them all and I find it so hard to find the balance of providing for my own family. I can't let my own children go hungry but the mother in me hurts when I see a mother desperately fighting for her children's survival."

"But you help so much. You employ people when you can. Mary works in your home."

"True. And we buy milk, eggs, and goats from the villagers. We in turn share the meat back to the villagers."

My twin so often undervalues the extent of her contributions.

I anxiously scan the brush for the AK-47 wielding warriors as we once again approach the dry riverbed. I am relieved to see the figure there is only an elderly woman digging in the sand for water. With a warm greeting, she stops dipping muddy water into her yellow plastic jugs to visit. Two women, each carrying a pair of twins on their back and yellow jugs on their head, join us. As the women visit, they swing their babies to the front and allow them to breastfeed. Linda immerses into their conversation, with animated gestures indicating the direction of their village, giving me time to reflect on the scene unfolding before me.

Yesterday I studied the intricate patterns of scarring on the foreheads and necks of the women grinding sorghum. Now I see that the scarring continues down their chest and breasts. I cannot imagine the pain they go through to be so "beautiful" as seen in their culture. I suspect they create the scars in the same manner as the Tanzanian women I knew in my youth, using crude knives to puncture the skin then filling the wounds with ashes to create infection and ultimately their "beautiful" scars. Pure beauty to the Karamojong but, viewing this through my cultural lens, all I see are the pain and risk. My own culture blinds me, but my culture has similar rituals with earrings, piercings, and tattoos.

The sun dips to the horizon as we reach the open field of scraggly sorghum. No longer having to walk single file, we are better able to engage in conversation, which has moved to third culture kids, children raised in different cultures from their own. The term refers to the world we live in when we keep one foot in the culture of origin and the other in the one in which we are raised. Somewhere in the middle, between the two worlds, is the rich path a third culture kid has the privilege to journey and garner the best from each world as they develop a different language and a unique worldview.

"I suppose a third culture kid sadly has many goodbyes in life but, on the other hand, they have a focus on the here and now instead of on the future—"

"And an emphasis on real relationship and entertainment built around socializing with friends," my twin finishes for me.

"My MK and African friends have fun with sticks, rocks, trees, water, and things around them," grins Ben, sword-fighting with a stick, "instead of toys, Xbox, or games."

Third culture kids that meet further along in life tend to pick up right where they left off. There is a wider view of the world and an acceptance of beliefs, dress, and culture that is different from their own. With fewer people of their own type, there is less segregation by age groups, gender, or race.

"I always felt it was strange whenever we returned to America," I admit, "that friends sympathized because they thought we had a hard life in Africa."

114

"Yep, they either thought we were stuck in a crevice between two worlds, or that we were American kids like them, but stuck in a foreign land."

"Shame they couldn't see we are just like them but Africa is home to us, not a foreign land. D'you think there are downsides to being a third culture kid?"

"Maybe a struggle for a sense of belonging?"

Linda is right. We never quite fit into the African culture and we all had difficulties immersing ourselves into American ways. I tend to remember the positives, but my heart aches as a remark from Seve yesterday wrenches some buried memories to my mind: "We can fit in anywhere, but we don't belong anywhere."

It's difficult to answer the question, "Where are you from?" Our roots are where our heart and family are, not a place or a country. We all greatly value the life experiences that make us who we are, but everyone does like to belong.

Returning to furlough in America every four years, Linda and I experienced America during our fourth grade, eighth grade, and college years. The adjustment in my college years was hardest because I didn't make the transition under Mother and Daddy's secure umbrella. Although belonging to Baylor's track and soccer teams gave me a solid step, I still struggled to belong. I moved from a life that was free, slow-paced, loosely scheduled and with low outside expectations to the land of the "free," but I didn't *feel* free, with confusing expectations, fast-paced schedules, and routines.

I was dropped into a world where my clothes were years out of date, but I'd been living in a land where what I wore didn't matter. Coming from a land with a greater diversity and tolerance for difference, I found that matters of faith, spirituality, and religion were narrow, divisive, and laden with others' expectations. In some ways, I lost some freedoms when I moved to the land of the free. I was fiercely proud of America and being American, but just as proud to be from Africa.

Restrictions and land mines riddled my life in Africa, but I knew the game. Our communication was censored. We knew not to voice negative opinions about the government, take pictures of the airport or the president, tear a currency note, or openly fly our American flag. I love my American homeland and appreciate its freedoms, it was just a culture shock when I first immersed myself in it. The sense of displacement is a small drop of negative in the ocean of benefits of being a third culture kid.

Hearing Ben talk gladdens my already grateful heart, although I'm saddened to hear the next generation's struggle with the sense of belonging as I did.

Seve's twelve-year-old wisdom strikes a resounding chord. "Any place can become home if I only loosen my grip on my previous home, and others can become family if I only open my heart to let them in."

25 Bush Clinics *Kliniki Misituni*
Tanzania 1960's

Linda and I lay snugly in our twin beds as our daydreams passed to night dreams of tomorrow's clinic trip. Forgoing the usual ski 'jamas, we went to bed in our clothes to be ready for the early morning start.

In the place between reality and dreams, Daddy scooped Linda in one arm and me in the other, our arms wrapping around his shoulders, faces nestled into his warm neck as he carried us along the narrow hallway into the cool, dark night to the Land Rover. I peeked over his shoulder to see Steve and Jim stumbling along behind. He made a return trip for Chipper. Mother carried the cardboard box packed with homemade cinnamon rolls for breakfast, our lunch, and cans of emergency food.

I awakened slowly at dawn to the jostling of the Land Rover, the feel of Linda's sweaty arm across my chest, and her stringy hair across my face. Daddy entertained us with stories and taught us the names of animals and birds and, as the day warmed, we took turns sitting on the roof rack, giving a bird's eye view of the scenery and an endless rollercoaster ride, bumping and jolting in the wind. The first few miles of the trip's paved roads quickly transitioned to rutted dirt roads, then small, sparsely-traveled roads, then footpaths and, at times, we just drove cross country. Daddy rarely used a map; somehow, he just knew where to go.

When we arrived at the mud-brick Baptist church, a boy rang the car tire rim hanging from a tree, drawing people from all directions as we helped Daddy set up for clinic. Steve opened the top of the medicine box and the familiar, strong scents of methylated spirits, liquid vitamins, worm medicine, quinine, and tetracycline mingled with the musky charcoal smell of the mud church as Mother began to arrange the jars of colored liquid and white plastic bottles of pills on the wooden table.

The sermon was always first and the patients had to listen to that if they were going to see the doctor. Sometimes the pastor gave the sermon and other times Daddy preached in Swahili while the pastor translated into his tribal language. I liked it when Daddy preached because it was short.

On the way to the clinic, Linda and I wrote numbers on a piece of paper from one to one hundred to use for tickets. Daddy charged five shillings (75 cents) for adults and two shillings (30 cents) for children to ensure they really needed medical care and to avoid the dependency cycle that handouts can set up. After the sermon, the patients saw the doctor in numerical order, which meant some waited until dusk. Daddy had a number system for all the pills and liquid medications so he could write, on the outside of a small envelope or on a bottle label, the medicine he wanted Mother, volunteers, or we kids to put in. An envelope with "24 (41)" meant 24 pills of tetracycline. He drew pictures of the sun and the moon to indicate how often to take the medicine.

Linda and I sat on the ground, enticing doodlebugs from their burrows in the mud floor. Some people called them antlions but I didn't think they looked like an ant or a lion. Across the small room, Daddy sat on a wooden bench talking to a woman, his stethoscope slung around his neck as he focused eye-to-eye, concentrating to cross language and cultural barriers. Swahili was new to him and was this woman's second language. They sat next to the window, utilizing the only light available. Her hollow cheeks and hot, feverish skin spoke more than the words they could find in common. Her *kanga* pulled down, she breastfed her infant from long, flat, wrinkled, dehydrated breasts as a child strapped on her back cried.

A small boy at her feet sucked on an empty vodka bottle brought to hold liquid medicine; he sported the reddish hair, huge swollen belly, and large protruding belly button of a child suffering from severe malnutrition. Daddy used his eyes and ears to diagnose; he looked, listened, smelled, percussed, and prodded since lab tests weren't available.

A pregnant woman was next. Daddy listened then translated for Linda and me. "This is her fourteenth baby, but she only has eight living." With one earpiece of the stethoscope in my ear, the other in Linda's, we strained to hear the sound of the baby's heartbeat.

"I can't hear it," Linda whispered.

I wasn't sure if I could or if I just wanted to hear it so bad that I imagined it.

Daddy flopped an old woman's flat, saggy breasts over her shoulder to listen to her heart and lungs. The old women had floppy, wrinkly breasts that drooped as low as their belly button. A woman could walk, with a large pot or bundle of wood on her head, and still pass her breast over her shoulder to feed the child strapped on her back with a cloth. Mothers carried their babies on their back and breastfed them until they were two.

As Daddy listened to her chest, he quietly began to hum a tune and we joined in with the words; a song about dog's ears, but we knew it was about breasts, which seemed so funny at the time:

Do your ears hang low? Do they wobble to and fro?
Can you tie them in a knot? Can you tie them in a bow?
Can you throw them o'er your shoulder like a continental soldier?

Do your ears hang low?

Using the same catchy tune, we added our own version of the lyrics. Daddy's patients laughed but thankfully didn't know what we were singing about.

We moved freely in and out of Mother's room where she dispensed medicine, but asked permission to enter Daddy's examining room with "*hodi*." The Swahili greeting asking for entrance works well in a land with few doors. With Daddy's stethoscope, we listened to the heartbeat of an unborn baby, a caterpillar crawling on the drug box, Chipper's breathing, and the heartbeat of the mangy, yellow dog outside the door.

As Mother dispensed medicine, she made furtive attempts to work homeschool math into our day. "If this lady needs two pills, three times a day for ten days, how many pills does she need?"

We held heads for dental work and limbs for suturing, kept records, counted pills, drew up medicine in syringes for Mother, and held bowls, flashlights, and instruments for Daddy. We watched more than we helped, but we felt like we helped. Daddy used whatever and wherever was available for his medical and dental work. He laid a woman on the front Land Rover seat, her head almost touching the ground, to give her a treatment of percussion-aided postural drainage as he thumped her back with his cupped hands.

Steve pestered him because he was bored. Daddy asked, "Steve, have you ever been here before?"

"No, Daddy, you know that."

"Well, if I were in a new place, I would not be wasting my chance to explore, find streams, climb trees, and see the birds. Now, I don't have time for that, so why do you waste your fine chance?"

That was the only prompting we all needed and off we went to follow the African kids into their bush world. My chest burst with pride as I felt my homemade slingshot bouncing against my bare chest as we followed single file along the narrow sandy path toward the river. Steve found Y-shaped sticks for slingshots, and sanded them to a polished smoothness while Daddy, when free, helped Jim cut strips from an old bicycle tube for the slings. Chipper helped me make the rock pockets out of shoe tongues cut from worn-out Bata canvas shoes the boys outgrew. I say that, but Chipper was only three; he just thought he helped. Linda didn't have a slingshot but I let her borrow mine.

She and I left the boys to their play to join the girls. We didn't get to play with them often because they were usually busy helping their mothers. They were so serious; we had to teach them to play. We made dresses from bark for dolls we made from gourds.

One of the mothers called the girls to the hut, causing an abrupt change of direction in our play. Linda and I followed them to the riverbed to dig holes in the sand with scoops made from split gourds. We squatted and waited for muddy water to seep into our hole so we could scoop and carry it in gourds back to the woman.

When the girls moved to help their mothers grind corn, we decided girls' work was too hard and drifted back to play with the boys. We built forts, herded goats and cows, played with mangy, tick-ridden dogs, threw sticks and rocks, ran, hiked, climbed trees, explored, visited villages, jumped creeks, dammed streams, and caught chameleons, tadpoles, frogs, lizards, bugs, and snakes. In the afternoon, we had a hot game of soccer using a gourd for a ball. The distant Land Rover horn or the setting sun were our signal to return to the clinic.

On the way home, we stopped at a small *duka* and sat on a wobbly wooden bench while Daddy studied the menu on the crooked black chalkboard. He settled for the known and favored cup of chai and a loaf of bread cut lengthwise and smeared with Blue Band margarine. Daddy bought fruit for the hospital because it was cheap and plentiful in that part of the country, buying 60 grapefruit-size oranges for fourteen cents and three stalks of bananas for seven cents. He bought tangerines, lemons, papayas, mangos, and avocados. Mother wrote about one of Daddy's fruit shopping sprees at Kyela:

> Last week John found an old woman who had oranges in her field. A group of young people gathered and waited for the wrinkled old grandmother to climb the tree. This shows the position of women. John was so embarrassed that this old grandmother would have to climb for him that he ended up buying every orange, lemon, and banana the woman had. His upbringing doesn't fit here, but nor can he forget it.

As we bumped along the dusty dark road toward home, the sky reddened as the sun melted into the hazy horizon, leaving us only a cone of light slicing into the darkness of the road ahead. With the darkness came monotony. Linda and I loved to read but the road was too bumpy to hold a flashlight so we occupied ourselves with trying to weave our fingers together as tightly as possible and by telling knock knock jokes.

In the headlights, we saw a man holding a boy in his arms, as he waved his hand up and down to signal us to stop. Steve said in America they stuck out their thumb when they wanted a ride but I didn't believe him.

The Land Rover engine whined as Daddy reversed through the thick dust and pulled over to examine the barefoot boy in our headlights. The boy looked away, trying to be brave as tears streamed down his dusty cheeks while Daddy examined his leg. He made a splint with some wooden dividers from his medicine box then settled both of them in the back between the stalks of bananas. It was a long, bumpy ride to the hospital where the boy would get a cast for his broken leg. He never complained but I could tell by the look on his face that he really hurt.

Dozing to the drone and monotony, I was startled awake as the Land Rover lurched to a stop, throwing me into the back of the front seats. "Daddy! Don't kill de kids!" Steve chimed before the dust even settled. Behind me, the boy cried out as his father quietly spoke to him in Swahili. Daddy grabbed the flashlight and jumped out to investigate.

The Land Rover rested at an angle, its front wheels dropped into an unmarked, deep trench across the road. Daddy worked most of the night jacking up the vehicle and packing rocks and branches underneath to raise the tires enough to get us out. It was still a dark, early morning hour when we finally resumed our trip homewards, bright lights again illuminating the arc of dirt road in front of us. My eyes blurred from fatigue as I strained to beat the light down the road.

Daddy gave us the job of watching the road for him and we took it seriously. Road construction was a constant, heavy equipment or ditches often left without warning signs. He often gave us jobs on these trips, usually giving Jim or Steve the task of watching the map, but many times we went places that weren't on it.

We rounded a corner and slid to a stop just in time to keep from running over a python stretched across the road. Against Mother's complaints, Daddy let us climb out to look, while the boy and his father silently watched through the window. The python, having recently eaten a dik-dik or small impala, could hardly move because of the huge lump in its stomach. Daddy drove into the bushes, around the python, to head on to the hospital then home, finally arriving at a tired 5:30 a.m.

*****

Clinic days were a mixture of fun and adventure but were also hot and boring. The long days were usually rewarded by a cool-off and campsite by a lake. Lake Masoko, one of our favorite stops, is a crater lake we called "Lake Me So Cold." It provided a chilling swim and the intrigue of finding old German Hellers in the mud. It's said that the German soldiers threw guns and coins into the lake to keep them out of the hands of the British when they lost Tanganyika in 1919.

Kyela Clinic was hot and humid in a region with heavy rainfall, mosquitos, and malaria. Mother described a clinic day:

After John had treated a one-month-old baby, her mother returned to my door with the baby gasping then becoming still and quiet. John massaged his abdomen, gave artificial respiration, and calmly asked me what we had given the baby. He was relieved to hear we had treated him for bronchitis so he was probably suffering from an allergic reaction to antibiotics. John was concerned because there is a narrow margin between the treatment and toxic dose for treating a baby for malaria. He remained calm, gave an adrenalin shot, and went on treating other patients while my own heart and breathing raced until the baby began to breathe quietly again.

One woman came in holding her baby upside down. With our language barriers, I couldn't figure out why. It turns out John told her to do that to tease me. Sometimes I think his humor doesn't help but it does break the monotony of the day.

Another woman had a series of parallel scars on her forehead and neck. The note from John gave the diagnosis as "bilateral headache treated by the witch doctor." Another, with scars cut on her abdomen, carried a note that commented "she saw a local gastro-entomologist before she came to see me."

We saw 70 patients — a light day. It seems that most suffer from malaria, malnutrition, and worms. In our clinics we see bronchitis, severe dental disease, asthma, diarrhea, hookworm, ulcers, goiters, bilharzia, infections, tuberculosis, and anemia. A recent blood test on a woman with hookworms showed a hemoglobin level of 3.6; values of five and six are common which are low when you consider twelve to fourteen normal in America and less than ten would be a candidate for transfusion.

This is a rice-growing area, which has kept the economy up. They had never had medical care until we started our once-a-week clinic. We loaded their payment of five, 150-pound bags of rice onto the Land Rover to bring to the hospital.

Kyela Clinic's campsite was about ten miles away on beautiful Lake Nyasa, also called Lake Malawi. The 360-mile-long, 50-mile-wide lake is the third largest and second deepest lake in Africa straddling the Tanzania, Malawi, and Mozambique border. Banana groves and small villages with straw-tufted, round houses lined the shore, with the Livingston Mountains providing a beautiful backdrop to the wave-washed sand where dugout canoes and fishing nets dried along the coconut palm lined shore. What I really cared about was that it had a beach and waves like the ocean. Mother continued:

> After the clinic, we went to the lake for lunch and a swim. As we were walking on the beach, I stopped and didn't want to go any further. "What's the matter?" John asked. I told him I couldn't go on because men were bathing. He said I wouldn't disturb them. After 34 years of my culture, it's not easy for me to pass by naked men and not feel embarrassed. Women bathe separately. They enter the water with their *kanga* without exposing themselves; their top doesn't matter. The bathers' routine seems unbothered by crocodiles and hippos in the lake.

We knew the drill well when we reached our beach campsite: unpack the tent and sleeping bags to set up camp high on the sand where it was level; match the color-coded tent poles, zip sleeping bags together, and then get swimsuits for beach time. Mother stayed at the camp to fix supper while Daddy took us swimming. We took turns climbing on his shoulders so he could launch us out over the water. I flew as I tried to arch into a dive, ending up in a clumsy belly buster — at least that's what Jim called it. I didn't feel my belly bust but it sure did sting.

Daddy called, "Time," and everyone headed out of the water toward camp, except for me. I was having too much fun so I ducked under the water and pretended I didn't hear. I felt the sand scrape along my legs as a riptide yanked me away from shore. I fought for the surface. The current sucked me under, filling my nose and lungs with water. I fought for the surface again to cough and gasp a precious gulp of air before the current sucked me under once more. Disoriented, I tumbled along the sand, bobbing up and down. I caught a fleeting glimpse of my family walking up the beach toward the tent before the current pulled me under again.

I was alone in a swirl of water and sand and I sensed this was the end. As in the pool on the Queen Mary two years earlier, I was sad. I didn't like being left behind. This time I struggled with everything I had to keep my head above water. I was in a desperate fight for life, which became more desperate with each glimpse of my retreating family. I knew how to swim, but my "swim" seemed to have escaped me, leaving me in a frenzied, panic-stricken struggle for air, life, and the family that once again was leaving me behind.

26 Striking a Balance *Kusawazisha*
Tanzania 1960s

I fought for a precious gulp of air before being tugged back under, over and over again. The grief of the loss of my family weighed heavily as I fought. Tumbling in the swirl of white, blue, and confusion, I felt a strong yank on my left leg. Still underwater, fighting for the surface, I felt my leg pulled, then yanked hard, pulled and yanked. Finally — air! I felt the coarse sand on my skin as someone dragged me by both legs onto the sandy shore.

I coughed and spluttered as I rolled to my knees, gasping for air. As my vision cleared, I saw an old woman standing above me, adjusting her wet *kanga*. She had left her laundry at the edge of the lake to rescue me. Looking between her bowed, gnarled knees, I saw Daddy running toward me. Conflicting feelings swirled; relief to be alive and with my family combined with the knowledge I'd disobeyed Daddy. The heavy guilt and dread of impending discipline melted away as he held me in his arms.

Back at camp, I immersed in the sweet chaos of family. We brushed the sand off our feet in a hopeless attempt to keep it out of the tent and sleeping bags. The faces of local kids filled our tent windows as Linda and I pulled off our wet swimsuits. Anywhere we camped, they were right in our face — no personal boundaries. They pressed their faces against the tent, car, or house windows to watch, laugh, and mock us. They followed us to the bush to watch us go to the bathroom or walked into our camp to watch Mother cook.

"I've got an idea," Steve jumped up, responding to our whines as he rummaged through the boxes of food. Linda and I watched through the tent screen window as he made a big show of bubbling Fizzies in a glass of water.

"What're you doing?" Linda frowned.

He poured the bubbly magic in a circle around our tent and told them, in Swahili, if they stepped across, it would bring bad luck. They didn't cross the line. Steve was my hero. As our local friends would say, "The wisdom of a big brother."

After a restless, hot, mosquito-buzzed night of bad dreams about drowning, I awakened to the sounds of Mother making breakfast. Daddy helped me put on my blue jeans, T-shirt, and red tennis shoes and we headed out across the sand into the bush. The walk to the village of the old woman who saved my life seemed to take all day. Finally, the narrow path approached it.

After a discussion in Swahili with the curious villagers, they showed us to the old woman's mud hut. The woman heated water in an aluminum pot on the fire in the center of the hut while she and Daddy talked in Swahili. The old, rough, hard-working hands that left her laundry and gave me life now offered me eggs.

Walking back to our beach campsite, Daddy talked to me about the importance of saying thank you to the people that help you in life; an early heartprint deeply engraved.

*****

Daddy's work at the hospital became challenging as he balanced medical practice, personnel issues, and a growing bush-clinic schedule. Then there was his real job — playing with us.

His scouting trips with agriculture and church-developer missionaries for places needing medical care uncovered much more need than means. A strong desire to be closely involved in his family life as well as providing medical, electrical, plumbing, and mechanical needs for the family and the hospital compound kept him in a fight for balance. Often he was the only doctor at the hospital so he didn't always return for breakfast or lunch. One day he said he hadn't had time to care for the sick, spending all his time ironing out disputes between nurses, and burying the dead because of a new law requiring a lot of red tape.

Mother described our favorite clinic, its remoteness offering us kids the sure promise of adventure:

> John has been sick for three days with malaria, his third case already and he gets it badly. He and Keith left for Matwiga where they did two clinics. He returned Wednesday and I had the children ready to go with him to his clinic at Songwe Ulambia. I had decided, if we were to see him, we would have to go along. I had heard it was a bad road and a faraway place, but I had to go to see it for myself. The place isn't even on the map! John has been giving smallpox vaccinations and seeing patients while working with an agriculture missionary to help the village with their crops.
>
> The people raise pyrethrum, used to make insecticide. Without public transport, the women carry the produce on their heads. The last time they went, the men were stuck for hours so I started packing canned food because, if the car broke down, it would take a week to walk out.

126

These people desperately needed medical care so Daddy told them they must build a bridge across the river so he could bring medical supplies. The roads were more footpaths than roads. They made a bridge by stacking loose logs across the river. Perfect if we were on foot.

The five of us balanced along the logs to join Daddy on the far bank as he directed Mother and the Land Rover across the bridge. Sensing the tension, we silently watched with gut-wrenching dread as Mother pleaded, "Oh, John. I just can't! Oh, John, John. No, John!"

I don't remember seeing Mother cry before, except when she said goodbye to Mema and Granddaddy. She cried then while Daddy sternly fussed at her. Putting the Land Rover in four-wheel drive, it roared and tilted at a scary angle. We stood there with dread in our hearts and lumps in our throats, pushing back the choking fear that Mother was going to fall in and drown.

Her letter only scratched at the emotions on that riverbank:

> When the logs began to roll, tilting the Land Rover, I lost my nerve and let it slip back. This caused the logs, which were just lying across other logs, to part, and the wheel slipped between the bottom logs, putting the Land Rover at a horrible angle.
>
> It was hard for me to follow John's directions because the spare tire, mounted on an already high front hood, kept me from seeing where I was going. It looked like John was directing me right into the river. He had to jack up the Land Rover twice and rearrange the logs before I could cross.
>
> I was tired before the clinic started and ready to stop after the first 25 patients, but we had 100 to see. One mother of six listened and remained to ask questions; two of her children's eyes were swollen shut and their faces swollen as if they were in the last stages of leukemia or nephritis. They were lethargic, had sores on their legs, huge swollen bellies, and red hair. They were dying. I saw three others dying of pneumonia, severe burns, and dehydration. The parents wouldn't allow the children to go to hospital. Oh, how my heart aches for them. Why won't the parents listen? I long to help more, but what can I do?

The birth and death rates were high. Women had a child every year of their childbearing years, losing a large percentage of their children. Their solution was to have as many children as they could so there would be some alive to care for them in their old age — a real deterrent to family planning efforts.

Our MK friends — the Laffoon boys and Oliphint girls — came along to the Songwe Ulambia clinic the next time we kids went with Daddy, magnifying the adventure and excitement factor.

Flop, flop, flop… The familiar thump of a flat tire, the third so far. Daddy pulled to the side of the washboard-rutted dirt road. Changing a tire was fun for us kids.

"Girls to the left, boys to the right."

Twelve kids bounced off the roof rack and hood and spilled out of the Land Rover, scattering to each side of the road for a bathroom break while Daddy unlocked the jack. As he fit the long handle into it, we searched the road and drainage ditches, racing to be the one who found the best tire chocks.

"When's it my turn?" I whined as Daddy fitted the wrench onto the lug nuts and balanced Linda as she stood and bounced on the wrench to loosen the nut. He cranked the long handle jack up and down while Steve bugged with, "Daddy, I want to do it, I want to help!"

Jim got to spin the iron wrench to remove the lug nuts then climbed up on the hood to loosen the nuts on the spare tire. Daddy pulled the flat tire off the axle and rolled it toward the boys as they jockeyed for position to roll it to the front of the Land Rover.

"Almost gotcha!" Jim bounced the spare off the hood, narrowly missing his target — Steve — so Steve could direct its wobble back to the rear where Daddy waited.

Squatting in the dirt, Daddy braced his elbows on his knees as he maneuvered the wheel onto the axle.

"Me, Daddy, Me!" Chipper got to start one lug nut while Daddy quickly hand-tightened the rest. Jim followed with the wrench, making several rounds to be sure they were equally tight. Steve lowered the jack and Linda and I got to take turns jumping with both our feet on the wrench to tighten the nuts, with Daddy doing the final tweaks.

He repositioned the flat tire on the ground in front of the Land Rover. With Steve directing from the front, Daddy drove onto the top of the flat tire with the front wheel to break the tire bead.

"Woah, Daddy! You got it!" Steve hollered as he motioned to him to reverse back off. Daddy pounded the flat tire with a large rubber mallet and used the tire irons to muscle the heavy-duty eight-ply tire to pull out the inner tube. I was amazed at his strength and loved to see his brown, muscled arms working. He rolled the inflated tube along his cheeks and lips feeling for leaks. Finding one, he used his Bic pen to mark a big plus then responded to our pleas of, "Daddy, I want to feel!" He then twisted a small handle, clamping a vulcanized hot patch over the plus mark on the tube.

Now the best part — lighting the match to set the patch on fire. A sweet, acrid, gray smoke enveloped us as we watched the fiery red cinders burn. Daddy worked the repaired tube back into the tire and wrenched the tire back into place with the irons and rubber mallet. Linda stood with both feet on the foot pump, jumping up and down, while I helped her balance. Daddy helped Jim lift the newly repaired tire to the hood so he could anchor it into place. Ready to go with a spare ready for the next flat.

Excitement built when Daddy switched to four-wheel drive as we crossed the wobbly log bridge made of stacked rolling poles. We made it across and began to accelerate up the winding, rocky escarpment but our wheels spun and dug into the sandy gravel. Scattered inside and on top of the Land Rover, we hung tightly as it roared, swayed, and kicked rocks as it once again dug into the sand.

"Yah!" "Faster, Daddy!" "Don't kill de kids, Daddy!" we cheered. He let air out of the tires and we tried repeatedly, each time reversing back down the escarpment, stopping just before the log bridge.

He jumped out to look over the Land Rover and the road. With a rear broken axle, he had to reverse up the steep, treacherous, rocky escarpment. With only the front axle working, he moved as much weight as possible to the front of the Land Rover to gain traction to climb in reverse. Steve helped him tie the heavy wooden drug box to the hood spare tire and we moved to the front of the Land Rover rack, hood, and bumper. Daddy tried many times to gain momentum to climb the hill, but the short distance between the wobbly bridge and the steep climb hampered his efforts. The road was loose and had many switchbacks, which he had to negotiate without visibility since he couldn't see the road with the Land Rover climbing in reverse.

Could it get any more fun than this? Some of us rode the roof rack of the bucking Land Rover; others ran alongside to jump on once we gained momentum. The journey up the escarpment was long and slow which gave us time to collect rocks, bugs, and plants, which we triumphantly showed Daddy. He knew the name and something about everything we collected, but seemed more focused on the road. Darkness came before we scaled the escarpment, which added to the visibility problems with the headlights pointing the wrong way.

With the excitement shared with our friends, we were in kids' heaven. The twelve of us talked about, and delighted, that our mothers must be worried.

A mother's perspective is very different:

By church time, John and the kids still had not arrived

129

and we began to get anxious. None of us could concentrate on the service. I can't even tell you who preached because we kept looking out of the window hoping to see Land Rover lights. Of course, there is no phone or vehicle services along the route, or any way for John to get our help if he needed it.

After church, we returned to the mission compound, but were all too worried to return to our homes. John can handle anything, but I began to imagine all the things that could go wrong. Our crew was long overdue as midnight neared and Keith and Frank began to organize a rescue. We gathered blankets, food, and made hot chocolate. Keith prepared to leave, as the only option was to backtrack along the lengthy route to find them.

Daddy made us feel like we were such a help. We were all in this together and we were going to make it. In the darkest of dark — African dark — triumphant conquerors topped the escarpment together and continued the journey home.

27 Song and Dance *Wimbo na Ngoma*
Uganda 2004

Our third morning in Kaabong and, as sleep fades and my mind awakens into consciousness, I struggle with, "Where am I? This isn't my bed; where in the world am I?" I savor a sweet snuggle with Stanley before we enter the busy world of family. We join the gang for chai around the warmth of the charcoal burner.

While waiting for the 7:30 a.m. daily radio contact with the Baptist mission in Nairobi, we take turns at the computer, connecting with our loved ones by email using satellite communication. It is as if we come up for air to connect with another world before we dive back into the world and culture around us. It makes me think of my girlhood years when the reel-to-reel tapes from Mema and Granddaddy connected me to another world.

The ache in my hips from yesterday's long walk fades a little with the early morning fog. This morning we are walking to Sit and Squat. I wonder how a small village in a remote corner of Uganda got the name Sit and Squat. I hope my personal needs won't require me to go behind a shrub to sit and squat because my still sore muscles may not allow me to stand again.

"Cinda, last night as I was going to sleep, I thought about the old woman that pulled you out of Lake Nyasa," Linda says as we walk. "Why d'you always get into trouble in the water? D'you remember in the fifth grade, when we lived in Kenya, you almost drowned in the Kisumu Club swimming pool?"

"What happened, Nuna?" Ben loves the thrill of adventure.

"Your mom and I pedaled our banana-seat bicycles down the jacaranda-lined road to the town club, our fins and masks tied to racks behind us," I tell him.

"I used to love our race down the steps to the dressing room, Sis. Frantically yanking on our swimsuits, fins, mask, and snorkel so we could clumsily clop to the pool."

"The finish line was at the other end of the Olympic-size pool, Ben. I led, with my legs burning and chest heaving as I swam, wearing the snorkel gear and Granddaddy's orange scuba gloves. I was wearing the gloves because it was my turn."

"So how did you nearly drown?" Ben asks.

"Somewhere in the deep end I lost my way. My world span as I sank and rose again to catch my breath then spin some more. I was confused, the world was a swirl, and I couldn't breathe."

"I was shouting, 'Cinda, what are you doing?' but I wasn't sure she could hear me."

"I looked up and saw your mom standing at the edge of the pool, peering over at me. Her voice was all I needed to steady my world. I couldn't believe I was in trouble in the water yet again. The hard part about this was… your mom won the race!"

As we approach the village, say our greetings, and settle on rocks and roots, the villagers gather around and Byron begins to tell the story in English of Sarah and Abraham as Tubo translates into Karamojong. "Sarah laughed to herself when the angel told Abraham that his wife would have many children." The people listen closely as he continues. "Scripture says Sarah was long past her childbearing years and, referring to Abraham, the angel says, 'From one man's dead and shriveled loins there will be people numbering into the millions.'"

Byron, in his boisterous, demonstrative way, stands behind and puts his hands on the shoulders of the oldest woman in the village. The old woman, toothless and topless, grins as Byron asks the villagers, "Is it possible for this woman to have a child? How could this woman have a child?"

There is much laughter and discussion before an elder speaks for the group. "Only by God Himself."

I look around at the people as they laugh and discuss this miraculous story. In a land where there is a constant struggle for basic sustenance, frequent drought, famine, disease, and death, there is hope in these stories of an all-powerful and loving God. Sitting on rocks or on the ground, covered in dust and flies, the villagers talk of how even their *imurans* could not bring a child to this old woman.

The chatter of kids, gathering at Linda's feet, interrupts the discussion. Wearing dirty, torn clothes, they jockey for position as they exclaim and point at her face. As I watch the kids' fascination at their reflections in Linda's mirrored sunglasses, it dawns on me they have never seen a mirror; perhaps they have only seen their reflection in the muddy waters of the river.

Linda, realizing the source of the distraction, quickly removes her glasses and tucks them into the pocket of her denim skirt. A loud "awww" sweeps through the throng of children as they point at her and chatter in a language foreign to me.

"Cinda, it's my blue eyes. They haven't seen blue eyes before."

So much for minimizing distractions for Byron's discussion. He smoothly guides us back to his story with a brief discussion on other things in life that distract us from hearing God.

As is the custom, the rifles, bows, and arrows are propped up against the only tree. I snicker as I see the hand-cranked cassette player against it too, among all the weapons. A tool that brings a message of hope nestles among fighting implements that bring hurt, despair, and loss.

It's amazing to see how stories connect across time and culture, as we see the light of awareness and discovery dawn in these people's eyes. A story, thousands of years old, about faith and God's miraculous power, has relevance for these people now, in this place. As Byron's storying mission progresses, these people will eventually hear of the coming of Jesus Christ over 2,000 years ago.

Jesus used stories to reveal Himself and God to us. Each of us has a story, is a story. They connect people in a real way at a heart-to-heart level, creating those lasting connections and truths drawn from real relationships. Our past is just a part of a continuing story of God's work in our lives and God uses these stories to reveal Himself to each of us and to each other.

Our stories combine to tell a big, awesome story — God's story. Every life is a tale, we just have to learn how to read it and allow others to read. Stories allow us to look back on a journey — ours or another's — to learn lessons and truths that let us move forward on our own life journey with wisdom, perspective, and purpose.

Tubo's chants, followed by the villagers' parroting repetition, interrupt our musings. The people follow Tubo's lead as he utters the story of Abraham and Sarah using the tune of a well-known harvest song. As it unfolds, the villagers, without prompting, naturally integrate movement into their song with clapping. Losilo uses the tape recorder to play Nakaramoi's rendition of the Abraham story as he challenges Sit and Squat to out-sing Nakaramoi.

The villagers transition to a large circle and begin to jump and clap as they repeat the song story. The rhythm intensifies as they add stomping, some with beads and rattles tied to their shins, to the rhythmic clapping and deep chants. Dust flies with the stomping, adding visual beauty to the rhythm. I can feel the deep pulse in my legs and chest like a bass drum.

One or two women take turns stepping inside the circle to dance, combining their foot stomps with impressive vertical leaps. They thrust their chests as they leap, bouncing their beautiful beads to the rhythm. Bright smiles light up the intricately patterned facial scars on the darkest of skin as they laugh, sing, and dance.

The old woman, the Sarah stand-in, pulls me into the dance circle with her. She takes strands of beads off her neck and places them around mine. There is much laughter as she corrects my dance. It seems I cannot make my beads bounce as they can. In my defense, my western clothing seriously hampers the flop factor, but I'm unwilling to dispense with it. Jessica steps into my place and jumps with impressive grace and height, her ponytail bouncing in rhythm. She is able to make her beads bounce despite her cumbersome clothing.

Jordan and Seve join in too, so easily spotted in the crowd with their white skin and blonde hair. Ben doesn't dance but young kids surround him as he sits on a rock with his *fimbo* in hand. He loves to crank the cassette player for them to join in and sing. My nieces and nephews connect in their own way, without a common language, better than adults do.

The women move outside the circle as the men merge into the inner one to dance with their vertical leaps, the ever-present *fimbo* in hand. A man invites Linda and me into the men's circle — an unusual invite. My dance partner across the circle looks familiar; a wrinkled old man with a white lip plug wearing a drab army-green jacket, green felt hat, and an ostrich feather. He is the *mzee* who connected with Stanley yesterday at Nakaramoi. His jacket covers his torso, but he is bare from the waist down again. I try to ignore the obvious as we bounce up and down to the rhythm of the dance. Oh, the beauty of cultural contrast and clash.

The Sarah stand-in makes her way over to the rock where Stanley sits smoking his pocket-size pipe. She admires it and shows him hers, crudely made from corncob. She begs for his pouch of tobacco, appearing to be pushy and demanding. With the language barrier, this is only a guess. Stanley gives her enough tobacco to fill her pipe bowl once. She grumpily accepts, allows him to light it, then turns and walks away without any recognizable gesture of gratitude.

The soul connection of music enhances the power of story to launch kinship and truths across barriers. Music is heard with the ears but it is understood with the heart.

As we walk later, I think about the mounting tensions in this area. "I love watching you work and the way your stories connect with these people," I call out to Byron, "but you're only at Sarah and Abraham. In light of the growing tensions around here, I wonder if it's time to fast-forward the timeline to get to Jesus Christ."

"These are oral people," he explains patiently. "You cannot make big jumps into the abstract. The story has to unfold just as a life story does. Words like the cross, mercy, salvation, redemption, hope, and heaven don't have a meaning to them. Truths come from the unfolding of the story."

"True. I sometimes forget that my life experiences are so different to these people."

"They cannot relate to many of our abstract words and concepts. Even the word 'love' doesn't have the same meaning as we give it. To understand the word, they have to see love as it unfolds in the context of a story."

My thoughts linger on how Moses, near the end of his life, summed up the Israelites' journey in a song. Songs bring life to a story and make it memorable and relatable. I wonder if they danced to their stories as these people do. As Byron extends his walking missions to distant villages, he finds that the songs and dances have already spread. People are touched, healed, and changed by real stories.

28 Cultural Delights and Challenges *Utamaduni*
Tanzania 1960s

As friction creates pearls in an oyster, collision points between cultures create precious heartprints. During childhood, I looked at the Africans' ways and was puzzled and intrigued, forgetting they perhaps looked at us and wondered the same. The intersection between cultures isn't smooth at best and can be stormy or even fatal at worst. The East African mother breastfeeds her baby until the age of two, giving her child nutrition on demand without the privacy and cultural restraints an American mother has. The multi-million dollar baby formula industry hit Africa when we were there in the '60s, with advertising linking bottle-feeding to the western world, which is enticing to the East African women because of its hope of a better life.

In addition to the obvious problem of the expense of bottles and formula, the babies lose the benefit of acquiring natural immunities from their mother's milk. A look beyond the beautiful, sophisticated women in the baby formula advertisement reveals insurmountable problems with infection. The African women don't have the knowledge or the resources to obtain uncontaminated water or to sterilize bottles. Most of the mothers don't speak English and cannot read the instructions on the formula labels. With limited resources, mothers often dilute the formula to stretch it further. The baby formula industry causes much illness and takes the lives of many children.

Mother and Daddy passionately fought a losing battle to counter the effects of advertising, as Mother described:

> I make rounds at the hospital with John when I can. Yesterday, when I saw a starving child sucking his thumb, I commented to the medical assistant that this was the first Tanzanian child I had seen doing so. They asked me why I thought this was. I assumed it was because the mothers carry their babies on their back, nursing them every time they cry. They were horrified to hear American mothers nurse their babies privately or only in the presence of close women friends. They are glad to be Tanzanian and think our custom mistreats the white baby, but I see their traditions hurt the children.

Today there were three who were bloated: skin with big open cracks, and eyes swollen shut due to starvation. All about eighteen months old, they came from the finest growing land in this region. They are starving because their mothers took them to the witch doctor with a minor illness and he told them to feed them only *uji* (white corn flour). The children starve among plenty because of the superstitions. The mothers bring them to our hospital as a last resort and they often die because they come too late.

Missionaries often focused on the person in front of them and asked about their children. The locals' culture was to be asked about their parents. The missionaries tended to group together and worshipped with other Americans instead of mixing with the nationals.

"We should shake hands in our greetings and spend a lot more time saying, 'Hello,' having a cup of tea, and talking about family, crops, and the rain before getting to the intended conversation," Steven Wanji, the African head medical assistant, told Mother.

"I know, but it takes ten minutes just to say, 'Hello.' My kids would go without supper if I greeted properly."

For my parents, it was as if they had one foot in America and one in Africa. They had America in them and wanted to teach us to love our home there, yet wanted to connect with the African people, to understand them, and to help them. Mother and Daddy knew they should worship with the locals, but how difficult it would have been to take us kids to a two- or three-hour service and try to keep us still when it was a language we didn't even understand. This is a missionary's dilemma.

The Foreign Mission Board sent summer or short-assignment missionaries for temporary help: doctors, surgeons, nurses, eye specialists, mechanics, dentists, and college students. The volunteers provided new ideas and services in the hospital and the side benefit was dental care for us. That summer there were sixteen college students as well as medical volunteers. Mother's time was spread thinly, trying to include the volunteers, translate, sightsee, house, and feed them while still trying to feed, school, and take care of us.

"If the Lord sends them out, we surely can find places to take care of them," was her motto. I often heard her exasperated complaint, "I think we should just move into the tent and let the volunteers have our house."

It was challenging for the newcomers to adjust to the sights and culture in order to get down to work but the locals saw their love and knew they cared. The mission trip forever changed the volunteers, altering their values and giving them a richer appreciation of their own country with its freedom and opportunities. Their new perspective on the needs of people in East Africa helped them promote mission support in America.

The cultural differences between them and our people was hilarious and embarrassing at times. The girls wore miniskirts, a shock to the missionaries and the locals. The miniskirt wasn't around when we left America and it was an eye-opener to see them here.

Mother's letter described the experience of some visiting volunteers:

> John and two other missionaries have returned from their ten-day trip to Masasi, near the Mozambique coast. It took two days of hard travel in each direction. They were scouting for the needs of churches, agricultural, and medical work. While they did three clinics in an area without medical work, I kept missionary volunteers busy, teaching quilting and nutrition at the hospital until John could get back to take them on a trip. We each drove a Land Rover full of volunteers and our kids to do medical and church work, and sightsee near the Malawi border.
>
> I had my hands full keeping the Land Rover on the slippery road as we descended the mountains from Tukuyu. Each time we slid, I started crying, "Oh, oh, oh." I think this disturbed my passengers. When we got into the flat lands, we slogged through one mud hole after another. The road is on raised ridges with rice paddies on each side; there is just no room for error. If you mess up, you get good and stuck. John dodged to miss a man on a bicycle, crashed into the banana trees, and did just that. The chains were passed back and forth as one Land Rover pulled the other out of the mud, only to get stuck and have to be pulled out by the other.
>
> Proceeding toward Lake Malawi, we approached the village of Ikombe where the trail disappeared in the ten-foot high grass. The villagers were extremely drunk and threatening. We tried to hurry, but we couldn't see the path because of the tall grass. John and Keith left us in the Land Rovers as they went to scout another way across the river. The drunken men swarmed and banged the vehicles with rocks and sticks, trying to break the windows. They pulled off our outside mirrors as they yelled and threatened us. I had to back the kids away from the windows as the men forced the small triangle vents open and reached in to grab us.
>
> John returned to find us swarmed. He ran, yelled, and

pushed people aside. He jumped in and began hitting the men's hands reaching through the vents, then drove through the crowd. It was frightening, to say the least, and a real shock to the visiting volunteers.

Finally, we found our way out and returned two miles back to a small concrete building that served as a demonstration farm run by our mission. The volunteer girls were horrified we were all going to sleep in one room, having never spent the night in a space with so many men.

The next morning, we were pleasantly surprised to find the village deserted so we forged the river, skidded, slid, and bumped our way toward our destination village, Ikombe. Lake Malawi is in low land so it is always hot and last night's rain made it steamy. Without roads, driving the twenty miles of walking paths seemed like a hundred.

A tribe in Malawi makes clay pots and transports them by dugout canoes to sell to the Nyakyusa tribe in Tanzania. Women tie ten to 25 pots between long split bamboo poles and balance the 150-pound loads on a tight, donut-shape roll of banana bark on their head as they walk barefooted as far as 150 miles into the interior. Each pot will sell for about five shillings (75 cents) so the 150-mile trip might net them about seven to fifteen dollars. I especially cherish the pot given to me by a woman I know from the hospital. Even with deformed and painful legs from elephantiasis, my friend walks to sell her pots.

We camped on the shores of Lake Malawi so we could swim and explore a big cave where the Nyakyusa leave sacrifices of chicken, birds, and beef. Because of high tide, we had to walk over a high mountain and then down to the lake's edge to swim around to the entrance. Monkeys made fun of us as we fought our way through the stinging nettles.

Mother apologized for being a grumpy mother as she had a bad attack of malaria. She had felt it coming, but didn't want to cancel the trip because she knew we were looking forward to it. Friday night she had chills that would have shaken the bed, had there been one, but aspirin and chloroquine gave her some relief. Malaria was something we learned to live with, along with constant upset stomachs.

We were up and out of our tents before the sun because Mother wanted to return to the Tukuyu leprosarium for the dedication of a new church for lepers and the baptizing of the first ten members. Again, the Land Rover slid into a ditch and hit an embankment, which rattled the other passengers. Even in four-wheel drive, she lost traction on a long, muddy hill and the adults had to pull with a rope. They would pull, slip, and get up to pull some more to keep the vehicle from sliding sideways. I was so afraid she would run over someone.

29 Collision Courses *Mgongano Njiani*
Tanzania 1960s

Visits to local churches, often combined with medical clinics, immersed us into local culture. On one outing, we traveled almost two hours over fifteen miles of rough roads to a bush church. We looked forward to the visit with mixed emotions because these people were extremely isolated and had strange ways, such as burying live goats with their dead. They rang the tire rim bell when we arrived and people appeared out of the bushes. The church was cold and damp. Linda and I shared Mother's sweater and the boys fussed about being cold. Meanwhile the naked local boys ran in and out of church unbothered. Mother wrote:

> We had the place of honor, sitting on a bench in the front of the church beside the preacher. How many women at First Baptist Midland have to make their kids be still right at the front?
>
> The pastor asked us to say a few words and a few words they were with only two months of language study. I memorized a prayer just in case, but I forgot it. I could only think of the Swahili saying, "God, thank you for loving me. God, thank you for loving all the people. Amen."
>
> John talked for ten minutes, but he didn't say much; it just took him a long time to say it. When he comes to a word he doesn't know in Swahili, he substitutes English or Spanish words, making his sentences flow, but no one can understand them.
>
> Church pews are narrow benches with the men sitting on one side, women on the other. I sat in this ten- by twelve-foot mud hut and felt contented. In the entire world, this was where I wanted to be. Around me, Tanzanians sang in their tribal language, my children played at my feet, and women sat with babies strapped to their backs. The barefooted pastor wore a woman's pink blouse, khaki pants, and a woman's three-quarter-length coat. How joyous to feel I am in the will of the Lord.

Oh, the long church services — hours long and in a language we didn't

143

know. I loved having a twin so at least I had someone to play with. Like any kid, I daydreamed a lot, but my daydreams came alive when I shared them with my twin. We played games with our hands —"Here's the church, here's the steeple, open the door and there's all the people." We elbowed each other, made faces at local kids to get them to laugh, trapped doodlebugs, and drew pictures in the dirt floor. Steve and Jim liked to sneak chameleons in their pockets to terrorize the local kids. What fun that was!

Mother fussed at us if we giggled when the offering plate came around. These people gave from a place of little, but sometimes I just couldn't help myself. Coins, eggs, rice, oranges, and bananas — that's fine, but how can you not giggle when there was a live chicken in the offering plate? As the plate passed by, Jim plucked a feather to get it squawking and struggling to get loose from its grass-strand leg bindings. When the plate passed Steve, he turned the chicken upright, which made it squawk as he stuck its beak into Jim's neck to give him a chicken kiss.

Once we brought Frisky on a bush clinic trip because we were going to be gone for several days. A man had his chicken tied up under his bench waiting for the end of the church service to pay for his medical care. Jim lost the battle holding Frisky, who chased the squawking chicken, creating havoc. He ran under the benches and between people's legs, until Jim finally trapped the chicken in a scuffle and a flurry of feathers in the corner of the church. The preacher just kept on preaching. Frisky had chicken feathers all over his muzzle. Daddy bought the chicken but ended up selling it to a man who hitched a ride with us, reducing the chaos of a dog, a chicken, and us five kids in the Land Rover.

Baptisms were a time of huge celebration and the subject of many MK's stories, some perhaps embellished; stories of blood-sucking leaches pulled off after baptism and rivers stabbed with poles to check for crocodiles. If a church wasn't near water, missionaries carried it on top of the Land Rover or dug coffin-size holes in dry riverbeds so enough could seep in to splash over a person lying flat. There were rumors of missionaries on the Kenyan coast spreading a circular fence around the baptism area to keep the sharks out. It sure would have been easier if our denomination's custom were to sprinkle for baptism.

Mother wrote of a one-week camping trip for clinic and church at a remote area near the Mozambique border:

> The journey to Masasi is 600 miles and two hard days each way. The last few miles aren't even a road at all, just a footpath. This is the furthest we have been from anybody or anything; we saw no vehicles and heard no planes. The pastor let us have his two-bedroom house for

the night with men in one room and women in the other. It was so quiet because they cannot even afford cattle. The next morning, when I returned from my walk, the other missionaries smiled when they asked how I had slept. They showed me my night visitors — bed bugs covered my orange sleeping bag and mosquito net.

The pastor asked John to baptize thirteen people so we walked three miles to the river. John learned Swahili words while I worried if I would ever finish the walk. A man carried Chipper. I wished he had carried me. I walk a lot, but the nationals do it all the time and travel at such a fast pace.

Ahead, Daddy walked fast with the men, forgetting they needed to slow down for us. I stepped as close to Linda's heels as I could, slipping my foot onto her footprint as soon as she lifted hers. She got annoyed if I timed it wrong and my toe rubbed down her heel.

The congregation walked, barefooted, while singing hymns with familiar tunes though I didn't know the language. We watched as Daddy helped the pastor baptize in the swift river while the congregation continued to sing, yodel, and cheer.

Linda whispered, "I think we should wait until we get back to America to get baptized so we don't get drowned or eaten by a crocodile." She made me giggle and we both got a "be quiet" look from Mother. Mother continued her account:

The pastor awakened us before daylight to say that people brought a sick baby for the doctor. John examined it and told the father he must have milk, but the baby died before he could return from the *duka*. The people in this area are all hungry. They planted their crops last year, but the rains did not come in time for them to mature. The corn is ten feet tall, but it died before the heads could mature, as did their maze, cassava, and groundnuts.

We carried three sacks of corn and rice on top of the car from the churches in Tukuyu. The people were all sick; the babies had runny noses, infected eyes, and bloated stomachs from malnutrition. The adults were suffering from malnutrition, worms, malaria, and eye diseases. Each time John told a mother, "This child needs orange juice, meat, and vegetables," he knew he was asking the impossible. This is the first time I have seen people that could not help that they were so hungry.

The problems are so big. I wish there were more I could do to help. The people have such a wonderful spirit; they never complain, are quick to laugh, and are generous with the last thing they have.

It took us no time to use the two buckets of water left at the house for our use, so I volunteered to go with the local girls to get more. We walked about a mile downhill to a hole they had dug. As the water drops, they have to dig deeper. The girls used a bamboo stick with a gourd on the end to dip muddy water from the bottom of the twelve-foot hole into the two buckets. I thought I would try to carry one of the buckets on my head but the weight just drove me to the ground. One of the girls, who was around seventeen, picked it up, put it on her head, and carried it up the hill. They thought it was so funny that I was all out of breath and panting.

After two large clinics, we drove to Lindi and stayed in a real hotel on the Indian Ocean. We had good food, an inside toilet, and cold running water — such luxury. We ruined four shock absorbers, one tire rim, three tubes, one tire, one overhead rack, and the exhaust pipe clamps. This is what these roads do to a new car.

*****

Mother and Daddy loved to travel and work together, but often their work took them to separate places, putting Mother traveling the rugged roads alone except for us kids. It also put her in a place where cultures collided because she was a woman in charge in a land where the woman's role was subservient. Her letters hinted at this cultural collision:

Last Sunday, I loaded up the kids at 8:00 a.m. to meet the pastor and a boy, Staryo, at 8:30 a.m. Silly me. Being stuck in an American custom left me waiting a half hour. The road to Songwe, near the Zambian border, was dusty and full of chug holes but we arrived on time. The chaplain asked me to stop by a store while he walked into the banana trees to a cluster of houses. The children and I waited for an hour in the car. He returned to find an impatient driver — another silly American custom. He said I was very brave to wait so long.

The service hadn't started because the people were waiting for the visiting preacher. Sunday school finally began 90 minutes late and the two-hour service an hour

146

later. The church is located 100 yards off the road and in a low area so we waded there. As I sat in Sunday school, my toes swam in the water in my shoes; the nationals don't have this problem because they don't wear any.

We questioned the candidates to see if they were ready for baptism and then set off toward the river. I foolishly asked if it was far. I already knew the answer would be, "No, just over the hill." We walked in the blazing hot sun about a mile and a half to the river. The pastor baptized nine people; when he lowered Staryo into the water, the swift current almost swept him away.

We returned to the same store where we waited earlier and walked into the banana trees to a small, two-room hut for a late lunch. Their one- or two-room huts are used for sleeping, mating, giving birth, dying, and cooking.

The men asked me to sit with them. If John and I are together, I am often invited to eat with the men; if not, I usually sit on a tiny stool or the floor with the women. The women prepared a meal of tough sinewy meat in a gravy with *ugali*, made from ground corn that looks like cold cream of wheat. They dumped half of the *ugali* and most of the meat onto a large tray for the men and me, giving the other half to the women and children. The men gathered around the tray, rolled the *ugali* into balls with their fingers, and ate with their right hands, reserving their left hand for unclean tasks such as toilet needs.

It tasted like wall plaster. I haven't eaten wall plaster, but that is what I think it would taste like. I tried to eat it to be polite, but was only able to swallow a bite or two. The women poured chai from big oil cans into huge wash pots then dipped their few metal cups which were shared by all. I was glad we were first. I began to feel uncomfortable in my honored place so I told them, in stumbling Swahili, there were too many men and excused myself to join the women. The men found this funny.

The women appreciated that I chose to eat with them. I noticed their tray of food had much less meat than the men had and the children, gathered around a small bowl of *ugali*, had none. The women nursed their babies as they ate. I entered the kitchen to tell the cooks I enjoyed the food and did the best I could to wind my skirt around my legs as I sat on the five-inch stool. The kitchen was a dark, hot, smoke-filled room with a cook pot on an open fire. The only window in the house was a small one where the women ate so the smoke had to filter through the roof. My eyes burned so badly I wondered if it would make me blind.

The Tanzanians treated us with honor and respect when we visited. We kids fit in well, sitting with the local children, and we knew not to complain. Mother packed sandwiches in case we didn't get enough to eat or if the food was too spicy.

The churches in America had so much and these people had so little. A widely-known pastor of an affluent church in Dallas flew to Mbeya to preach. He droned on and on, bragging about the size of his church, the bowling alley in the basement, and activity building with racquetball courts, things these people couldn't imagine. The translating missionary used pauses perfectly as he gave a simple talk on who Jesus Christ is and what it means to know and follow Him. Someone who has footstepped with another culture long enough is able to smooth the collision between upbringings.

*****

Culture collided when America met Africa, when new met old, and when Christianity met tribal traditions. Police in Tanga, a heavily Muslim area on the Tanzania coast, jailed a pastor, the only Arab Muslim we knew who had chosen to follow Christ. He married an Arab Muslim girl and moved to attend the mission's seminary. The Muslim tradition requiring killing the Muslim girl because she married a Christian had begun to find disfavor with Tanzanians so their people beat, then jailed, both. It was easy for us to live out our Christian lives. For these people, it meant they would be stoned, beaten, and disowned, the latter being the worst because belonging was a big thing for them.

Old and new clashed when Daddy traveled with his medical assistant, Joel, to his village soon after his grandfather died. Joel's father was a chief and had six wives. Joel proudly introduced Daddy to his own mother and a few of his siblings. Each of his father's wives had her own hut. The husband was supposed to show no favorites and visit a different hut each night for supper and to sleep. When Joel's grandfather died, Joel's father inherited his father's eight wives. Their huts were in a semi-circle behind the huts of his first six.

Joel, being the eldest son of the first wife, would eventually inherit his father's fourteen wives. From my cultural perspective, it seemed that would make Joel's former grandmothers and mothers his wives. It didn't translate well into our traditions. Joel, caught between culture, generational values, and faith, wasn't interested because he was an educated Christian.

Mother described the collision of the old ways of polygamy and arranged marriages with the expectations of Christianity:

> The two main tribes in the Mbeya region are the Safwa, a primitive tribe, and the Nyakyusa, who are more educated and accepting of Christianity. A group of Safwa youths from the slopes of Mbeya Peak expressed an interest in Christianity so a missionary helped them build a church. The adults want no part of the religion; they stay drunk on *pombe* and persecute the young Christians. In spite of opposition, the church has grown and they baptized twelve teenagers.
>
> Last week, a father promised his fifteen-year-old daughter in marriage to an old man who already had one wife. She refused. The father wouldn't return the six cows he had received for a bride price. When the husband-to-be reached out to grab his intended bride, she fled, leaving him with only her *kanga*. She took refuge at Mama Mary's home, a Christian woman in Mbeya.

Cultural collisions not only occurred between missionary and Tanzanian way of life, between old and new, and between African tribes, they frequently occurred between African countries, as Mother described in a letter to my aunt:

> A serious situation has arisen here I want you to know about in case something happens. You can decide whether you should pass this on to John's parents or hold it until you receive more news. Some months ago, Malawi declared Tanzania took some areas from her. Malawi has demanded the return of this land. Of course, Tanzania refuses.
>
> Today is the day for the showdown, army trucks and troops are on the move. Nothing may happen—it may all be a bluff, but then again it may be serious, endangering our Christian friends, missionaries, clinic, and church work.
>
> Please copy this letter to my parents, for I will not risk another letter past the censor. I shall write in a couple of days if possible. Best not answer this letter.

It was a difficult time for many of our friends as Tanzania moved from colonialism to nationalism and socialism, transitioning farms, businesses, and services from Europeans, Indians, Asians, and Afrikaans into the hands of black Africans or the government. Many of these people had been in Tanzania for several generations and many may have had Tanzanian passports but now they didn't belong in their ancestor's home or Tanzania.

The world around me was secure and full of fun because we were never far from Mother or Daddy. We had a lot of independence, but we were under the umbrella of their security and that of the other missionaries. The locals liked kids and weren't a threat unless they were drunk. Little did I know the rug would be pulled out from under me as I faced the most traumatic collision of cultures in my early girlhood years.

30 Sparks Fly *Cheche Huruka*
Uganda 2004

"Do you remember the trouble we had when you visited us in Matapato a few years ago?" Jessica asks as we make our way back from Sit and Squat. "When all eight of us traveled in the pickup to Mombasa?"

"Dad's driving was the best!" Ben's current enthusiasm wasn't matched by my own at the time. Byron's driving style had become fast and aggressive through his years driving the Kenyan roads. The trip began at sunrise and was hard and furious as he tried a new route recommended by a Maasai friend. We all laugh now at the memory, knowing the friend had never been in a vehicle in his life.

The tired, dusty, rattled crew hung on as Byron bumped his way on the pothole-ridden dusty road to Rombo, through Amboseli Park, past Mount Kilimanjaro, into Tanzania, and back into Kenya. At least a foot of soft powdery dust hid the heavily potted road, covering it as a muddy river obscures the obstacles beneath.

Hours passed like days as the suffocating dust filled the car, caking our bodies and lungs. At one point, we stopped to ask directions from two men, a rare sight on this desolate route. Gesturing with a nod and puckering their lips toward the road they said, "Oh, it's just there, but you'll find there's dust on the road ahead."

Linda and I looked at each other and the kids squeezed in the back seat with us. We saw tired eyeballs peering out from a thick mask of dirt and we began to laugh until tears streamed through the coat of dust on our cheeks. We laughed, more out of frustration and fatigue than humor.

We finally made our way to the Mombasa ferry as the sun was setting behind the palm trees. Twelve hours of bone-shattering, dust-suffocating adventure — closely approaching misery — with stops only to find a bush for the necessaries, refuel, fix flats, and reattach the battery. We never stopped to drink or eat the picnic prepared before dawn or to ogle the elephants, giraffe, and zebra with the rare opportunity of a clear Mt. Kilimanjaro in the background.

Traveling the roads of Africa is a higher risk to life and limb than any other threat a missionary faces; a far greater threat than any wildlife present. Defensive, offensive, and aggressive driving skills are necessary for survival. Years of enduring East African roads can transform a gentle, mild-mannered "you go first" missionary into a hard-driven competitor or a survivor. The differences blur.

Once, in congested traffic in downtown Mombasa, Byron passed on the inside lane and bumped up onto the median. Our pickup connected with a two-ton truck, locking the bumpers and doors together in the inside lane. Byron got out of the car to negotiate. The irate driver began to incite the anger and aggression of the rapidly gathering bystanders. The throng of passengers riding in the back of the truck spilled over the edge of the truck bed and grabbed rocks as they shouted and moved toward us. The chaos, anger, and threats escalated as the crowd rapidly grew.

Byron jumped back in, put our pickup into four-wheel drive, and then reversed to lurch backward and forward, wrenching the vehicles apart as the irate crowd banged on ours. Chaos and the sounds of rending metal mingled with the smell of smoking rubber. Our pickup lurched forward, bounced off the curb, and dodged between the bystanders, leaving behind the bumper and taking with it shocked passengers and a demolished rear door.

In East Africa, crowds can gather quickly, turn violent, and dispense their own fevered justice. Linda, sitting next to the door of the back seat, reached her arm through the window to hold the mangled door closed. With tension still high, Jessica cried, "Mom, there's something wrong with your door. Mom! Mom, what's wrong with your door?"

"Shhh! We'll talk about it later." Thus, the training trickles down to the next generation.

Stanley, having spent a full career in law enforcement as a game warden, found the idea of fleeing the scene of an accident inconceivable, but couldn't argue with the mounting tension and risks of impending, perhaps fatal, crowd justice. Byron did what he had to do to ensure the survival of his family.

"Nuna and I seem to attract more than our fair share of driving mayhem," Stanley tells the kids, as we approach their Kaabong home once more. "Remember on my first trip to Africa, Babe, when you were driving us from Matapato to Nairobi, on our way to Mount Kenya?"

"The armed police check? Not something that's easy to forget."

"Spikes had been extended across both sides of the road at the checkpoint," Stanley tells them. "Instead of slowing for the officers, as I expected, Nuna maneuvered through the spikes and sped on as I sat speechless in the passenger seat."

"After my adrenalin settled down, I explained it was the end of the month so the police officers would be looking for a bribe and would have made trouble because the insurance papers were in Nairobi," I finish for him.

What I couldn't explain was that there was more underlying the decision to accelerate through the police stop. Growing up in East Africa, we were wary of police and military. Capping the distrust was the influence of Daddy's anti-authority, challenge-the-system attitude so potently infused into the next generation.

"Nuna, didn't you get shot at one time on a date?" Ben asks.

"Yep, in my high school years, my boyfriend and I sped along a remote Rift Valley road and topped a hill to find a game warden check with police spikes across both sides of the road. We were speeding too fast to stop. My boyfriend, a competitive dirt bike and car racer, put the car into a slide, maneuvering between the gaps in the spikes."

Ben is wide-eyed with misplaced admiration, despite having heard the tale before.

"Kenyan game wardens are national police in a raging war against poachers, heavily armed with rifles and ready to shoot them on the spot, not bothering with the courts. As we slowed to pull over on the other side of the spikes, we looked up in the mirror to see the officers raising their rifles to fire. My boyfriend shouted, 'Duck!' and shoved me toward the floorboard as three rifle rounds banged our trunk."

"How did you escape, Nuna?" Ben fires an imaginary rifle. "Blam! Blam! Blam!"

"We swerved and accelerated away, taking our chance of a getaway over that of a peaceful resolution with officers that would shoot so quickly," I grin, relishing the excitement of the moment.

Daddy wasn't happy to find three bullet holes in the trunk of the car when his sixteen-year-old daughter returned home from her date. Ironically, that sixteen-year-old girl would later become a Texas game warden.

31 Fight for Health *Kushinda Ugonjwa*
Uganda 2004

Our times in Africa are often plagued with problems. Death and illness have sadly been regular features throughout the times we have spent here. I'm glad that Stanley and I, along with Linda and her family, are all fit and healthy and able to revel in our brief time together in Kaabong.

During our high school years in Kenya, Daddy fought depression and dark thoughts with his recurring battles with malaria. It often hit him when stress was high and his resistance was low and always with the strain of preparing to return to the States every four years for furlough. Mother and Daddy had to close down a house and sort possessions, keeping open the option of never returning to Africa because furlough was a time of reflection and re-evaluation. On one unforgettable occasion, his malaria progressed to black water fever. His urine turned dark, indicating distressed kidneys, and his illness dropped him to the lowest of low depression.

Mother once had to go to a farewell dinner without him because he was too sick with malaria. He lay on the bed, covered with a wet sheet to stay cool, and then crawled under the covers with bone-shaking chills. He knew he was losing control of his thoughts and secluded himself in the bedroom, warning us not to open the door. We were extremely concerned for him but knew when Mother came home everything would be OK. We had no way to contact her.

When Mother arrived back, she rushed Daddy to the hospital. He didn't stay there long; he doesn't make a very good patient.

The regular battle for his health has left Linda and me with a particularly painful memory. Jim and Steve had returned for college in America and Linda, Chipper, and I were in high school at the time. Mother went to America to take care of Granddaddy, who she thought may be dying, leaving us at home with Daddy. We thought at first he had malaria but, when he turned a sickly yellow, he knew it was hepatitis. As his illness progressed, he was unable to go to work or drive so we drove ourselves to school. We were only sixteen at the time.

As Daddy's fever continued to rage, he became extremely dehydrated and unable to keep any food or fluids down. He forbade us to call Mother or take him to the hospital. He ruled in our house, but we knew he was getting into trouble and wondered if he was thinking clearly. Each day after school, we stopped at pharmacies to beg them to sell I.V. (intravenous drip) fluids. We changed to different pharmacies, as they would deny our requests, saying if he were sick enough to need an I.V. he needed to be in the hospital.

I watched as Daddy patiently taught Linda how to start the I.V. "Be strong, baby gal, you can do this." Her only experience was giving shots in the clinic. Her heart pounded as she dug for his vein with a needle. She missed several times but he remained calm and patient as he encouraged her. She tried to be strong, holding back her tears and panic as she blew precious, dehydrated veins trying to get something to work. Finally, she got blood back in the needle, attached the tube, and hung the bag on the burglar bars above the bed. This nightmare followed her into her dreams for years and revisited her many times in nursing school.

As his dehydration progressed, she could no longer get needles into his hands and had to switch to his feet. Eventually we ran out of pharmacies willing to help and began to beg fluids at the hospital where they pushed us to admit Daddy. One night he told Linda, while she was trying to start an I.V. in his foot, "Baby gal, if my liver doesn't start working in the next 24 hours, I will die." She swallowed hard, blinked back her tears, pushed that thought out of her mind, and focused on what she had to do.

There it is again — "did what she had to do." That theme carries through the generations. Mother and Daddy passed that message to us loud and clear — buckle down the emotions and just "do what you have to do."

Daddy finally decided it was time and allowed us to admit him into the hospital where they determined his liver had quit functioning. Against his wishes, we called Mother. The accents changed as the call transferred from country to country until finally, with relief, we heard Mema's familiar southern drawl. Mema was hugely puzzled, telling us Mother was already on her way and would arrive at 8:30 a.m. our time tomorrow.

When Mother arrived at the airport, she wondered how she was going to get home because she thought we would be in school and Daddy would be at his clinic. Scheduled to arrive in two weeks, she was surprised to hear the familiar call, "Ssskk, Ssskk," and see our white faces in the sea of black.

She had had a sleepless night in Texas, sensing something was wrong at home. She had to tell her parents she was going to cut her trip short to return. The hardest part was saying an early goodbye to Jim and Steve who stayed with our grandparents while attending college. Mother clearly sensed God's lead to return home because she knew something was badly wrong.

She had no idea that Daddy was in critical shape without his liver functioning. It was such a relief when she got home; a huge burden off our shoulders and we could just be kids again. After her return, Daddy made a miraculous turnaround and the lab tests began to show liver function. It took a long time for him to get his appetite and strength back, but he did come back. This family needed their Daddio for many more years and for many reasons.

The experience gave a further treasured glimpse of Mother's strength. My chemistry teacher at high school was furious with me because I arrived late each day as we went through this ordeal with Daddy. Linda was lucky and not in that particular class. We were trying to manage his illness, driving on our own, begging I.V. fluids, and trying to run the household without help. My teacher's punishment for my tardiness was the requirement to type a 50-page, single-space report about water before I could return to class.

I had trouble pulling this off with my school responsibilities and team sports, so Mother sat at the dining room table for days and typed my paper while she nursed Daddy back to health. She wrote about water, water pumps, water bugs, water buffalo... I remember hearing the clicking of the typewriter as I drifted off to sleep at night and would awaken to the same sound, finding breakfast already made, lunches packed, and Mother clicking away. She didn't think the punishment was fair. Nor did I, but it gave me the gift of seeing the generosity of her heart.

As I look back on this desperate time, I wonder why we didn't ask for help. Our missionary aunts and uncles would have done anything to assist us. Maybe if I'd confided in my chemistry teacher the reason for my tardiness, he would have extended some compassion. Our family is a tribe of its own that takes care of its own. Taught to be self-sufficient, we are self-reliant, stubbornly resistant to show vulnerability, and unwilling to ask for assistance. I think Daddy modeled helping others, even at a huge cost, but to ask for or need help was weakness, or at least unnecessary. Stubborn heartprints traveling through the generations.

*****

Looking at Linda's girls snuggled under a *kanga* as we now sit on the rooftop in Kaabong, I remember my twin fighting for another family member's life.

"Seve, you may have been too young to still remember now, but a few years ago you got sick with excruciating belly pain," I remind her. "Your dad was out of town and your mom had all you kids herself."

"We were in Kisumu, on Lake Victoria," Linda adds. "In fact, we lived in the same house where you and I were in the fifth grade, Cinda."

"Oh, Nuna, I do remember little bits. My stomach was hurting so bad I couldn't even stand up. Mom told me to go lie down on the couch. I felt like I was being too much trouble."

"She had the typical symptoms of appendicitis with pain in the midline that moved to the right lower quadrant of her abdomen, followed by the

157

development of midline rebound tenderness," the nurse in Linda tells Stanley. "When she turned down popcorn, it hit me she was in deep trouble! She had a low-grade fever too. I knew what was wrong and I had to get her to Nairobi quickly."

"Wasn't there a Russian hospital in Kisumu?" Jessica chimes in.

"Yeah, but I wasn't going to let them open one of you up!"

"Where was Byron?" Stanley asks.

"He had the car and I had no way to contact him. I left Jessica, Jordan, and Ben at home and got a ride to the airport with my friend, Nancy. I knew my other kids needed someone too but I had to figure that out later. Seve's life was on the line."

"I remember Nancy waiting with me in the car while you ran into the airport to try and get us on the plane."

"The airline wouldn't allow Seve to board because she was so sick and she didn't have a doctor with her. I went back to the car to get my thoughts straight and update Nancy. I remember her saying, 'Well, we'll just pray Seve onto that plane right now.' I went back in and told them I was Seve's doctor and would sign whatever I had to. She needed urgent surgery or she wouldn't get better. It was a fight every step of the way, but I got on that plane with her. They were not going to leave without us. This was my girl and her life was in danger."

"I tried to pretend I wasn't really that sick as Mom was so tense. But when she pushed her finger into my abdomen then released it quickly, I yelped a lot. It was *so* painful!"

"It really wasn't that I was trying to prove to you, it was more to justify in my own mind this drastic action was needed. Poor Seve, you got big ole tears in your blue eyes." Linda strokes her daughter's hair. "I felt bad for hurting you. Seeing you respond so classically doubled my urgency to get something done before your appendix burst."

"Mom said I couldn't eat anything because I was going to have surgery," Seve giggles. "I remembered the last time I was on a plane was when we came from America. That was a long trip. Since I couldn't eat for what I thought was another long trip, I thought I would die of starvation."

"When I finally got her to Nairobi Hospital, her doctor misdiagnosed her appendicitis as malaria," Linda shakes her head. "I knew she had appendicitis and insisted on seeing the surgeon. I had to throw a fit to get him called."

"I bet you weren't going to back down, Mom!" Jessica knows her mom well.

"When he finally arrived, he berated the doctor who insisted it was malaria. It took a fight every step of the way to take care of my girl, but a mother is going to do whatever a mother has to do."

"You sound just like Mother," I laugh.

Our three generations have endured so many diseases. Beyond the basic childhood illnesses of chicken pox, colds, and flu there are hepatitis, malaria, boils, and anthrax. The tropics also offer exotic ailments of intestinal worms, hookworms, and jiggers that crawl under the toe nail and fill up with eggs. The worst are the disgusting mango worms that start as eggs on your wet laundry then enter your skin to exit as live, squirming worms. Yuck. Enough of that visual.

"I can remember being at the hospital with you, Mom," Ben chips in, "when Dr. Mark asked you to help him amputate the boy's arm that had gone septic." He sticks out his tongue. "Bluah."

"All caused by a thorn," Linda tells me. "It was only Dr. Mark and I, so we had to handle both the surgery and the anesthesia."

"I had to sit at the boy's head, Nuna," Ben adds proudly. "Every now and then, Mom would ask me how our patient was doing."

"He would look up from the little car he drove over the edge of the operating table to say, 'He's fine, Mom.'" Ben and his mother erupt into giggles at the shared memory that time has thankfully mellowed.

Throughout the evening routine of family life, I sense a strange contrast of feelings. I'm so grateful to be with family and I feel the sweet satisfaction of "all is well," contrasting with a sense of foreboding. What is it? When I finally crawl into bed, I spoon all the closer to my man. I feel my body ache with the day's exertion and feel his restlessness, finally falling asleep to the sounds of gunfire and distant artillery.

32 What a Fuss *Namna Gani*
Kenya 1960s

A feeling of adventure grabbed us as we made a temporary move to Nairobi, where Mother and Daddy were to do a five-month assignment. Daddy wrote:

> Closing house for five months requires many details. It was early evening when we finally got the Land Rover loaded and off to Mbeya for fuel and a few errands, so we decided to slip back and sleep in our own house. Martha and I slept in our bed, with the girls and Chipper on the floor below us to keep from having to unlock the bedroom doors. The two older boys slept in the car to keep thieves out of our things.
>
> We weren't able to take a roundabout route, as I would have liked, because many roads were either impassable due to river rises or so muddy it made four-wheel drive passage laborious, time-consuming, and treacherous.
>
> We had an enjoyable trip, camping four nights under the intensely star-lit and near moonless African sky. The third night, a blustery wind lashed and eventually downed the tent, leaving us undisturbed in the collapsed tent with heads under the netted windows. The kids and I had camped like this on an earlier trip when we inadvertently left the tent poles at home. We spent our third night outside the crater entrance to the Ngurdoto National Park. Martha had misgivings since, fifteen minutes before pitching camp, Chipper, who was riding on top of the Land Rover, spotted an elephant foraging on the flat, clear area, which was best suited for tenting.
>
> After all those months in the bush, we were wide-eyed as we entered Nairobi with its six-story skyscrapers, jets, television, freeways, streetlights, traffic, and parking problems. Martha hasn't stopped talking about the supermarket she visited. Nairobi's contrast with the rest of East Africa is unbelievable.

Mother had different recollections:

I got a tsetse fly bite on the inside of my leg, which made me sick for the rest of the day and uncomfortable throughout the trip. They bite like a horse-fly and leave a welt that itches like bedbugs or chiggers. My leg swelled so I couldn't walk and itched so badly I wished I could scratch it off. On top of that, I had the worst headache I have ever had. On the road to Ngurdoto Crater, the children saw an elephant cross the road by our camp and, in spite of all my fussing, pouting, and all the things a woman uses to get her way, John wouldn't move camp.

We settled into our new home on Jogoo Road in Nairobi. Daddy said it was the house where we spent our first night in Africa, but I couldn't remember that. Missionary Aunt Hazel helped Mother find some used school uniforms and hemmed Linda and my blue and white checked dresses, which we had to wear with matching panties. Horrors of all horrors, not only did I have to wear a dress to school, I had to wear it with blue knee socks. Our brothers' uniforms were gray shorts, gray shirt, blue and gray striped tie, and gray knee socks. They got mad when we laughed at them.

The laughter abruptly ended as we stepped into the harsh environment of the British school. The bullying and belittling began at the top with the dreaded and feared headmaster, Mr. Percy, and passed on through the hands and mouths of the teachers who overlooked and tolerated bullying by a few students. Unable to connect well with our African, British, and Asian classmates, Linda and I found refuge in each other. Oh, the priceless blessing of a twin who walks by my side.

Our first day began like all the others, but was memorable because of its ugly contrast to the homeschool environment we knew and loved. General assembly began with all of us standing by the flagpole in rows with our class. Mr. Percy swaggered onto the raised platform and surveyed us with steely, gray eyes and an ugly scowl. He sent shivers through me with his harsh voice and frowning, scraggly eyebrows. "Right... Now! What's all the fuss about?"

He gruffly commanded kids forward from their class line to belittle them for crooked ties, untied shoelaces, or sloppy clothes. Infractions, such as needing to go to the bathroom, allowing your knee socks to droop, or misspelling a word, earned marks and stripes that accumulated to the punishment of a whipping by a *tackie* (tennis shoe), a cane, or a cricket bat with holes. Mr. Percy belittled kids then sent them for punishment to his office during general assembly so everyone knew.

It made me cry inside when I saw their humiliation. I walked in fear of punishment, but also carried the greater fear of my sis, Jim, or Steve being next. Steve and Jim struggled to be good at the best of times and, in this school, it was easy to get into trouble. The first day, Mr. Percy turned his belittling attention to Jim, calling him out for standing with his hands in his pockets. Poor Steve, he really caught the heat for not wearing a tie. It really wasn't his fault because Mother and Daddy hadn't bought him one yet.

Steve accumulated marks quickly and had to go to Mr. Percy's office for the *tackie*. Kids described Mr. Percy taking his time to demonstrate the three levels of punishment. He seemed to delight in watching students squirm under his emotional abuse. Steve said that dropping his gray uniform shorts for the punishment wasn't as demeaning as the verbal lashing.

In homeschool first grade, we learned to write in cursive; here we were berated for it and punished by having to fill out many exercise books with printed letters. We learned the multiplication tables all the way to the thirteenth. An error or an infraction was a "mark" in the punishment tally. Accumulated marks meant having to stand in the front corner of the classroom in shame.

Changing for P.E. was one of our real dreads. We had to quickly strip off our uniforms and put on blue shorts and T-shirt while standing next to our desk. It was painfully embarrassing and the teacher made fun of those who dressed the slowest. Afterwards, Linda and I would run to the bathroom and push our stomachs hard to pee fast so we didn't get in trouble for arriving late in the P.E. room.

That school was the worst collision of cultures I experienced during my childhood. Linda and I were lucky to have each other; I don't know how Steve and Jim got through without a twin. We only saw our brothers at general assembly because our classes were segregated. Later in life, Jim said what he remembered most about that time was excruciating loneliness. He would get to know this loneliness later at boarding school, but Kilimani created it in a day-setting by ripping away our individuality, separating us from our brothers and sisters, and setting up a harsh environment of controlling authority using fear and shame.

*****

With the dread of school temporarily shelved, the excitement mounted one weekend as we loaded up in the mission's "Blue Goose," our Volkswagen van, for the first camping trip from our Nairobi home. We joined other members of a naturalist club connected with the East African Museum to collect poisonous snakes for the snake park so they could milk them for anti-venom.

As Mother made supper at camp, Linda and I chased each other around the tents we called Tent City. Linda tripped over a tent stake and fell face down.

"Eh! What's all the fuss about?" A harsh, heavy British accent from the tent sent tremors of recognition and fear — the dreaded schoolmaster, Mr. No-Mercy Percy. Who would have thought he was a member of the naturalist group? The fun of the trip immediately dissipated and we were keen to go home, but Daddy distracted us with adventure.

We camped out three nights under the full moon with all the comforts of good camping: sleeping with the sounds of hyenas, lions, leopards, and bush pigs. We explored the mountain forests, vast undisturbed savanna teaming with big game, and gazed in wonder at the 4,000-foot vista dropping to the floor of the Great Rift Valley. We could see as far as Lake Rudolf to the north and Lake Baringo to the south. We were as far north as we could go without military escort due to the *shifta* (bandits) and Somali terrorists who have caused Northern Frontier border disputes ever since Kenyan independence in 1963.

The game department had adopted a baby elephant and cape buffalo that followed us wherever we walked. The buffalo liked to bump us with his bony head; he was clumsy and stepped on our feet. The baby elephant liked to smell our ears and curiously explored the world with his trunk. He wore a burlap bag over his back to keep him from being sunburned since his Mama wasn't around to provide shade for him. We wanted to take them home so were disappointed when our parents said we already had a dog, rabbit, and hedgehog and they didn't feel the need to add buffalo and elephant to our family.

Mother added a different perspective of the trip:

> I had an interesting talk with a Kikuyu game warden, the tribe in the Mau Mau uprising of the '50s. The Mau Mau used oaths to bind these people together and get them to do horrific things to tribe members who refused to join the uprising. Part of the oath involved eating goat eyeballs and human organs. Many Christian Kikuyu faced punishment for refusing the oath. The Mau Mau often forced the father of the family to watch each of his children chopped to death by a *panga* (machete) before they slaughtered him.
>
> This young man told about hiding in the bush while the Mau Mau confronted his father. He heard his father, a Christian, refuse the oath because he wouldn't take the life of another. He saw men he knew in his own tribe chop him to death, starting with his extremities so that death would come slowly. What a humbling experience. I wonder how many of us would be so brave if our Christian

walk came with such a sacrifice.

Back at school, Linda and I balanced on the beam of an overturned soccer post. Our arms outstretched, we challenged each other to be the last to fall. Linda fell and cried as she hugged her knee to her chest. Forgetting that her fall made me the winner, I dropped to the ground and held her as she, mouth wide, silently screamed. Oh no... I finally got her to open her fingers, revealing a deep wound, ripped open by a screw, just above her kneecap. I thought I could see the bone. I held her tight in my arms and put my hand over her mouth to keep her from crying. "Shhh, Linda," I pleaded. "We'll get in trouble. Shhh…" Warm tears flowed over my fingers as her chest heaved silent screams of agony.

My worst fear came true as I heard the English growl behind me. "Eh! What's all the fuss about?" I looked up at the monster, his thick eyebrows meeting above his cold, gray, steely eyes. Mr. Percy growled at Linda for being a "foolish little tyke" and made her march to his office. I was surrounded by uniformed kids but, for the first time, all alone. Mr. Percy wouldn't allow me to go with Linda. Back in class, I couldn't focus on school. All I could think was, "Where is Linda? What has happened?" For all I knew, Mr. Percy had eaten her. I discovered later that she was taken to the hospital for stitches and thankfully recovered well from the physical wound, although the emotional trauma stayed with her much longer.

Mother wrote:

> Sometimes it is harder to adjust to the Englishman than to the African. Each morning the kids hated to face the day with so much newness. They look funny in their uniforms; the only thing that looks American is their haircut. Jim came home saying, "Everyone has long hair except for me." I explained he was American and they just wear their hair different. He said a boy in his class has such long hair that his mother has to braid it and tuck the rolled braids in the back of his head. He said, "At least I think that was a boy because he wore a boy's uniform." The boy was Sikh and could never cut his hair.

Chipper became a British kindergarten dropout — he lasted only three days. Maybe he was the smartest of us all.

Mother and Daddy went to school a lot longer than we did. An *aya* (nanny) looked after us until they finally got out of class. Well, she was supposed to look after us, but we liked her because she didn't. She left us to do whatever we wanted while she sat in the shade, spinning sisal to make baskets. She spat in her hands and rolled the sisal up and down her black, smooth, polished shins while we had the run of the place. The five of us climbed trees, played monkeys, hunted chameleons, and had wars. No adult supervision, how fun was that!

Thankfully, there were many pleasant memories of this temporary home in Kenya that overshadowed the misery of British school. We kids didn't comment on the agonies of school because we had learned to endure, without complaint, and find the positives in even miserable circumstances.

33 Love Leaves a Hole *Shimo la Upendo*
Tanzania 1960s

Excitement built to nervous anticipation as my parents' graduation drew near, scattering butterflies in my stomach, because Mema and Granddaddy were coming from America for it, to see Africa, and go home to Mbeya with us. Their voices on the reel-to-reel tapes exchanged across the ocean had kept us connected since the time we said our goodbyes to begin our new life.

After graduation, we loaded up in the Blue Goose and headed with them for a long camping trip into Uganda to visit Murchison Falls, the Nile, and the Congo border to see a small pocket of pygmies.

I was as tall as the old pygmy man and woman that stood under Daddy's outstretched arms. I guessed they were older than Mema and Granddaddy because they had many wrinkles. Their smiles lit up their entire wrinkled faces, especially their shiny eyes. They wore very little clothing and what they had was dirty and torn.

On a fishing trip, Granddaddy caught a 62-pound Nile perch, more than I weighed at the time. We ate fish for days. Mother wrote:

> In the middle of the night, all four adults sat up in our sleeping bags. It wasn't anything we heard that awoke us, just the sense of danger. We peeked out the door and there stood three elephants between our tent and the kids' tent. One of the elephants was six feet from the door, so close we could hear his stomach rumble. John made a low whistle and two turned away, but the big daddy stood there and stared while we held our breath. He finally turned and lumbered away. I had slept well while camping because I thought I would be able to hear an elephant long before he got near our camp, but they got close enough to unzip the tent door with their trunk.

Packing for the trip home to Mbeya, Daddy removed the back seat from the Blue Goose so we could pack, squeeze, shove, and fill every inch of space. Chipper spoke my thoughts when he asked, "But Daddy, what about the people?" We still needed to squeeze in nine people, Frisky, and Spiny, our pet hedgehog.

He was a timid little guy, about five inches long with an overcoat of three-quarter-inch brown, white-tipped spines. He was usually a tight ball of spines but, when he got comfortable, he slowly unfolded, revealing a cute, long, pointed nose, delicate twitching whiskers, and bright, shiny black eyes. Contrasting sharply with the spine coat he wore on his back, he had a silky soft underbelly and tiny feet that tickled your hands when he walked.

For as small as Spiny was, he made noise worthy of a mischievous 50-pound animal as he foraged at night, rustling behind bookcases and under beds, scraping his spines as he snooped. He always returned to his small cardboard box home to sleep in his tight spine ball during the day.

As we approached the Kenya-Tanzania border, Daddy told us we might have to get out of the car for an inspection. Temperature, tempers, and tensions were high at the border but, out of respect, they didn't ask Mother or Mema to get out as they searched our car. Spiny made it through in his little hiding place under Mother's dress, but sadly didn't survive the rugged trip home.

Losing him made me sad; there was an empty hurt deep in my stomach. About a month earlier, we had lost another pet when Frisky ate Eupe, our rabbit. Usually they played and even slept together but, one day, we came home to find blood splattered on the glass patio doors and white fur strewn across the yard. I couldn't understand why Frisky would eat his best friend. We watched through the blood-splattered glass as Daddy buried Eupe in our patio yard.

Pets held a special place in our family's heart, bringing warmth, love, amusement, intrigue, and even understanding. Perhaps the love for a pet is as rich as the love for a sibling or a best friend, but without all the baggage. The loss of a dear friend and pet was a wound, but nothing like the wound created by the collision of an American in a British school. Our family hit another culture clash when we faced the challenges of boarding school.

Steve had finally convinced Mother and Daddy to let him join his MK friends at the RVA boarding school for missionary kids, run by the African Inland Mission (AIM). Steve had begged to go and Mother and Daddy resisted for some time on the basis that "Steve may be old enough to go to boarding school, but his parents aren't old enough to let him do it."

Mother cried all morning the day we dropped him off and turned our Land Rover toward our Mbeya home. Steve did well at RVA at first then his grades and his satisfaction nose-dived. His upbringing and his loving environment of home and family collided with the ultra-conservative rules of the AIM boarding school.

His absence affected all of us. For the first time, our family wasn't together and I really missed him. Who would have thought? He picked on Linda and me all the time. I admit I missed that. Thinking of Steve made an empty hurt, a longing in my stomach, as it did when Spiny and Eupe died, but at least we got to see him every three months. Mother talked a lot about missing him and often cried when she prayed for him before we ate. Jim moped around and kept asking when he was going to come home. Daddy covered his longing for Steve in humor as he wrote to his parents:

> Guess who? I have an absent son who I wish would write home. This makes me ever so much more conscious of how long it has been since I wrote to my own parents.

Mother and Daddy felt they made the right decision to send Steve to boarding school and wrote of how happy he was. They worried how they would send four more kids that way next term. Steve's pushback against the rules, his declining grades, and dissatisfaction made them later regret their decision. The impact of boarding school issues on family were a major challenge for missionary families in rural settings. Luckily, most cultural collisions were not as painful and even provided a source of growth, intrigue, and humor.

34 Hospital Horrors *Maafa ya Hospitali*
Uganda 2004

Laughing with exhilaration, I straddle the motorcycle, my arms wrapped tightly around Linda's waist, as we career along the dirt road toward Kaabong. Years ago, I would be on the front and I sure wouldn't have been wearing a skirt. Feeling the vibration of the motorcycle and my body synchronizing with the movement of the machine brings back a flood of memories of riding together in our teenage years, our hair whipping as we rode on the winds of freedom and fun. I savor the memories of the two of us motoring through the Ngong Hills and the Rift Valley as we chased animals, dreams, and adventure. We giggled our way through our teenage years. A twin is a gift of connection and joy. Even the most serious of moments somehow transforms into insuppressible, embarrassing, and unexplainable giggles.

"I'm glad you still know how to ride double," Linda hugs me when we stop. "Last time I took some local girls, they hung on to convenient handles — my breasts!"

"One of those awkward clashes of culture and personal boundaries, huh? Like the male habit of holding hands with other men. I wonder if an African ever tried to hold Daddy's hand."

The dusty town of Kaabong has a filling station and *dukas* selling dry goods such as beans, onions, potatoes, Coca Cola, candy, yarn, and eggs. A side, dirt road has a lean-to shanty with used tires and shoes crafted from the treads of worn tires for sale.

As I look around, I am struck at how there is next to nothing, no green produce for sale and few fresh goods of any kind. It's a lazy little village with people hanging around waiting... for what? A vehicle to drive by?

The Wittes buy milk, meat, and eggs from their neighbors in the *manyatta* next door in order to support them without starting the endless cycle sparked by handouts. They buy Blue Band, potatoes, onions, and soap from Kaabong shops.

A goat purchased weekly from the village adds to the blend of Friday dawn sounds. The kids enjoy playing with it, but then there's the inevitable sad reality as they watch Sera, the guard and helper, slit its throat to prepare it for cooking. The kids are used to the stark reality that pets may become food. I, on the other hand, have become used to buying my meat packaged in a clean, clear wrapper with a label on it, giving little room for thought about the animal providing my meal.

I recall, on a previous visit to the Witte's home in Kenya, the girls telling me I was "sitting on Kwanza." Kwanza, meaning first in Swahili, was the Witte's first calf that became their beloved milk cow and pet. She became several meals for the Wittes when she died, her meat shared with their Maasai neighbors, whose friends then hand-tanned Kwanza's hide and made the chair I was sitting on. Seve asked one night, while we were eating hamburgers, "Are we eating Kwanza now?" We were.

Tomorrow night, Friday, we will enjoy the Witte's treasured traditional Sedar, a time of family connection and worship modeled after the Jewish celebration with a focus on family, prayer, and gratefulness. We will roast the goat on top of the charcoal stove and serve it with homemade rolls and the week's treat of a can of corn and peas. Throughout the following week, the goat will become stir-fry then pot pie. Byron will give its head, organs, and some of the meat back to the village.

The family's diet also includes *ugali*, a firm, tasteless version of corn meal we called *uji* in our girl years. A tow sack of dried greens, softened by water, provides the only green in their diets except for the produce from their small garden.

The drinking water collected from the roof is rationed in collection cisterns. A well at the bottom of the yard provides water for showers and toilets. Solar panels heat water for buckets hand-carried to showers. The locals dig deep holes into dry, sandy riverbeds to gather water to carry back to their homes. Water is a precious commodity.

After passing through the scant village, we approach the cinderblock government hospital built by the Swedish. A closer look shows there has been little maintenance and the infrastructure is crumbling in on itself — a repeating story in East Africa. Many call it "AWA," meaning "Africa Wins Again." Volunteer organizations and international countries construct buildings, hospitals, roads, wells, and toilets but there isn't a culture of accountability to maintain the infrastructure — AWA.

The hospital has a solar system that no longer works and water pumps for towers that no longer hold water. The staff use pressure cookers on charcoal fires to sterilize equipment because the autoclaves no longer work. Three separate concrete buildings contain an operating room, a male ward, and a combined female and child ward. I am appalled at the number of patients with gunshot wounds in the rows of beds in the open men's ward.

Linda introduces a new mother as she places a pair of tiny twins in my arms. Unaccustomed to handling babies, I awkwardly balance them.

"I remember their C-section delivery," Linda tells me. "I placed the babies in the hands of a nurse but, as she walked away, I noticed one was lifeless. I broke scrub and chased after her, took the baby, and started resuscitation."

"Lucky you realized so quickly."

"I've done it many times, but doing it on a baby is vastly different to a manikin. I don't think I took a breath until the baby did. I was so overwhelmed when the child finally let out a cry."

"How do the mothers cope afterwards? It all looks so primitive compared to the care women get back home."

"Elaine, my missionary colleague, runs a feeding project for babies, providing powdered milk, cornmeal, and cribs with mosquito nets to put a stopgap to malaria. Once the babies are well enough to take home, the mothers bring them back once a week to get milk and cornmeal."

I admire my twin's dedication to helping this community with its sparse resources.

"During their return visits, they hear Elaine's Bible stories and the songs that go along with them. We try to go beyond treating illness, so often caused by malnutrition, and work beyond the physical to bring hope and life by touching them on the spiritual realm."

The resources are desperately limited and the problems are huge, yet these people in this remote, almost forgotten, corner of Africa still find love, hope, and care.

I am overwhelmed as I see the great needs and how little there is. A woman lies in a fetal position on the bed, her skin the blackest of black, wrinkled, and stretched thin over her bones. She appears to be about 80 but is probably around 35. Her eyes, sunken and sad, show more life than the rest of her body. Her husband gave her AIDS, then he and his family deserted and ostracized her because of the stigma. The hospital doesn't provide food for the patients. Their families stay in small huts and cook for them. She has no place to go and no one to help, feed, or love her.

The grief of seeing this woman all alone, having to beg food from other families, weighs heavily on me as we walk to the huts in the TB village. Patients stay there for three to six months so they can receive their daily shot of streptomycin.

All my life I have been haunted by the question: "What can I do?" I have seen people in hopeless poverty and desolation contrasting so sharply with my own life. I carry a nagging sense of unfairness, which keeps me unsettled. Maybe that is a good thing.

*****

After their first furlough in Texas, Byron had returned to Africa to set up their home in Kaabong while Linda finished closing their house and packing the plywood crates to send to Africa. She traveled with her own four young kids, their dog, one of Chipper's girls, and the luggage through Europe to Kampala then finally on a small plane to Kaabong. At a layover in Paris, the airline personnel told her she must pay an astronomical and unforeseen price for Noel to continue her journey. She couldn't pay it. The only other option offered was to let the dog out on the Paris streets. The kids began to cry while Linda cried inside. The airline employee ended up paying the fee herself and they were able to travel onward.

"I remember being excited and bone-deep exhausted when I first set foot in the hospital the night we flew into Kaabong. I assisted Dr. Mark perform surgery for a man with a small bowel obstruction," Linda tells me. "We had to use a flashlight to find the way to the operating room to fire up the generator for surgery. The man had visible loops and ripples in his abdomen from obstructions. Putting him under with ketamine, we opened his abdomen to find his hugely dilated bowels were full of masses of goat hair."

"Goat hair?!"

She nods. "The Karamojong put their goats on the fire and eat everything; nothing is wasted. Goat hairballs obstructed his intestines. Surgery went well. We turned the generator off and wheeled him to the unlit, male ward where we found the male nurse drunk.

"We transferred the unconscious patient, with his I.V., to his bed and left him with the drunken nurse who had no light. It was a real shock to me. Thankfully, it all looked a little better when I saw it by daylight."

"It must be hard to know where to begin when people's needs here are so great."

"Yep, it is. Most of our work was caused by preventable illnesses and injuries caused by custom, raiding, or the witch doctor."

"So sad that so many problems are exactly the same as those that Mother and Daddy fought when we were kids."

"Too many things are identical, Cinda. One of the worst times was when I went to the hospital to help after the village raid when I saw my people sifting through their charred possessions. The day I told you about, when I went to the men's ward to find the gunshot patients and found it empty because the men were gone during this raid. They shot women and children."

I can't help but wince.

"I'll never forget the sight, sounds, and feelings of seeing a two-year-old girl crying, her legs suspended above her at 90-degree angles because bullets had shattered them both. She looked at me with such big, dark, sad eyes." She shakes her head as if to dismiss the heart-rending images. "Enough of the gloom and doom. The work thankfully has its funny side too sometimes.

I remember accompanying Dr. Mark as he consulted at the bedside of a new patient. As he began to unravel a blood-soaked rag wrapped around the man's penis, he described how a bullet hit him as he squatted during a raid. I asked Dr. Mark if he thought the shooter purposely hit the man in the penis. 'I sure hope not,' Dr. Mark said. 'I would hope they aren't that good a shot.'"

Her stories are gripping, heartbreaking, and gut-wrenching but they often have a funny twist, making me belly laugh through my tears.

I remember Mother describing her first night in her new African home when she assisted in amputating a boy's arm decades ago at Mbeya Hospital in Tanzania. My heart aches for the depth of hurt and struggle. At the same time, it bursts with pride over the way my twin is making a difference, relieving suffering in at least this one small part of the world; making a difference one life at a time.

I am proud of Byron for meeting these people and bringing them hope and life through story, the medium they understand. I am impressed at his willingness to walk as they walk, and to eat and meet in their way.

Motoring through the gates of my twin's home, I enter an oasis, briefly leaving behind the great needs and struggles to immerse back into family. We head to the yard for a snack and, as we settle into the depressions in the rock, I look around at Linda's children and marvel at how she continues our parents' legacy. She homeschools, develops meaningful family rituals, connects with her children and the local people on a real heart level, and finds the tricky balance between family and ministry. Finding the balance, too, of bringing American culture in the home, but still connecting and cherishing the Africa around them.

35 Trouble in the Air *Shida Imekuwa Imekaribia*
Uganda 2004

I thought life would move slowly in this corner of the world, but I find one day seems like two or three. It is quiet without the noise and distractions of TV, phone, electrical appliances, or music radio. As I rest between our outings, Linda plays catch-up with laundry, homeschool, housework, and the many needs from neighbors who want to visit or need medical care.

A gentle, warm breeze blows through the window, bringing in the sounds of birds, sheets popping in the wind, the rooster's crow, and Ben's hum as he pushes a homemade mud car around Byron and Stanley's feet as they visit on the outside porch. I'm enjoying the sweet lull in activity as we wait to hear the goat bells entering the next-door village. I feel obligated to accept the invitation for chai, but hope to make an early exit to slip in a treasured run with my nieces before sunset. I'm tired from the morning's walk to Sit and Squat and the afternoon outing to Kaabong hospital.

Joseph, a polished, well-respected Karamojong, motorcycled by the house this afternoon delivering the "local newspaper" or as close as you can get to one here. That means he brought the most recent news and gossip on the wind. Engrossed in the walking ministry and plugged into family life, we haven't kept up with local news. Gunfire in the village is a common night sound, a way to vent frustration while soaking in the home brew. Recently we have sensed the climbing frustrations as the gunfire increased in intensity.

Joseph has been working as negotiator between the local tribal warriors and the military ever since the warriors broke into the barracks and killed a commander. This spark ignited the powder keg while we were making our way to Africa. He is persistent, but hope is ebbing for a peaceful outcome. The Ugandan military has demanded the Karamojong warriors turn in their weapons. Joseph has heard the military is sending reinforcements from Kotido, but there's no way to get news or to distinguish news from hearsay or gossip.

We finally make our early exit from the village after "saying our manners" as Mother would tell us. We run with an easy rhythm along the dirt road. Jessica and Seve lead, both long-legged and graceful, their ponytails keeping an opposite rhythm, one swinging left while the other swings right. My mind wanders without the distractions of music, traffic, or signs. Jordan strides in step beside me. Built like Linda and me, she is shorter, stockier, and stronger than her sisters.

I love to run — always have. I love music and wish I could sing, but I can't. When I run I feel like I am moving inside a song — a praise song. This is when I feel most connected with my creator. A few minutes into a run, my body hits a rhythm of breathing and foot strikes that become the rhythm of a song. My spirits soar and my thoughts fly. Adding to the joy, I am also running in Africa, the land I love, and with my girls I have so missed. Without cars to dodge or curbs to step off, I relax and savor the peace, joy, and gratefulness for health and family.

The cherry at the end of the run is a race to the top of the rocky hill overlooking their house and the village. I challenge the young ones and the race is on as we scramble over the loose rocks and large boulders. My lungs feel as if they will burst as I shift gears, using every ounce of my energy and ability to hold my own. My nieces are young and fit, but my years give me wit, wile, and wisdom. I tug the back of Jordan's T-shirt and muscle past her. As I grab Seve's shirt, she catches the hem of Jessica's and we all collapse in deep belly laughter.

Sitting on top of the rocks, the sounds of the village below reach us with surprising clarity: the jingle of goat bells, children playing, shepherds calling, and a woman shooing a chicken out of her hut. We watch the women pull the thorn barrier over the entrance to the village.

The kids there hear us on top of the rock and begin to call out, "Chevy, Chevy." They all love Seve. We watch as they run through the village maze to the entrance, already closed by the thorn barrier. A woman tugs it aside, allowing them to slip through and scramble their way toward us.

"I love these friends," Seve tells me. "In America, my friends avoid me because of my dorky clothes. Here they accept me. I belong."

"Mom says it was like that for you two when you were kids," Jessica adds.

"Yep, it sure was, but we always had each other."

"Most of my friends are boys because they can go play. The girls are serious and are busy helping their mothers work. It makes me sad to leave Kaabong. I love living here and I'll miss my friends," Seve continues.

As she and Jordan dive into a long discussion about whom they will give their possessions to, I reflect on my precious treasures sitting next to me. Sitting side by side, leaning back on our arms with our legs extended, I notice Jessica's legs far out-length everyone else's. It seems just yesterday she was barely a toddler riding on my shoulders, gripping my short hair, as I walked through the shoulder-high grass along the Mara River in Kenya. Her contented baby babble would change and I would feel her stiffen with alertness as she exclaimed, "Doooggg!" in a strong West Texas accent that followed her to Africa. "Doooggg" was her only word for all animals. My heart would race as I strained to peer over the grass to see if she had seen a dog, zebra, buffalo, lion, or hippo.

Jessica, arriving in Africa as a toddler, prefers green slimy *sukuma wiki* (boiled greens), and cold-water hose showers to the conveniences and fast food a fifteen-year-old American girl takes for granted. The first-born claims respect and, along with it, responsibility. In fact, a mother's identity is tied to her first-born. Linda's name was Mama Jessica even after Jordan and Seve came along. It is a boy's world, however, and her name changed to Mama Ben when he joined the family.

Jessica, elegant, athletic, and quiet, leads, loves, and fiercely defends her younger siblings. She has make-believe tea parties with her sisters then easily crosses into the adult world for grown-up conversation.

Jordan's entrance to the world was surrounded by turmoil. Linda, home alone with young Jessica, alarmed by a persistent high fever, festering boils, and an absence of fetal movement, snagged a ride to the Mombasa Hospital where a nurse induced labor without fetal monitoring, a doctor, or an estimated due date. Jordan's first glimpse of life was of her mother fighting an antibiotic-resistant systemic infection in a steamy, hot hospital room with no air conditioning, overlooking the Indian Ocean. Her father wrestled a mind-wracking malarial fever in the emergency room of the same hospital. After Linda's post-delivery, hot curry meal — complete with a roach — and hot chai, my twin returned home to care for her toddler, newborn, and her malarial-fevered husband.

Then there is Seve Lil Lynn, born in Nairobi Hospital. Byron, busy orienting American mission volunteers, gave me the honor of sharing the double bed with my sis and the newborn child. Seve loved to sleep on my belly, her legs and arms tucked under her like a tree frog. The cutest tree frog I had ever seen. The quiet one, Seve is a sweet alloy of tomboy, girliness, boldness, and shyness, connecting with others but content to play and sing alone in her own world. Jessica's announcement of her baby sister's entrance into the world twelve years ago — "Seve came home!" — hints at strong family bonds even before birth.

As I savor the memories and my eyes feast on the sun melting into the horizon, I notice a large dust storm gathering to the south. The sounds of distant gunfire have intensified, but there is more… There is a new, ominous sound, the deep boom of mortar or artillery fire. I feel the deep percussion in my chest and a sense of foreboding creeps in as my thoughts whirl. What could that be? Just stay calm. Do not overreact.

We clamber down the rocks in the dwindling light. Frenzied villagers gather outside their thorn fence, searching the southern horizon and calling their children back into the thorn enclosure. Some say the explosions are bombs; others say it's the Jia stealing their cows again. That doesn't sound like the sound of cattle raiding to me. Not that I would know.

The villagers return to their village, reclosing the thorn barrier. We withdraw to our compound and have dinner on the rooftop. There is one thing unusual about tonight. There is no singing or dancing in the village next door. Intermittent, distant artillery punctuates an eerie quietness throughout the night.

36 Under Fire *Katikati ya Vita*
Uganda 2004

I lose track of time and days in this land. The first conversation, on awakening, is a disagreement with Stanley over the day of the week. For the first time since I arrived at Kaabong, I dig out my watch from where I placed it four days ago, on top of our passports in the bedside table of our quaint little guest house. It confirms that I am right — Friday August 27, 2004.

It was a restless night with little sleep, especially for Stanley.

"Babe, I have a bad feeling about this," he frowns. "The last few days we heard AK-47 fire close by, but it was only intoxicated, angry men letting off some steam."

"What d'you think we're hearing now?"

"The sounds in the distance are entirely different. The locals say it's the Jia raiding their cows, but this is big artillery and the distance is closing. I'm almost sure, Babe. Don't forget, I've been in the army. I couldn't help but notice the sounds getting closer during the night."

Stanley served in the army in Germany during the building of the Berlin Wall. One of his primary responsibilities was to drive an armored personnel carrier in an artillery battery for the Second Armored Calvary Regiment. I don't know what's ahead for us but I'm confident he knows heavy gunfire. During the night, I brushed off his concerns and turned over to put my good ear on the pillow to retreat into my dreams. I'm deaf in my right ear from an infantile attack of meningitis. Now his concerns have my ears, or ear.

The morning begins like the others. We sit on stools, watching the milky chai steam in the blackened aluminum pan. We hold the hot metal cups by the rims, waiting for the liquid to cool enough for that wonderful first sip of sweet, milky tea laced with spices. I notice the village boy has already tied the goat to the fence in preparation for tonight's Friday Seder meal and celebration.

While we discuss the plan for the day, we take turns at the computer, writing emails to our loved ones. In my email to Mother, I update her on all the happenings but leave out my gut-level concerns. I'm more upfront with my worries in an email to my friend, Georgia:

> Bud, all is well here, but I feel there is trouble on the way. I've mentioned gunfire at night but last night it was different. There's an intensity and persistence in the

small-arms fire and there's distant, heavy artillery. Although it's way off in the distance, Stanley believes it's moving this way. There's no way to get news.

The talk of the village is that it's only cattle raiding going on. Stanley's concerned it's a lot more than that. Byron guesses it may be reinforcements coming because our warriors attacked and killed a commander at the military base. He isn't concerned because we're not the enemy or the issue; the conflict is between Karamojong warriors, the people the Wittes minister to, and the Ugandan army. It may not be a big deal but just wanted you to know.

Today I will go running with my sis then we will walk with the kids to the bridge to build sandcastles again.

Byron is to walk to Lochom, seven miles to the south. He and his ministers are always vigilant, walking abreast so one bullet cannot take out the whole group as they pass through no man's land. Several months ago, one of the ministers was shot in the hand on this journey. Lochom is the direction of the dust storm and gunfire. Linda and I decide this is a good day to call in sick and I do have some sizable blisters to justify my position.

"Aren't you worried about the artillery fire, Byron?" Stanley asks.

"We are not the enemy or the issue," he emphasizes. "Tubo's son is at Lochom, which gives me the opportunity to model pastoring and concern to my mentees by going with them."

Stanley isn't easily appeased. "When the bullets fly it doesn't matter whose side you are on."

"I'm not sure we will get to Lochom," Byron counters, "but I want to make the effort and I want to get the newspaper. You know — the news."

We watch Byron, followed by Tubo and Locilo, head out of the compound with a hip belt containing lunch and water. Linda and I strategize our own plans. We'll grab the opportunity to do what we love most — run together in Africa. We reassure the kids that afterwards we'll go with them to the bridge to build sandcastles, and make them promise to wait until we return from our run. Jessica and Jordan volunteer to make sandwiches for a picnic and Ben chimes in that he will carry the backpack. Stanley contentedly sits on the porch, smoking his pipe. I say contentedly but, as I look closer, I notice tenseness in his jaw and a worried look on his face that I'm not used to seeing on my man.

Linda and I have played and run together all our lives. In grade school, we ran and giggled our way around the hospital compound in Mbeya, Tanzania. Our fifth grade year, we lived in Kisumu, on the shores of Lake

Victoria, where we played, ran, swam, and looked for monkeys and hippos. During our high school years, we lived in the village of Karen, named after Karen Blixen, best known for her memoir, *Out of Africa*, at the foot of the Ngong Hills outside of Nairobi. We competed to see who could run the fastest across those hills. Only now do I grasp what a feat that is on a mountain range at 6,000 feet.

We shared our imaginations, fantasies, our own twin language, and had our own ways. Often when we ran, we pretended to be different animals. We would run and bound like a Super Ball to mimic a kongoni, or thrash our way through the thick, magical forests of the Abedare Mountains pretending to be buffalo. A twisting trail along the trout streams at the base of Mount Kenya became a roller coaster or, when tired, we pretended to be tortoises. We were born to run, built to run, and given the gift to run together.

All that to explain what may seem to be odd behavior — 44-year-old sisters running and jumping along a dry riverbed in northern Uganda, giggling and pretending to be warthogs. The concerns of the morning long gone, smothered under delight and giggles, we run to Sakatan. We climb and challenge each other to chimney to the top; a technique to maneuver up a crack in the rock where I put my back and one foot on one wall and a foot on the other rock slab to work my way up like a ratchet.

We were avid rock climbers, beginning in fifth grade year when we climbed at the sugarcane fields near Lake Victoria and on through our high school years. Our rock climbing has taken us from the depths of Mount Suswa volcanic caves to the icy cliffs of the 17,000-foot Nelion Peak on Mount Kenya. The techniques and the memories return to me.

We scramble onto a south-facing ledge, sitting shoulder to shoulder with our legs swinging over the precipice as we savor the precious moments together. A burst of distant artillery fire wrenches me back from my reflections. Linda and I feel the percussion deep in our chests like a rumbling bass drum. The dust boils in the direction of the explosions.

The magical moment is gone, replaced by concern and an ominous foreboding. We meet village women and children hurrying toward the rocks as we frantically scramble toward home. The anxious women tell us we must go. Go home now. A crisis turns on a switch for Linda.

"The women say men with gunshot wounds are arriving at the hospital. Hurry, Cinda. We need to go there to take care of these wounded people. We're going to get to do surgery together today."

We run hard toward the house, meeting more women and children as they run toward Sakatan. Stanley is no longer sitting contentedly on the porch smoking his pipe. He was alone at the house with the kids and we have been gone for a long time. Time melts away when the Twindas are at play.

Byron is gone for the day to Lochom, the kids have lunch packed and are ready to hike to the bridge. Linda is pumped and ready to go to the hospital. As I stand in the middle of the living room, trying to put the pieces together and figure out what is best to do, Stanley pulls me aside to express his concerns privately.

"Babe, you can't go to the hospital. That leaves me alone with the kids. They need a parent here."

"You think it's really serious now?"

"The sounds in the distance aren't just rifle fire. It sounds like 105 Howitzer rounds. Something big is developing and it's moving our way. I think we need to stick together because I'm not sure what's going to unfold."

My husband's words convince me, but Linda isn't easily swayed into staying at the house when needed at the hospital. The hold on the trip to the bridge is not a popular decision with the kids.

"Mom, if we can't go there, may I go play with my shepherd friends under our tree?" Jordan pleads. She responds to Linda's negative response with a roll of her eyes in a manner that can only convey annoyance as she sulks off with a parting complaint. "I'm not going to get to see them much longer."

Byron surprises us when he walks through the gate. The military wouldn't allow him to continue toward Lochom. He makes radio contact with Nairobi and Kampala to check on flight possibilities in case the conflict threatens us. Linda and I, busy playing warthogs, had missed the usual 7:30 a.m. radio contact.

Byron contacts the Missionary Aviation Fellowship and tells them we don't think we're going to need to leave but want to check on the possibility in case our situation escalates. MAF informs him their planes have left for the day and they're unable to help. We can radio after 2:00 p.m. to see if a flight can be arranged for tomorrow.

He tries repeatedly to contact Laurie, "Lima Mike," the missionary in Kenya they contact each morning. He alternates his radio calls between Laurie in Kenya, and Jonathan Parsons, "Juliet Papa," a short-term relief missionary covering for a regular in Kampala. Byron calmly and methodically repeats the calls, "Lima Mike this is Juliet Whiskey, Lima Mike this is Juliet Whiskey. Juliet Papa this is Juliet Whiskey, Juliet Papa this is Juliet Whiskey."

In the tenseness of the moment, my brain still twists to see humor in the fact that John Byron Witte's radio code is Whiskey and, in his work, he cannot partake of alcohol. All we get is silence.

Accustomed to constant silence on the other end, we are startled when the radio crackles, followed by Laurie's voice, "Juliet Whiskey, this is Lima

Mike. Go ahead."

With no radio contact at the routine 7:30 a.m. time, Laurie had gone about her routine and was carrying a laundry basket down the hallway when she heard Byron's radio call. At his request, she immediately calls Jonathan in Kampala who makes radio contact from a mission vehicle. Radio communication, usually difficult to hear, is as clear as if they are standing across the room.

Byron radios, "We have fires developing to the south of us, and they seem to be moving in our direction."

"Fires," code word for trouble, is a word carefully chosen since anyone can hear the radio communication.

"The fires started last evening and continued through the night, moving in our direction," he continues. "We don't think we will need to leave but just want to let you know of the developing security issues."

All agree it's wise to begin a contingency plan so we will know of the available resources in case the "security issue" escalates. Jonathan and Laurie drop whatever they're doing to make connections for us.

The two missionary air support organizations, MAF and AIM have their Cessna Caravans out of the country for servicing. Laurie works with AIM on alternatives while Jonathan contacts Byron's boss, Tim Gillihan, and the American Embassy in Kampala.

AIM have no planes in Uganda, but two available in Kenya. They put their MU-2 plane in Nairobi on standby with two pilots. Jonathan requests prayer support for us. No little matter — one phone call activates a prayer chain connecting missionaries to a worldwide network of people who care and pray.

At this time we don't think an evacuation is necessary, but we begin to make preparations to cover three possibilities: hunker down until the fires pass, evacuate by foot to hide out in the bush until they do, or leave by foot to the runway, six miles away, for an air evacuation.

Byron calmly and logically gives updates and instructions from his vantage point, crouched down by the radio below the dining room window, as he works through negotiations and logistics with Jonathan and Laurie. I am to help the kids fix backpacks with filtered water, sunscreen, a *kanga*, and their essential items. Stanley patrols the perimeter of the yard and climbs on the roof to watch for the fires. He gives periodic updates to Byron on the status and position of the security issue. Linda calmly makes decisions, organizes, and moves toward closing down her house.

The gunfire and heavy artillery become louder as they move closer. Stanley's return visits to the house, with updates on position and approximate distance, become more frequent. Meanwhile, Jonathan strategizes with the US Consulate to get authorization to fly a plane from Nairobi direct to Kaabong.

Time becomes a blur. Around 10:00 a.m., we hear the intensity of the fires increase significantly. Distant, heavy artillery blasts percuss in my chest along with the sound of rapid, automatic gunfire punctuated by the occasional high-pitched whistle of rounds whizzing overhead.

I cross the yard to the outside storage rooms serving as bedrooms to check on Jessica and Jordan's progress. Their backpacks need a little tweaking, but are almost ready. We plan to put sunscreen on just before leaving — if we leave — and pack only one bottle to share. As I work with each of the kids on their essential items, I am acutely aware of the need to keep the packs light in case we need to run. I remind them about the basics of sun protection and water. There seems to be an endless string of decisions.

Jessica claims her makeup is sun protection and is therefore essential. Her Dad nixes the idea, but I slip it into my essential bag for her. I think if he can consider his golf sand wedge essential, Jessica should get to take her makeup; besides, it's essential to me. The kids linger and finger their most prized personal possessions; many are handmade gifts from siblings. How do you determine essential from non-essential items when it comes to those deeply sentimental possessions?

As I watch Jordan finger the contents of her wooden box from Dubai, I realize the pictures, candy wrappers, handmade jewelry, colorful rocks, and magazine scraps are the only few treasures that have made the move to more than fifteen homes in her short life. They are pieces of constant in a world of change. It is these things they treasure the most. What do you do? They may never return to this house. My heart hurts for them, but there isn't time to dwell.

Although the rounds are high overhead, I crouch as I run from their rooms back into the house. Finding Seve also stuck in a mode of treasuring and reminiscing, I gently bump her along. With the sound of gunfire approaching, we crouch below the level of the windows.

Ben makes his decisions quickly, packs his two bags, and is soon underfoot whining, "Mom, I'm bored, what can I do next?"

"Ben, go clean your room."

As he spins and heads off, Linda's list trails behind. "Put all your sticks, *rungus*, and spears in the bucket, pick up your dirty clothes, don't forget to make your bed, and, oh, did you pack your cap?"

I look down the hallway and see Ben standing upright in front of his bedroom window as he moves around his room. Tied up with helping Seve, I holler at Stanley to deal with him. Unable to hear me, Stanley quickly gets the message when he looks in the direction I point. When I look up again, I see them both on their bellies in a military crawl. His essential items approved, Ben amuses himself by bugging his sisters as he wriggles across the floor with his homemade AK-47 rifle.

For a mother whose babies are threatened, Linda remains surprisingly calm as she focuses on her tasks, leaving the big picture to Byron and Stanley. Her experience and expertise as an emergency room nurse honed the ability to focus on the job right in front of her, as she trusts the team for the rest of the picture. She shelves her emotions, as our parents modeled, as she calmly makes decisions. With twin dynamics, there is comfort and confidence in a crisis we face together. This is not the first crisis we have faced jointly, and I can only hope it is not our last.

37 Mission Meeting *Mkutano wa Misheni*
Kenya 1960s

July each year we reconnected with our own people, journeying from Tanzania to Kenya for the annual gathering of East Africa Baptist missionaries for spiritual refreshment, mission business, and to restock supplies.

Linda and I were newly and proudly six in July 1966 when we made our first journey there and our first overland trip to Kenya. Although we had dreamed of going for months, we really didn't know what to expect. Pieces of stories from other MKs, aunts, and uncles, merged into dreams of an ultimate slumber party.

Our trip to Nairobi was, as Daddy wrote, for "the official combined purposes of supply procurement and new missionary orientation." Daddy had his own agenda — to play and explore Africa along the way. The trip was extra-long because there were Serengeti, Ngorongoro Crater, Lake Manyara, and Ruaha National Parks to explore for the first time.

Preparation began several days before departure. Mother planned the menu and cooked as much as possible ahead of time. There was bread to make, food to buy, meat to grind, laundry to do, and camping gear to pack. Safari menus were macaroni, spaghetti, sloppy joes, cereal, canned ham, and Vienna sausages. Mother bought passion fruit, mangos, a gunnysack of oranges, and a stalk of bananas that reached my chin and was too heavy for Linda and me to lift.

With all the missionaries heading to Kenya at the same time, our homes became targets for thieves. Closing down the house meant turning off the water heater in the back bathroom then working down the hallway, locking every interior door and, of course, the exterior doors so, if a thief gained access to a room, they couldn't get very far. This tedious process reached annoyance level when, with everyone and everything loaded up and ready to roll, Mother said, "John, did you turn off the water heater?" Oh, no! The big ring of keys came out and the unlocking marathon began, only to find that it was, indeed, off.

With final packing and checks taking longer than expected, two Land Rovers, our family of seven in one and the Oliphint family of five in the other, left the last pavement at the outskirts of Mbeya and headed north along a ridge toward Chunya. The road from Mbeya to Chunya followed the Rift

Valley, with breathtaking views as it climbed to 8,000 feet into the eucalyptus and pine forests.

Daddy did most of the driving, with Mother in the passenger seat and Chipper in the makeshift middle seat. He built a plywood bench behind the front seat for the rest of us. A foam mattress, doubling as a camping mattress, padded the bench. The "back back," the space on top of the luggage and camping gear, was a coveted position. The novelty soon wore off when the roads required the riders there to lie on their backs and brace their feet against the ceiling to prevent bangs and bruises. The roof rack was a place of refuge and welcome relief, but had the downsides of requiring a lot of bracing, sitting on a hard rack, and a great deal of sun exposure.

Our first campsite was only 30 miles from Mbeya, a two-and-a-half hour trip, on the banks of the Great Ruaha River. Daddy and Uncle Keith began to unpack camping gear while we anxiously waited to help put up the tent which we did by holding the poles to match the tape color-coding. We were such good help that Uncle Keith rewarded us by hanging a rope swing in a tree nearby. He tied a piece of twine to a rock and the other end to the end of a thick rope, threw the rock over a high limb, and pulled the twine which raised the large rope over the limb to make our swing. We all took turns on it while Uncle Keith returned to help Daddy finish erecting the tent without our expert assistance.

All twelve of us shared one tent. Daddy zipped two orange sleeping bags together for all the girls and a double for the boys. We checked our bags for bugs and scorpions before sliding in, and the slumber party began while the adults sat under the car-battery-powered, bug-covered light bulb, playing Forty-Two dominos. Our tent was full of giggles and ghost stories.

The next day was a long, hard road to Ruaha National Park, 250 miles from Mbeya. The game park, a promised 30-mile side trip, turned out to be a hot 75 miles and four additional hours. With seven in the Land Rover, we fiercely defended our space. It was scorching and dusty, my skin was sweaty, and the tsetse flies were a constant nuisance. Our family trips were amazing adventures, full of excitement, but spiced with the sheer misery of heat, sweat, dust, bugs, and monotonous, body-jarring roads. For the most part, our miseries went unvoiced because of our family's intolerance of whining. We silently defended our space to avoid sweaty contact with a sibling.

Daddy stopped often to let us out for adventure, challenge, and to let the boys fight. A race up a nearby mountain served as a good diversion from the rigors of the trip. Our excitement bubbled over when we topped the hill and saw the ferry crossing into the Ruaha National Park. It was a wooden float with cables on each side, pulled by six men and carried one Land Rover at a time so we got to ride it three times. We helped haul the cable but quickly lost interest, choosing instead to run up and down the ferry looking for crocodiles and hippos. We watched people bathing, naked kids swimming, and people doing laundry, but saw no wildlife.

We kicked aside the elephant droppings from the grassy track in front of the Land Rover to set up our next camp further along the Great Ruaha River. The period between stopping to set up camp and sunset was playtime. We bustled from the new swing Uncle Keith hung near camp to climb termite towers, collect bugs, and wade in the river.

"Hey, kids, I need some water for cooking and doing dishes, please," Mother called.

Steve jumped off the rope swing, slinging it behind him in a blind attempt to hit Jim, while Linda and I tagged along behind.

"Watch out for hippos and crocodiles, Twindas, they're all over the place," Steve warned, as he led down the narrow path through the reeds. We thought he was teasing.

We startled with delight, tinged with an edge of wariness, as a hippo snorted spray into the air and bellowed, showing off his enormous mouth and teeth. Steve filled the pot with muddy water as we watched humps, eyes, and big flared noses.

"There's a crocodile sunning!" Daddy exclaimed amidst his tent constructing.

"I can only see crocodile-looking logs." Linda was disappointed.

Watching warily, I told her, "It's OK, they're all in the water." OK, until I felt a grabbing bite on the back of my leg. I screamed, and Linda screamed because I screamed. I almost peed in my pants, although Daddy never allowed us to say that word. I guess I should have said I almost micturated in my pants. Linda and I grabbed each other's hands and spun around to find Jim rolling in laughter. Intensely focused on looking for crocs, we hadn't seen him slip up behind us. I thought how much I would like to feed him to the crocs. I didn't mean that but it would have made more room in the Land Rover. The red muddy water we brought to Mother came out surprisingly clear after it was filtered and boiled.

Daddy and Mother had a system. At dusk, we helped Daddy select a level spot for a campsite so that we wouldn't end up in a pile at one end of the tent; a spot that didn't have animal trails or animal holes. He rigged the light from the car battery so Mother could make supper. While she washed dishes from water heated on the Coleman stove, he brought a pan of hot water into the tent to bathe and pajama us kids. He gave us each our own hot washcloth for us to clean everything from our head to toes.

Daddy tossed us our pajamas and helped Linda, Chipper, and I get our feet down into the footed garments with the pajama feet facing the same way as our toes. One pot of water provided a bath for all of us then boiled to sterilize the cloths for the next night. I awoke before daylight to the sound of Daddy pumping the Coleman stove to build pressure before he lit it to get the hot chocolate going. The car-battery-powered light provided illumination for him to fix the flat tires from the previous day's travel. While Mother prepared breakfast and a picnic lunch, Daddy helped us get dressed so he could fold up the tent and sleeping bags.

Stops along the way to fix flats or refuel from jerry cans were times to run and explore. Africa offered a wealth of things to see, check out, and collect — weird insects, birds' nests, lizards, and rocks. Often Linda and I would run along the road to see how far we could get before we heard the horn behind us.

My muscles tensed and my spirit soared as I gripped the roof rack, watching for animals alongside my twin and brothers. Linda and I, with our long, stringy hair whipping in the wind, took in the changing sights and scents. We delighted in the way each animal had its own kind of run: tommie, topi, waterbuck, jackal, hartebeest, warthog, kudu, giraffe, and several kinds of monkey. A list of the birds we saw was like reading an index of one of Daddy's big bird books: openbill stork, hammerkop, malachite kingfisher, great kingfisher, lilac-breasted roller, flamingo, egret, spoonbill, wood ibis, turaco, weaver, starling, silver-cheeked hornbill, guinea fowl, crowned crane, ostrich, secretary bird, bustard, ground hornbill, and marabou stork.

It was a rough, dusty, 300-mile day through Dodoma to our sunset campsite south of Babati. We pitched the tent behind a ten-foot high termite hill. Termite mounds housed more than termites. You could find busy ants, lizards, birds, snakes, insects, and monstrous monitor lizards. The termites altered the red dirt in their construction business, making it like red concrete. The Maasai dig the dirt from the anthills to mix with cow dung to make strong walls for their *bomas*. Jim and Steve discussed their plans to build a house out of termite dirt one day because it would be indestructible. Mother said they would have to sweep because she didn't want to try to keep a dirt house clean. She described the final leg of our adventure:

> The Tanzania and Kenya border cuts right through the Maasai tribal country. The Maasai are the tallest men in Tanzania and Kenya. They are nomadic and follow their cattle, which are their prized, and almost only, possessions. The men have long, droopy earlobes with large holes that carry a plastic film container with tobacco, a bottle, or a rolled piece of paper.
>
> Sunday we bumped our way to Arusha, past the fog-covered 19,000-foot Mount Kilimanjaro. The kids'

excitement escalated as we approached the big city of Nairobi with its tall buildings, traffic, and ice cream stores. We traveled another 25 miles into the foggy highlands of Limuru then turned into the Brackenhurst Baptist Assembly having traveled five days and 1,100 miles.

The other missionaries were worried because we were almost two days late and both our families are new to travel in Africa and the mission field. Mission meeting was strange and exciting for us, especially for the kids. They couldn't remember ever seeing so many white kids in one place.

An old English colonial hotel and golf club, converted to a conference center, hosted missionaries from Uganda, Kenya, and Tanzania for a week of mission business, worship, and socializing. Nestled in a tea plantation close to the equator at 7,300 feet, it was lush, foggy, and cool.

For MKs it was all about fun, like a family reunion with all our cousins. As we chugged up the winding hill, all noses were at the window, looking for the first glimpse of our new friends. Sure enough, a game of American Eagles was already underway on the big green lawn beyond the dining hall. We tumbled over each other to join the MKs in the traditional tackle game and to share inflated stories of our trips.

Brackenhurst offered a wealth of fun with ponds to fish, frogs to catch, chameleons to find, tea plantations in which to play hide and seek, and manicured hedgerows to climb. We explored an underground network of dark rooms below the hotel, our imaginations fueled by rumors of people hiding from the Mau Mau in the bowels of the building. The tea bushes in the surrounding plantations looked like a beautiful, smooth green carpet, its green leaves providing a shaded canopy for a network of forts, passageways, and getaways.

Our lodging was two rooms converted from horse stables at the top of the hill. The rooms at the conference center ranged from converted stables, rumored to be a refuge during the Mau Mau days, to hotel-like rooms and big, British colonial houses.

During our stay, we traveled to Nairobi to restock on groceries, car parts, and take care of business as well as enjoy ice cream and the excitement of immersion in a busy city with tall buildings, throngs of people, and a jillion shops. Business in Nairobi was no easier than business in Mbeya, where neither customer service nor efficiency was known or valued. Those who have walked the streets of Nairobi know the press of people, the frustrations, and the constant threat of pickpockets and purse-snatchers. They also know the excitement of the mix of tribes and cultures from all over the world — truly an international city.

With mission meeting and new missionary orientation in the rear view mirror, the trip home to Mbeya started with a final trip to Nairobi to finish stocking up supplies and food for a year, then cross the border into Tanzania to camp at Lake Manyara on the floor of the Great Rift Valley. This park stretches between the wall of the rift and the shore of the brackish lake with its vast terrain varying from jungle and grassy plains to marshes, and is home to a captivating variety of animal and birdlife. We gripped the roof rack for a ride and view of a lifetime as we journeyed the meandering, grassy tracks.

The first campsite was under a huge baobab tree, one of the oldest and oddest trees in the world. Our African friends called them "upside-down" trees. Some believed the baobab tree asked the creator to make it as tall as a palm tree and to give it pretty flowers like a flame tree. God, tired of its whining, turned it upside down. These trees, some as old as 1,000 years and 70 feet around, have a small root system and store a lot of water in their trunk. We met a man who lived inside a baobab tree that even had a door. Its fruit, called monkey bread, is a large, coconut-size gourd that hangs from a leathery cord. Locals use the bitter, white spongy pulp of the fruit for drinks, medicine, and as a base for cream of tartar.

Our adventures at Lake Manyara continued to nearby Ngorongoro Crater where the twelve of us squeezed into one Land Rover to save park entrance fees. Although already packed with people, the park rangers insisted we couldn't enter unless we had a guide. After a heated debate, Daddy put the unhappy ranger in the back corner of the Land Rover, making thirteen of us. We climbed the steep side of the volcano into the fog and jungle then twisted downward from an altitude of 7,500 feet to the floor of the crater, 2,000 feet below, where its 100-square-mile crater teemed with wildlife.

We watched elephants stand on their hind legs to tear bark from upper branches, and baby elephants wrestle with each other in the shadow of their moms. As the elephants ate, white egrets mingled around their feet to catch bugs stirred from the tall grass. As if by a signal, the elephants stopped eating, turned toward us, spread their ears, and bellowed their protests. We decided we'd seen enough elephants and headed on down the grassy track.

The day's treats were large herds of buffalo, zebra, and wildebeest, but the prize was three rhinos. Two stayed close together and slept while one stood watching from a distance, ready to charge. The tension was high as Daddy edged closer, with Mother and Aunt Peggy fussing, and the unhappy ranger in the back. As we whispered, Daddy let out a war whoop that would awaken the dead. The sleepy rhinos startled to their feet and stared, steaming mad. One ducked his head and charged toward us. With Mother worrying, Daddy accelerated away as the rhino thundered ever closer. We all knew the familiar, "John," said with a drawn-out musical scolding tone. Suddenly, Daddy stopped, turned off the engine, and the rhino froze.

Circling vultures are the signpost to a kill. We followed their signal to a grassy meadow where we watched the pecking order transition from the lions who slowly waddled their full bellies away, to foxes, then marauding hyenas and finally to the vultures who ripped and fought over the intestines of a zebra. Another circle of vultures led us to an elephant carcass whose leg bones were bigger than I was and whose teeth were bigger than Daddy's feet.

We hung tightly to the roof rack as we bumped cross country next to three giraffes, their heads rocking in rhythm with their long, loping strides. I could smell their musky scent, see the whiskers on their chin and their big eyes with long, sweeping eyelashes swarmed by flies. Chasing ostriches turned our giggle boxes upside down but angered the ranger in the back. The ostriches put out their left wing if they were going to dodge to the right and their right wing to turn left, as if their turn signal were broken. We giggled at kongoni running and bouncing like Super Balls as they bounced off their watch on top of termite hills.

At our first rest stop, we scattered our separate ways — boys to the left, girls to the right. Deep ditches alongside the roads for wet-season drainage provided cuts into the thick undergrowth, making good places for a rest stop. Chipper rode Daddy's shoulders as he walked down the road to an unoccupied ditch. Startled by a crash overhead, Daddy looked up to see an elephant towering above him, trunk in the air bellowing and huge ears flopping. Daddy turned and ran, hollering, "Elephant!"

At first, I thought he was teasing but, when I saw his face, I knew he wasn't. All twelve of us ran back to the Land Rovers from all directions like a movie in reverse of someone stepping on an ant bed. Daddy said he wasn't scared, he just wanted everyone to know there was an elephant nearby if anyone wished to see it.

Mother fussed as he drove off the grassy track to get a closer look at a herd of buffalo. He was like a hunter, but hunting for a better look instead of a kill, and seemed to love bumping the boundaries of safety and rules. The buffalo turned toward us, showing their massive horns. As if there were a silent signal, they thundered in our direction with dust flying. I felt the rumble in my chest of their pounding hooves as I gripped the roof rack.

"John, John, oh, John!" Mother pleaded. Suddenly, the Land Rover lurched as one wheel dropped into a hidden four-foot deep, three-foot wide hole.

Daddy let out a whoop as I had heard Granddaddy do when he called his cattle to feed on a winter day. The startled buffalo slid to a stop, circled around us, and stared. They watched, just like Granddaddy's cows, with their proportionally small tails swatting at flies while their tongues picked their noses. White egrets resumed feeding from their backs and their feet.

Daddy jacked up the Land Rover while we warily gathered branches and chunks of wood from nearby bushes to fill in under the tires. All the while, the arc of buffalo watched. Daddy pushed the Land Rover off the jack, rolling it forward to land on the other side of the hole. We left the watching buffalo behind to move on to the next adventure.

We developed a greater respect for the buffalo after the death of one of our missionaries soon after.

38 Betrayed *Tumedanganywa*
Tanzania 1960s

The last stage of our journey home from missionary meeting, Daddy joined us on the roof rack while Mother took our adventure from Ngorongora Crater into Serengeti. It was a hot noon as we made our way to the only shady tree in view. As we pulled under our picnic tree, Steve looked up and loudly whispered, "Lions!" Six full-grown lions lounged with paws dangling and tails slowly swinging with a twitch of the tip.

"Every one of you get into this car. NOW!" Mother hissed. We did. We slithered over the rack and down into one of the open windows. Mother's tone of voice took the linger out of our scramble. We left the lions to the only shade and settled for a sunny picnic.

Our stops to refuel in the dusty little villages of Babati and Singida were welcome breaks from the rugged travel. A man pumped fuel, trucked to these remote little towns, manually into a liter measuring glass that emptied into our tank and jerry cans. The tedious process allowed time to buy bubble gum and enjoy the treat of a warm Coca Cola from the *duka*. Men sat on the porch, surrounded by colorful cloths hanging from sticks that protruded from the tin roof, as their feet pumped Singer sewing machines. We restocked with bread, fruit, and UHT milk.

During the day's travel, we only saw five trucks, two buses, and very few people. We stopped at a well to watch women lower a gourd tied to a 75-foot, braided sisal rope to draw water. As usual, Daddy visited with everyone while he practiced his Swahili and learned about them and their tribe. The villagers were from the Wagogo, Wataturu, and Maasai tribes. The women were ebony black with large disks in their ears and lips. They carried babies on their back as they scrubbed their laundry on rocks and carried firewood and water on their heads. There was so much life going on around the well with people, cattle, goats, lizards, birds, dogs, and bugs.

We rode the roof racks of the Land Rovers as we chugged into the cool uplands above Chunya, six hours from home. With five miles to Chunya, both Land Rovers spit, sputtered, and stopped within 100 yards of each other. All twelve of us loaded up into, and on top of, one vehicle. Daddy poured all possible sources of fuel into one tank — white gas from the cook stove and kerosene from the lantern. With two miles to go, there was no fuel left. Uncle Keith and Daddy walked to find gas while the rest of us stayed with the Land Rover.

"I'll take you back in my car for ten shillings (a dollar and 50 cents)," a man offered, as they walked back.

"No, if you needed a ride, I would take you free," Daddy told them. "This is two days' hard work's pay, and I will not give you money."

They climbed the mountain in the noon heat. Can you imagine, not one gas station in 407 miles?

Our round trip travel tallied up to 2,300 miles with ten days and eight nights of camping en route.

Finally arriving home, we found that, despite all our efforts, a thief still broke into our house. He was only able to get into one room and the hallway because we'd locked the interior doors. The thief took some soap, Daddy's medical bag, and a bicycle, but the worst was he took Linda's doll with the scraggly haircut. Donut, our yardman, didn't show up at work and was seen in the town with our bicycle. My friend had double-crossed me.

When I later saw Donut walking along the path outside our fence, I told him what I thought of him stealing Linda's doll. He admitted he took our things but didn't apologize. He told me not to tell my parents I'd seen him, but I didn't keep that secret very long. Eventually the police caught him and I had to go testify at court.

At six years old, I couldn't see over the tall, ebony wood walls of the witness stand. I could hear the judge's booming voice above me but was unable to see him. I was feeling pretty small and afraid. My pounding heart found relief when I stood on my tiptoes to peek through a crack in the wood to see Mother sitting in the row of black faces.

"What were you doing at the fence when you saw the man you call Donut?" the judge asked me. I got a glimpse of the judge when I walked to the witness stand. He was fat, black, and had a long, flowing, curly, white wig like George Washington in my homeschool book.

"I was pushing a stick through the hole in the cement post, where the wires go through, to push lizard eggs into a box on the other side of the hole. I put the eggs in cotton-lined matchboxes and put them on top of the fridge to hatch them." I couldn't imagine what this had to do with Donut admitting to stealing Linda's doll.

The judge was annoying and asked many questions.

"Can you point to the man you call Donut?"

How was I to see when I couldn't even touch the top of the wall, much less point over it? "I saw him get up from the back seat of the courtroom and walk out."

A low murmur rolled through the crowd when they turned to see the bench was empty. "How could you see Donut leave when you cannot see over the wooden wall?"

I pointed to the crack I had peered through to spot Mother, then see Donut leave.

Mother always fussed at me if I tattled on my brothers, but she said it was OK to tattle on Donut. We never saw him again.

*****

One year, the trip to mission meeting was different because Daddy felt he couldn't leave the hospital without a physician. Mema and Granddaddy's visit was so exciting. They brought warmth, love, presents, kisses, hugs, and a piece of America, but the trip to Nairobi without Daddy was miserable. Mother wasn't happy about going without him. Granddaddy was there to help change the flat tires and to refuel the Land Rover and jerry cans but he didn't have Daddy's experience and language. Mother, Granddaddy, and Mema sat in the front seat of the short-wheel-base Land Rover while we had the back, on top of the luggage and camping equipment.

When there was a dispute, as in when the boys fought, Mother would pull over and just start spanking legs… all legs. Mema and Granddaddy sat straight up and never looked back. It was amazing Mother took on this responsibility, but she always did whatever she had to do.

39 A Bullet Strikes *Risasi Imepigika*
Uganda 2004

"She always did whatever she had to do." That strikes a note that resounds down through the generations. I look at my twin, my beloved... and see Mother. In both I see a mother in all the sweet contexts and images that brings up. I see an amazing mix of unfathomable love and compassion, tenderness, love of family, and fierce defender. I see the same strength and undying loyalty to their husband's mission while they still manage to squeeze in their own as they impact lives as no other could. I see them put their own needs last in line behind husband, kids, and mission. I see an amazing ability to compartmentalize, to put personal, unspoken feelings on the shelf to do whatever they have to do, a trait that journeys through the years and generations, providing resiliency when things get tough.

A woman's determination and fierceness to protect family runs deep. Perhaps I have some of those traits in me but I believe it is easier to see with clarity into others' lives than it is into one's own.

Linda places a large red duffle bag in the center of the living room for the family's non-essential items; all the essentials go in each of the backpacks. I have no answer for the kids as they place their cherished possessions in the red, non-essential bag and ask me how they will get them back. Linda hopes that, somehow, someone will forward these items by vehicle.

"Mom is being weird," Jordan mutters. "It's annoying how unserious she thinks it is, and Seve is just as bad."

"Which friend should I give this toy to?" Seve asks Jordan, who just looks at her as if she were crazy.

Linda goes into pack and clean mode. I am puzzled as I watch her mop the floor then walk into the yard to remove the sheets hanging on the line. We shuffle around, crouched low, but she purposefully stands upright as she attacks her tasks.

"I've got to send one of the kids to the village to pay Mary for the eggs. Oh... and I've got to somehow get these Coca Cola bottles to Joyce," she mutters to herself as she stacks bottles next to the door beside Byron. He turns from the radio with a puzzled look then focuses back on his task.

Her intense focus on the tasks and the effects of the stress around her make her unaware, or what seems to me to be under-aware, of the danger around us. It works well for our team because I am highly distracted by the dangers while she is able to stay on task. Although she takes care of some tasks that seem unimportant during this crisis, her calm demeanor helps to keep the kids calm.

"The conflict is now about a mile from us," I hear Byron report by radio call.

"The whole family must depart as soon as possible," Jonathan tells him. "The evacuation is mandatory."

AIM, unfamiliar with the Kaabong airstrip, questions the safety of landing and taking off the MU2 on the small, underdeveloped airstrip. Jonathan relays information as AIM studies its files on the airstrip.

At 10:30 a.m., the tension escalates when Stanley comes in from his patrol saying the firing is about one mile away. We can hear heavy artillery just out of sight over the hill. There is only one road. We guess they are now at the bridge where we would have been building sandcastles and picnicking if we had stayed with today's plans. The artillery is between the airstrip and us, currently closing the possibility of evacuation by foot.

Byron and I work together to prepare the generator storage room for a place to take cover. Next to the stairs that lead to the roof is a tiny room used for storing the generator, fuel, and batteries. We quickly haul propane and jerry cans of gas to another storage room, replacing them with water, food, flashlights, and sleeping bags. I don't like this room. The door, like the other storage room doors, has bolt locks on both sides. I have a vision of rifle-toting men locking us in as they throw a torch or stick a rifle through the only small barred window. I feel better since we moved the fuel, but I still don't want to be anyone's captive. I wish we had time to remove the outside bolt.

Linda has so much to do and so many decisions. I really don't know how to help her. She asked me to take care of the kids to free her up to do what she needs to do. They are full of questions.

"Can I bring my teddy bear?"

"Nuna, what about She-She? I've had this sheepskin all my life. Can I bring it?"

"Do I have to wear a *kanga* around my legs or may I run out in my shorts?"

"Ben made this for me; can it be my essential item?"

With a jillion small decisions to make, I feel calm and confident as I roll through decisions related to tasks and the big picture but lock down in dealing with smaller ones with big emotional impacts.

Stanley returns and points as he reports, "They are close, on the horizon. Look."

Peering over the fence toward the bridge, I am startled to see soldiers walking alongside a tank, a large army truck, an armored personnel carrier, and a tracked, self-propelled Howitzer. Stanley estimates they are a quarter-mile away.

Now some of the loose pieces begin to fall into place. Tensions had escalated between the local warriors and the army just before our arrival three days ago. We heard approaching sounds of artillery last night. It would probably take three days to get military personnel, armored vehicles, and artillery to this remote corner of Uganda. Unbeknownst to us, storm clouds of trouble brewed on the horizon while we walked, storied, hiked, and played.

At Byron's prompting, I move with the kids to the screened back porch where we sit, holding hands with our backs against the wall, while I pray aloud. I can hear his voice, "Lima Mike, Juliet Papa, the fires are in sight now."

Linda walks through the doorway with a book in hand. "Cinda, we're reading this at naptime, maybe you could read it to them now. There's a marker where we last read." I am astonished she thinks I can focus on the book. I flip it around to read the title; a book set in WWII with a leather bookmark at the chapter, "Bloodbath." I reject her idea.

As Linda turns on her heel to return to packing, she stops dead in her tracks exclaiming, "Byron, look at the tanks out there!"

He responds with a tone of tolerance, "Yes, Linda, everyone else has seen them."

Linda returns, this time with a camera in hand. "Cinda, would you go take a picture of the tanks? I'm really busy packing." Is she kidding? I don't think she is.

Hearing the high-pitched scream of bullets overhead, I duck as I scurry toward the far fence. I refuse to go to the rooftop as she requested. Sera, having heard Linda's plea that I get a picture from the roof, moves the wheelbarrow to the fence for me to stand on. Picture snapped, I quickly retreat to the house.

As I rejoin the kids, Byron updates me on the progress: concerns for personnel in the plane, safety for us on the ground because the plane may draw fire, and the MU-2's ability to lift ten people at an altitude of 5,000 feet on a short, underdeveloped, and unfamiliar dirt runway. With the decision made, everything moves toward evacuation, but the current location of the tanks prevents us from running to the airstrip. The plane heads our way in case the tanks move, as the process of authorization to land continues.

Byron instructs me to shift the kids to the master bedroom to keep as many concrete walls as possible between us and the tanks.

"We're going to get the family out if the path to the airstrip clears," Linda tells me. "Byron told me he wants to stay. He felt he would desert his people if he left. It's fine with me because I know he can run fast."

"But—"

"Don't worry, he'll be fine," she reads my mind. "I really want him to make his own decisions because I'm making as many as I can handle right now with my packing."

"Mom," Jordan goes to her mother in tears.

"Everything is fine. We are safe," Linda reassures.

"I'm not worried about *us*. I'm worried about my friends. I feel bad I can leave but they have to stay in danger. It doesn't seem fair."

Byron is incredible, very cool and logical. He stays crouched at the radio where he calmly talks and plans. No one panics. Linda stays totally cool, just too cool; she seems unaware of the danger.

Her brain clicks through all the things left undone just as an emergency room nurse would check off a pre-op list. "Did we lock the neighbor's guesthouse door?" she asks.

We can't remember. Earlier, I brought my backpack down to the main house, packed with our money, passports, and Jessica's makeup. When gunfire came close, Stanley and I agreed, with the change in events, there is nothing we now consider essential in his backpack on our bed in the guesthouse. We have been barraged by decisions and can't remember if we locked the door. It seems days ago we walked out of our room this morning.

"Linda, what if we didn't lock it? Is it essential that it be locked?" I am concerned we may be in the crossfire as we run uphill, but she feels responsible for the security of the borrowed guesthouse. Bullets whine overhead, punctuated by a solid hit in the tree above us, as Stanley and I crouch and run to grab his pack and lock the door.

Returning at last to the house, I find that Seve is missing. With panic rising, I hurry to her room. No Seve… To Ben's room. No Seve…

"Jess, where is Seve?"

"Nuna, she said she was going to the village to take some toys and clothes to her friends."

Crouching, I run toward the gate to look for Seve at the village, my mind tormented over why Linda would have allowed her to leave.

Sera, seeing my panic, stops me at the gate saying, "But… you shouldn't pass here." Sera assures me he has been standing there and Seve didn't pass. Panic chokes my breath as I run back toward the house.

"Nuna, I found Seve!" Jordan calls from the front door.

"Jessica and Jordan told me you were looking for me, Nuna," Seve says as I gratefully hug her. "I want to go give some of my things to my friends in the village but Mom won't let me. Will you go with me?"

"Seve Lynn, we just can't do it, we've got to be ready to go," I tell her as I hug her tighter.

The shift in position of the conflict makes our decision whether to leave by foot or hunker down. As the tanks shift to the northwest, moving toward Kaabong, the warriors approach our house with rifles in hand saying, "We are ready for battle." They move close, probably assuming the military will not fire on the mission compound.

The tanks are on Lomusian hill near the bridge and the warriors are at our house and on the hill behind us. When the tanks engage the warriors, we will be in the crossfire. The choices quickly narrow to leaving the house to hide out or walking to the airstrip for evacuation. My regret that we have no vehicle disappears as I realize it wouldn't have helped because the tanks are on both sides of the only road. The only way out is by foot across the country toward the airstrip.

Around 11:00 a.m., there is a pause in the firing.

"You have fifteen minutes," Byron tells us.

"Fifteen minutes to what?" Linda still doesn't seem to get it that we are going to walk out of here. Byron physically holds her by her shoulders.

"Put your shoes on now. For the sake of the people taking us out, we need to leave. Now."

That finally gets through to her brain. We gather outside to leave, each of us with our backpack.

Standing under the big tree, for some reason I notice the weaverbirds are silent. Byron turns to Stanley then me to get a final decision. We prepared for three plans: hunker down while the crisis passes, leave on foot to hide in the bush until the crisis subsides, or leave on foot for an air evacuation.

A bullet strikes the tree overhead, solidly emphasizing that the battle approaches. Questions whirl through my mind. Will bolting ourselves behind the storage room door make us safe or corral us in the middle of battle and at the mercy of others? Or do we run into the bush, under the relentless equatorial sun, losing vital contact with possible rescuers? The room is ready and our essential possessions packed. The kids look up, poised to move; their eyes full of trust, courage, and a thread of fear. The decisions and consequences whirl through my heart. My answer chokes on the lump in my throat.

40 It is Necessary *Ni Lazima*
Uganda 2004

We must leave. I stand ready, in disbelief that we really are going to depart on foot. I still favor the idea of being out in the bush and not someone's captive in the tiny room though.

This is it. Byron is to stay by the radio since negotiations continue to get authorization for the plane to fly direct to Kaabong. He also wants to keep the option open for him to stay with "his people" and rejoin his family later.

He quickly and calmly reviews the plan. We are to leave the gate and circle the compound clockwise to keep the house structures between the tanks and us. We will then run to the dry riverbed and follow it as far as we can toward Sakatan, then pass on the far side of the rocks and continue the six-mile trek to the airstrip.

Time to go… This all seems surreal and time appears to move in slow motion. I look around and see Linda striding purposefully from the house to the storage room, where she proceeds to unlock the door.

"Byron, what's Linda doing?"

With a roll of his eyes, he responds, "She is getting Jack; she says Jack is an essential item."

"You've got to be kidding."

Jack is the nickname for the sourdough bread starter fed by Jack Potato Flakes from America. Granted, making bread is a major part of the family's diet. I think the latest turn of events might supersede that priority, but who am I to say? She puts the bread starter in a black and yellow, soft-sided cooler and clips it to her backpack with a large carabiner.

With Jack secure, we are ready to roll. The time is now. Disbelief fades quickly to "yes, this is really happening." Byron interrupts Linda's mutterings about undone things with a quick peck on the cheek. I shove the negative fleeting thought away — "Will we see Byron again?" Throughout the day, I've battled to keep the negative thoughts and "what ifs" out of the way to keep focusing on the next step.

Sera leads out of the gate, carrying a backpack and stick in his hand. Jessica, Jordan, and Seve, each carrying a backpack, follow single file close behind. Jordan carries one of the family's most essential items, Noel, in her essential item, her doghouse. I follow close behind Stanley and can see the toes of Ben's shoes right behind me.

We stride hard, just short of a run. As Byron instructed, we hug the fence, moving clockwise around the compound, keeping the house between the tanks and us. With a lull in the gunfire, the atmosphere is tense with anticipation.

Pushing hard, I wasn't aware Ben had dropped back. I hear a heartbreaking cry behind me. Swinging my backpack around, I see him lying in fetal position under a scraggly bush. His cries shake his whole body. There is no sight of Linda. I run back and ask, "Ben, where's your Mother?"

"Nuna, I forgot one of my backpacks, the one with my CD player. I was afraid I would never see it again so Mom went back to get it. She told me to wait here. She'll be right back."

Mom usually rules but, under the circumstances, I pull auntie rank. "No, Ben, you must come with me now."

Ahead, Jessica hears my command and returns to negotiate. "Nuna, if Mom told Ben to wait for her here, I think he had better. I'll wait with him."

I unsuccessfully reassure distraught Ben as I grab his hand and tug him along. There's no time for emotional needs right now. I'm puzzled by Linda's decision and concerned about her safety, but I must focus on getting the kids to the cover of the riverbed. Relief floods through me when I hear Linda hurrying up behind me.

"I ran back to the house to get the pack with the CD player," she explains breathlessly, "and headed back to catch you all. Then I remembered we have no money. I knew Stanley hadn't had time to exchange any and Byron was planning to stay, so I went back. Byron got a little impatient with me."

I don't have time to tell her I'm not surprised. Linda holds Ben's hand, encouraging him to run a little faster as she settles into an awkward jog with her old blue backpack bouncing on her shoulders. I notice Stanley's limp has become significantly worse and his need to stop to rest his hip is becoming more frequent.

"Linda, why are you carrying the heaviest load of all of us? Here, let me carry one of your packs," Stanley chides.

"I'm doing fine, thanks, Stanley. I have the packs well balanced on my shoulders. This cooler, though, is driving me crazy. Would you mind carrying it for me?"

"Of course," he responds as he slings the yellow and black cooler over his shoulder. "What's in it anyway?"

Avoiding eye contact, I toss him a vague answer. "You don't want to know. Just keep going. Hurry."

"Look at my kids all bounding through the tall grass with Noel right behind them," Linda diverts his question. "It reminds me of a scene in the *Sound of Music*."

I giggle to myself at Linda's masterful change of subject. Stanley wouldn't want to know the annoying cooler banging his side with each step contains sour dough starter. As he limps ahead out of earshot, Linda and I discuss heavier issues than Stanley's limp and the contents of the cooler. She is concerned about his previous heart attack, particularly as the temperature is now burning hot in the noon equatorial sun.

"And I must say, we appear to be somewhat under a bit of stress," she adds in an exaggerated British accent, understating in a typical British way.

In front, I see my beloved nieces walking hard with their packs. Behind me, Stanley, my twin sis, and Ben push to get to a place of refuge or to the airstrip for an evacuation. Will we make it?

I shift my load to my left shoulder for some much-needed relief as I clumsily fight my way across the African red dirt to the cover of a dry riverbed. With distant automatic AK-47 rifle fire, my thoughts dwell on "how did we get here?" How did a day, which began with a sunrise cup of tea on the porch in the magnificent northern Ugandan vastness, deteriorate to a run for our lives?

The answer to that question goes far beyond last week. How the past prepared me to handle this conflict began even before my trip on the Queen Mary to begin my life in Africa.

41 A Chapter Closes *Kufunga Sura*
Europe 1960s

Like many missionary families, we compartmentalized the memories of our lives by our terms on the mission field. Each three- or four-year term in Africa, followed by a ten- to twelve-month furlough in America, brought a new stage in life, a new direction in medical missions, new friends, and a new place to live. They also brought more sad goodbyes. These shifts, marked by a move, kept the landscape of home and friendships changing, which tightened family bonds. Furlough ushered in a mixture of feelings like walking through a door that you know you can never walk back through; leaving behind a good life, saying goodbye to dear friends, and stepping into an exciting world laced with a thread of anxiety.

I guess it was more like a walk through a tunnel than a door because each transit across the world was a month's journey through a different part of Europe. Our travel by rental car or public transport, and camping in parks, roundabouts, and barns, gave us a lot of family togetherness and further forged family bonds.

Stress escalated as the curtain closed on each term with the many decisions around belongings and treasures. In addition to Mother and Daddy's copious speaking engagements and professional training, furlough was a time of reflection and consideration whether to return to the mission field or stay in America. Preparation required shutting down a house without knowing if we would return.

We divided our belongings into several groups: things to sell immediately or give away, things to carry in our suitcases to America, things to squeeze into one barrel to ship, things to store but give away if we didn't return, and things to ship if we didn't return. Where, in all these decisions, did my black monkey with the banana go? What about my rock collection and sling shot? What about Mother's silver and the china plates Mema painted? Who would keep our dogs and what would happen to them if we didn't return?

July 19, 1969, we rode the Land Rover roof rack to the airport, retracing our steps as we walked across the pavement and climbed the steep aluminum stairs into the East African Airlines DC3, closing the curtains to our first four-year term.

At our initial stop the next day, we shopped the windows of the sweltering Dar es Salaam streets and lingered in front of an electronic-store window display to watch, on a black and white TV, Neil Armstrong's first steps on the moon. Although I was interested, I was as intrigued with seeing a TV as I was with the moonwalk. I had dim memories, as a five year old, of when I last saw a TV. I wondered if Tarzan came to Africa too.

From Dar es Salaam to Nairobi, the excitement climbed as we drove to the edge of the Rift Valley to pick up Steve from boarding school. His hair was long, his clothes dirty, he smelled, and his voice was deeper, but my big brother was back. Our family was once again together and we could move on to our one-month journey to our first furlough and get a Dairy Queen Milkshake.

Our trip, with the ever-present orange sleeping bags, took us to the Egyptian pyramids, sphinxes, ancient temples, tombs, and a boat ride along the Nile. We traveled to the tourist sites by bus since taxis wouldn't carry all of us. Mother wrote:

> In Luxor, a man told me that people were staring at us because of the size of our family. He told me he also had five kids and confided that his wife went to a clinic to get medicine so she wouldn't make any more children.
>
> We had to catch a flight from Cairo to Athens but ran into trouble at the airport. John declared all his money when we entered Egypt. We changed money as we needed, at the going rate. We didn't realize there were heavy fines for changing money anywhere except at the bank. We were $50 short and, boy, were we sweating! I couldn't imagine life in an Egyptian jail and I worried about the kids. We stood in a huge custom line as they checked all the money and the bags. We knew we were in big trouble. I thought my children could help so I brought them all around us in the line. This added more confusion, as you could imagine, so the customs man from another office came by, put a check on our bags, and told us to go on.
>
> As we traveled, Chipper kept asking, "Where are all the Africans?" It seems strange to see all the people dressed nicely and wearing shoes. We loved shopping stores with things worth buying.

Our journey took us to the sights of Greece where a self-appointed, unpaid, walking guide was delighted to find that the wine served with our family's seven meals would all be his. In Rome, we fished coins out of the Trevi Fountain and toured the Colosseum, the Roman Forum, and the

Vatican where the boys got in trouble for fighting. Years later, I learned there were not fifteen other chapels — we saw the Sistene, not the sixteenth, Chapel.

Two weeks in, we rented a car and camped through Germany. Although I remember seeing castles, palaces, and museums, it is the memory of Dachau Concentration Camp that followed me. Haunted me.

Linda and I held hands and skipped along the sidewalk to the entrance as we chimed back and forth, "512... 555... 0124." Daddy made a game of memorizing Mema's phone number which would be the only way to reconnect, via an operator, if any of us got separated or lost. At each new place, Daddy designated a meeting place in case one of us strayed. The iron entrance to the barbed wire fence was the agreed venue this time.

At nine years old, the skip in my step waned and my heart became heavy as we walked through the barbed wire fence into the dark dorms, the gas chambers that prisoners believed were showers, and to the incinerators where they burned bodies. The long hallway, with its squeaky wooden floor and lined with black and white photos, affected me the most. I cut my eyes high and right to keep tears from escaping down my cheeks as I saw with horror the photos of rooms full of hair, gold fillings, shoes, and hollow people with big, baleful eyes.

A picture haunted me for decades: a woman walking away, holding the hand of a little girl, a boy in the other hand, looking back over her shoulder at the camera. Contrasting with the striped pajamas of the other prisoners, these three were nicely dressed. The caption said the mother told her kids they were going to church, as they made their way to the "showers" — the gas chamber.

Memories of visiting Anne Frank's house four years earlier on our way to Africa merged with the stories from Corrie ten Boom's book, *The Hiding Place*. The Nazis sent Corrie, a Dutch Christian, to a concentration camp when they discovered her family's secret room and their work with the Dutch underground. Like me, Corrie had a sister she loved. I connected with their bond and the way they sheltered, protected, comforted, inspired, and loved each other in the most inhumane and inconceivable circumstances.

I remember Corrie's sister, Betsy, saying, in her final words before her death in the concentration camp, that there is no pit so deep that God is not deeper still. Through Corrie's story, I learned more about forgiveness and faith than I learned in church. Stories speak to me. I found that even a fleeting thought of losing my own sister was excruciating.

Mother wrote of another painful memory in Germany:

> At the world's largest science and technology museum, I lost Chipper. I was beside myself. Here we were in a

213

foreign country, in a multi-story museum with 50,000 square meters of exhibits. The guards finally succumbed to my requests to call Chipper over the loud speaker but they spoke in German. Now, how was my six year old supposed to understand that? John and I told the other kids to stay put on a couch while we searched everywhere. After three hours of frantically trying every floor in the place, I stood in the main lobby trying once again to get the guards to call Chipper in English or let me talk.

Our designated meeting place in case of a lost kid was the rental car. John had checked and rechecked the parking lot for Chipper. With the front and back entrance almost identical, Chipper had gone to the parking lot on the opposite side of the museum. Not finding our car, he assumed he had been left behind.

I held it together until I heard his quiet little voice behind me, "Mother, why did you leave me?" Then all I could do was cry.

Difficult moments were interspersed with fun. On a Rhine River trip, the boat had a Coca Cola machine that filled paper cups. We found, if we sipped the drink through a straw while it was filling, we could get about a cup-and-a-half for the price of one. Who really cared about castles?

We journeyed onward into the magnificent Alps in Austria and on into Switzerland. Hikes across the beautiful heather land at the base of the Matterhorn were a highlight but I was most intrigued by the underground fortresses built under the mountains in defense of the Nazis' threats.

Retracing our steps to America, how fitting that we would travel from Southampton to New York City by ship. We sailed on the S.S. United States during its last year of service just as the Queen Mary almost four years earlier had been nearing its last year of service when we sailed on it. Maybe my fighting brothers shut down their shipping lines.

Three days in, Category 5 Hurricane Camille stole the fun of the voyage. At first, the high waves were exciting. We played in the strong winds and leaped off stairs, timing our jumps with the wave crests to give us more flight time. We knew a storm was brewing but didn't realize how big it was. The crew closed down the pool, the movie theater, and all food service so everyone could go to their room.

Mother wrote:

Sunday morning at 3 a.m., the night porter banged on our door saying we were in for "a little rough weather" and asked us to close the porthole. I got up to go to the bathroom, the last time I would stand upright until four that afternoon. The rest of the time, I lay flat on the bed or crawled to the lavatory to vomit up nothing. Sick! Never have I been so sick. The waves lifted this big ship up and slammed it down like a small motor boat. As it rose, it lifted me out of bed and left me in the air, then pressed me down into the thin mattress as if a heavy weight were pressing on me. I could last about three of these then I'd crawl for the bathroom. I devised a bed out of chairs so I could stretch out and still keep my head in the lavatory.

Everybody on the ship was sick. All the children were in the cabin next to ours, except for Chipper. John said he himself was doing fine but when Chipper vomited, he didn't even raise his head, just threw him a towel. About 4 p.m., we were out of the storm. Supper that night was our first meal of the day.

The sink in our room and the plumbing in the hall bathroom clogged with vomit. When the storm passed, we walked out of our rooms to a real stinky mess. The vomit-soaked carpet in the theater didn't keep us away. After watching a movie about America, we were full of questions. Daddy pulled out American coins and taught us how many shillings were in each coin and how many coins it would take to buy a milkshake.

The final paragraph of Mother's letter was an apt conclusion to our '60s life in Africa:

August 22, 1969, over a month after our departure from Mbeya, we sailed past the Statue of Liberty into New York City Harbor. I remember so well how it felt to leave America and all I knew as we sailed past the Statue of Liberty four years ago. What a feeling to come home. The port at New York City was dirty and the air smoggy. Woodstock ended four days earlier and I believe all the hippies went to New York City. Chipper held his nose and whined, "Oh, Mother, I didn't know America was going to be this bad!"

42 More Trouble Than a Setting Hen *Shida Zaidi*
Uganda 2004

With relief, we drop into the semi-cover of the shallow dry riverbed and settle into an easier pace as we push toward Sakatan. Although our feet slip in the loose sand, we are appreciative of the cover of the riverbed. The gunfire is distant and the pressure is off. I choose not to think about how Byron is doing. I do what I must do.

With a six-mile journey ahead, we settle into a steady rhythm, making our way along the same riverbed Linda and I ran hours ago, or was it days ago? A call behind us interrupts my thoughts. Tubo runs toward us, his tire-tread shoes gripping surprisingly well in the deep sand. The message from Byron is for us to wait at Sakatan where he will either meet us or send a messenger with further instruction.

He has hashed out the logistics and options with the decision makers — the mission, AIM, the US Embassy, and Ugandan authorities — who are covering all the bases. The MU-2 turboprop is en route from Nairobi but, when we came under fire, they decided to get the Cessna Caravan headed straight to Kaabong too since its base at Lokichogio is near the Kenya-Uganda border with a shorter distance to cover.

With the discovery that there is a plane but no pilot at Lokichogio, hope now rests on the MU-2 heading our way. With the escalation of the conflict, the efforts intensify to get authorization for the MU-2 to bypass Entebbe, the entry point to Uganda, and fly direct to Kaabong.

The authorities insist that under no circumstances may the plane bypass Entebbe. Unable to get authorization, they decide to do what is necessary to save lives, which means crossing an international border and landing a plane in the middle of a military operation. Jonathan, along with the pilot and all those who are collaborating, has his hands full and a lot resting in them. This would be like quickly trying to get authorization for an American plane to cross the international border to land in a tiny town in Mexico in the middle of a military operation. Byron remains at home for radio contact to coordinate the logistics.

"Tell Byron if he comes, to please bring my bag with the toothbrush," Linda requests, as Tubo turns to leave. She really wants to be sure he brings an essential item — her eyelash curler she still has from her high school years in Nairobi — but doesn't want to try to explain an eyelash curler to

Tubo.

We will hide out in the Sakatan rocks, where we played hours ago, until we hear if they are able to coordinate an air evacuation. Waiting at the airstrip would put us in the noon equatorial sun, with the risks of no man's land and the possibility of drawing fire upon us or the plane.

Unaware of all the logistics and those making decisions on our behalf, my thoughts whirl as I put one foot in front of the other. With Sakatan to our right, I regret that we must leave the cover of the riverbed, although there is comfort in the distant sounds of artillery. Sera leads us up the gentle slope toward the refuge of the rocks. "Be strong, baby gal," Daddy's words find their way through the praise songs playing in my head. Praise songs… in the midst of battle...

BOOM! My thoughts, my heart, and time itself almost stop.

The ground shakes as I wheel around to see dust clouds over the town of Kaabong. The battle has moved to the west and the village of Kaabong is under fire or, as the locals say, it is being "bombed." One of the "bombs" appears to have made a direct hit on the hospital. My mind briefly lingers on the fact that the hospital is where Linda and I would have been if Stanley hadn't insisted on us sticking together. The decision to do surgery, at best, would have separated us from family during this critical time. At worst… OK, I must focus on the next step in front of me.

With a sigh of relief, we drop our packs at the foot of a large tree at the base of Sakatan. Positioned higher and behind a rock outcropping from the battle, we have time to rehydrate, rest, and wait for Byron or his messenger. I feel like I weigh 250 pounds as I drop to the dirt and prop my feet on Linda's dusty, blue backpack.

Karamojong women and children scramble out of the rocks and surround us. Sera's wives and children and many of Linda's friends are excited to see her. A time of reunion. I vaguely remember women and children moving toward the rocks when we returned to the house from our morning run, but I didn't understand the significance of that at the time.

Linda boots up her laptop and shows video of these people dancing to the stories and songs of Noah. They had heard themselves on the hand-cranked tape recorder, but this is a first for them to see pictures and video of themselves. Enthralled, they surround Linda while they sing, clap, and laugh. I wonder where she is getting all that energy and enthusiasm. As I scan around my group, drained of energy and propped against the packs, I notice Seve curled up in a fetal position at the base of the tree.

"Seve, are you OK?"

"Yeah, Nuna, my stomach just hurts."

No tears, just a stomachache. It doesn't require much of a stretch to imagine her stomachache might be stress related. The kids never complain; I wonder where they get that? I am aware our bodies desperately need water. I don't know what lies ahead but I know rehydration is a priority. Not wanting to drink in front of the villagers, I use Linda's diversion to pull the kids and Noel aside.

Ben is worried about his Dad. He climbs from his perch, midway up the tree, to a lower limb where he reaches to pull Linda's hair to get her attention. "Mom, I'm going to go back to the edge of the hill to see if I can see Dad."

Linda grunts approval and turns her focus back to her friends. Although Linda is a nurse, she is like their doctor: delivering babies, performing surgery, treating illness, and suturing wounds. Their bonds are as tight today as Linda has ever made with this tribe. She finds the Karamojong the most difficult to connect with out of all the people they have worked with in Kenya, Uganda, and Tanzania.

Jordan and I run to catch up with Ben. We are both concerned he might go beyond the rock, putting him in the line of fire. We walk to the edge of it where we can look down upon Kaabong and see the mission compound. I pass my binoculars to Ben and Jordan so they can watch for their father. Finally, we see Byron run from the compound with Tubo and two other men. All four carry packs, but Byron is easily spotted with his red shirt and Aussie hat.

Relieved and excited, Ben runs back up the hill. "Mom, Mom! Dad is on his way. I saw him. He's coming!"

As Jordan and I watch the foursome's progress, two warriors, rifles slung over their shoulders, walk up beside us and demand my binoculars. As they are looking through them, we see Byron "bombed" then hear the blast as a blanket of sand obscures our view of the foursome. I exclaim a word, appropriate for the occasion, but not found in the Bible.

"Oh no. Where's Dad?" Jordan cries.

"Nuna said a real bad word," Ben giggles, having arrived back at just the wrong moment.

"What about Dad, Ben? There's no sign of him." Jordan grabs my hand.

Fear and dread grip me as we wait and search. I grab the binoculars from the warrior. Seconds seem like minutes, maybe hours, as I scan for movement. The dust finally settles and still I see nothing. Anxious minutes we watch.

"There he is!" Jordan whimpers in relief, close to tears. "See his red shirt climbing out of the riverbed? He's running this way."

The warriors ask for my binoculars again. Standing beside them, it dawns on me — these are our friends but they are the enemy of those in the tanks. This is not a good place to be. As I spin to head for the rocks I shout,

"This is not my battle. Go fight your own battle." I'm glad they don't dispute this because they have firepower.

"Babe, I'm getting confused here," Stanley mutters, joining us as we make our way back to the tree. "When the kids talk about the enemy, they're talking about the army. Who is the enemy here?"

"The kids' connection with the locals makes the lines blurry. Their friends are the villagers; the warriors are their friends. To these kids, the Ugandan army is the 'enemy.'"

"When Mom told Dad it was OK if he decided to stay with his people, I thought she was crazy," Jordan explains. "Then I agreed with her and actually thought about asking if I could stay too. I'm with Dad, I feel we're deserting our people in time of need."

Family traits run deep.

The mass of people surrounding Linda has thickened. "Everything cool?" she asks. Words cannot escape the lump in my throat.

I silently mouth, "No," and gesture a sideways swipe of my bladed hand; a signal from our past meaning "don't go down that path any further." She continues to look at me for an explanation but I still cannot form my words. Finally, I hoarsely whisper, "Linda, you almost lost Byron." Without a word, she turns, shuts down her computer, and gathers her things as she moves into default mode. Doing what you have to do.

The high-pitched "whizzzz" of rounds overhead sends Ben quickly down from his perch in the tree and the villagers running to the rocks. Ben crawls into his mother's lap and begins to cry for his Dad. The villagers look at him curiously, but their faces change when Linda speaks to them.

"I told them he was worried about his father. They were also worried about their men folk. I think this is the first time they see I am like them."

When Locilo sees Byron coming closer, he lifts Ben up to see his father's hat. Seeing his dad appeases Ben.

Byron arrives, breathing heavily as he gives us an update. The MU-2 isn't going to stop at Entebbe; it's coming straight to Kaabong. At 12:15 p.m., he shut down the radio and started toward the airstrip, a six-mile trek away; a lot of ground to cover before the 1:50 p.m. arrival. The plane will only land if the pilot sees Byron with his hands raised on the airstrip. All communication was over when Byron and his three friends left the house to meet us at Sakatan and continue to the strip. We are busy, but to those that wait and care, this will be a long communication blackout period. We know people all over the world will hold their breath, wait, and pray.

"We have to move fast," Byron tells us. "We still have over four miles to go."

The adults exchange a look of admiration as Seve puts her head down and wordlessly heads on toward the strip, followed by her sisters.

"Let me go first, kids," Byron has to insist as he and Tubo take off, covering the land as fast as they can while Sera and Losilo hurry along with Linda, Stanley, the kids, Noel, and me.

We push through the brush as hard as we physically can. The intense sun shifts to a steamy rain. Thick steam curls around our feet as we fight for footing in the slick red clay. The intensity and heat of the sun seem only to increase with the rain. Stanley has to stop often. "Babe, you go on with the kids, I have to rest this hip," he tells me.

"Are you kidding? Leave you behind?" The dilemma tortures me. Do I push forward to be sure the kids make it or do I stay back with my husband, my love? I would stand by him even if it meant we do not make it out. This event would certainly fall under the "worse" in the "for better or worse" vows I made a decade ago. I feel the weight of the world on my shoulders as if my decision will have a lasting impact.

With no words exchanged, Linda senses my dilemma. With a squeeze to my shoulder that speaks volumes, she wordlessly steps around and moves ahead of me to keep the kids moving while I stay with Stanley.

Sera respectfully nods his head as he hands Stanley his *fimbo*. These people have a lot of respect for the *mzee*, the old man. The meaning of this gesture, this gift, does not translate across cultures. It is a gesture of deep respect. A man doesn't part with his stick easily; it is a part of him, one of very few possessions. Stanley walks hard then rests, leaning on the *fimbo* until the pain and numbness subside so he can continue. As much as I want him to, it is physically impossible for him to gut it up and work through the pain.

Without a path, we follow Sera's lead across country. The precariousness of our position fades into the focus on footing as we push hard, slipping and sliding through the wet clay. In front of us, I see Linda struggling along with Ben. The physical exertion and the stress seem to have come down on him. He cries for Buddy, the neighbor's dog left behind. In the brush ahead of Linda, I get glimpses of the three girls making good progress with Noel bounding by their side.

At 1:50 p.m., we hear the plane approach, circle, and crisscross low overhead. Our focus is head down and thrust onward. We never wave or signal to the plane. We are just putting one slippery step in front of the other. I sense that time is critical but we are pushing as hard as physically possible. We assume the pilot has seen us.

"Oh, no," I hear Stanley mutter. "They're heading toward the house. Maybe they can't see us."

We push onward.

Byron and Tubo reach the airstrip, drop their packs, and run along the airstrip to be sure it is clear of animals, logs, and rocks. At last, the pilot seems to spot our weary bodies snaking through the rugged bush close to the edge of the strip. Byron raises his hands overhead for the OK signal.

I hear the plane low overhead as it circles in for a landing. With relief, we finally break through the brush and see the plane shimmering in the waves of heat at the far end of the airstrip. We are exhausted. Time has stopped. It seems that no amount of physical effort brings us closer to the plane. There it sits, shimmering in a lake of heat — a mirage. We walk and walk. The plane still shimmers in the distance.

43 Touch and Go *Wasi Wasi*
Uganda 2004

The wariness of knowing it isn't over taints the relief of finally reaching the plane. I haven't forgotten that it may draw unwanted attention. Pilot Jim and co-pilot, Chris, meet us on the far end of the runway, their concern professionally but not completely hidden from their faces. They quickly approximate the weight of the people and bags. With concerns for the plane's ability to take off safely on this runway, Jim decides it's worth the time to make a reduced load takeoff to ensure the plane can safely haul out the weight of the entire group.

They leave behind four jerry cans of jet fuel and ask for two volunteers for a trial takeoff. Stanley and I, the obvious choice, climb aboard, crouching as we make our way to our seats in the rear.

"When we return for you to board, it may be a little noisy, windy, and confusing," Jim tells the Wittes. "Just follow Chris, walk behind the engines, and he will help you get on board."

As we pull away, I see my family and their friends huddled together under the bushes beside the runway. A flood of emotions conflict me: concern, gratitude, fatigue and relief. There is another emotion, but I cannot find the words. My heart is ripping out of my chest.

Separated for the first time, we have worked through this crisis together until now. I'm acutely aware that any or all of us could become targets and that I'm on a trial takeoff. As we taxi down the bumpy red dirt airstrip, I hold my breath and take another look, perhaps my last glimpse, at my family tucked in the bushes. I feel comfort as Stanley tightly holds my hand as we bounce along the rugged strip and lift into the air. We circle at a seemingly impossible angle to land again.

As we taxi back to my family, I see the three girls leave the tight knot of the group and dart toward the Karamojong boys huddled in the nearby brush. Bracing on each other for balance, they pull off their running shoes and give them to the boys, then turn and walk barefooted toward our plane. The girls are grateful to them for accompanying us to the airstrip and for helping to carry our bags. It is more than that. The kids have bonded with their friends and they fear for their lives. Shoes are all they have to give.

The roar is deafening as Linda climbs on board with Noel in one arm and her cage in the other. The four kids quickly follow, single file, with

Byron taking the seat closest to the pilots. Our belts buckled, Chris barely gets the door closed as we taxi along the runway. We bounce and bump. For how long? It seems impossibly long. Mud splatters the windows and we still bounce along the ground. I take a deep breath and hold it, an unconscious attempt to make us lighter.

The engines roar, the scraggly brush flies by, but we still bounce along on the rough strip. No one speaks. I can see the brush at the end of the runway approaching rapidly. The thought briefly crosses my mind — this may be the end.

I look at Stanley, my love, and down through the narrow aisle at each of my precious family members. I silently plead a prayer for a miracle. The plane briefly lifts then bounces back to the ground, lifts again, and then bounces again.

I don't know if the pilot makes the plane bounce to get some lift to fly or if the bounces are failed attempts to get into the air. All I know is that the agonizing seconds seem to drag into many minutes. Are we going to make it or is this the end? It seems I have plenty of time to think about it. If this is the end, it has been a good ride, a great life. I feel a twinge of regret if this is the end for the young lives in the plane. They have so much to give the world.

We finally clear dirt, barely passing over the top of the brush and flying low for a long time before we begin to climb. Clapping finally breaks the silence.

"Well, that was ugly," Jim says over the intercom. "I'm going to have to clean this plane when I get back."

"Yes, look at the mud on the windows," Linda points out.

I suspect Jim is referring to cleaning upholstery in the pilot's seat, not the exterior of the plane.

"Ohhh… man… the blast blew my hat and sunglasses into the bush." Linda ruffles her windswept hair, a little more relaxed now we're in the air. "Still, on the positive side, there is some Karamojong wearing them now." I admire her ability to be thinking of others even after what we have just gone through. "When the blast blew the door open on Noel's cage, she yelped and ran to the bushes," she continues. "Byron knelt and called her name. She sheepishly walked sideways to his waiting arms. It would have been terrible to lose her. I'm so glad Jim recognized the importance of the dog as he prioritized our cargo. She's definitely an essential item for the kids. Well, for me too."

The plan is to land at Entebbe. Missionaries will meet us at the airport with the Wittes' passports so they can continue their flight to Kenya. Stanley and I will catch a ride to Chipper's house in Kampala. I'm just happy to be on our way out of Kaabong, but sad to think we will be parting company early with Linda and her family.

The co-pilot passes out cold water and cookies. How could he have known how badly we need that? We didn't even know we did. There have been a lot of hours, exertion, and stress since our cup of tea this morning. It seems like days ago.

As I gulp down my cookies, I peer out of the window, trying to get a glimpse of the house we left behind, the hospital, and the battleground. Seeing the circular village compounds below, my mind skips back four days when we flew over these same villages. I was full of anticipation for an adventure, time with family, and Linda's promised relaxing vacation with the greatest stress being the wait for the hen to leave her clutch of eggs.

I can't see people below but the faces of the people we got to know flash through my mind like a stack of colorful pictures. Life isn't fair; they are still there with their families, just trying to survive. I think of Tubo, Sera, Losilo, and the boys separated from their families during the crisis to help get our family out. My heart is full of gratitude.

The noise of the plane is loud and conversation subdued. Numbness, exhaustion, and a feeling of disbelief at what we just walked through begin to seep into the overall feeling of relief. Seve sits with her knees pulled up under her chin. Tears well over from her big blue eyes and streak down her dusty red cheeks.

"Seve Lil Lynn, can you talk to me about it?"

"Nuna, I'm just so sad. We get to leave but my friends can't. I'm muddy, hungry, and tired but I get lifted out of trouble. My friends are muddy, hungry, and tired but they may have had their homes burned too. It just isn't fair."

"Seve, I love that you care. This is a dilemma we have all faced… how can we help more? All you can do is love and care and help where you can."

Linda, the most animated of our gang and always positive, is already planning the next step of where they will go and when she will resume homeschool. She is shocked to hear the schoolbooks didn't make the essential cut to the backpacks. All of the schoolbooks lay in the non-essential red duffel in the center of the living room floor. Detecting a little chide in Linda's voice, I come to the girls' defense, admitting I was in on the decision. We have no idea when, or if, we will see the books.

Jim calls over his shoulder to Byron as he hands him a pair of earphones. I am curious about their long conversation, drowned out by the engine noise.

As the noise subsides, Jim tells him quietly, "I'm not sure what we will be facing here in Entebbe because of my landing in Kaabong. I will need to move on to meet with the authorities pretty quickly."

Officials wait on the ramp as we taxi into the airport and disembark. They kindly welcome us and patiently wait as we say our thanks and goodbyes under the shade of the wings. Words cannot express my gratefulness.

"Incredible guys," Byron tells us as we leave them.

"They sure are!"

"They risked their lives and careers to pull us out of harm's way. They're still grieving the loss of their own colleagues, AIM missionaries in northern Uganda, who were shot and slaughtered five months ago."

"You had a long talk with Jim on the plane, Byron," I say to him. "I'm dying to know what that was all about."

"He said his supervisor waited until he was near Kaabong to tell him the authorities had said that, under no circumstances, could he land there. He waited to tell Jim so he could make his own decision. Jim made the decision to land anyway and pick up our family."

I am gratified and stunned.

"He told me, when the decision was in front of him, he knew he would do whatever it took to keep that from happening on his watch."

Pilot Jim and co-pilot Chris are a rare breed of men that have left the lucrative world of American corporate aviation to support missionaries in a dangerous part of the world. They risk their lives to provide aviation support to them in tumultuous weather and treacherous terrain in war-torn areas, without the technology of the developed world. Driven by the passion to spread hope to Africa, the thought "the need outweighs the risk" has probably been a deciding factor in many of Jim's decisions as he flies from Kenya into Uganda and southern Sudan supporting missionary and relief efforts.

The plane is part of the Samaritan Purse ministry supported by Franklin Graham. I have put together gift shoeboxes for Samaritan Purse to distribute to children in third world countries for many years. How ironic that my family and I are now a recipient of their generosity and ministry. Next Christmas, my Samaritan Purse shoebox will have a new meaning.

The pilots slip away to the airport offices to deal with the aftermath of their decision to bypass the international border to land in the middle of a military operation, and begin the logistics of forming a flight plan for their next leg of the journey, to fly a missionary with a medical emergency from Entebbe to Nairobi.

"We're gonna go to Chipper's house for now," Byron updates us.

"Uncle Jonathan and Uncle Frank are here," Jordan cries excitedly, spotting them at the airport where they thoughtfully wait with ice-cold water and hugs. "I wish I could give some to our people we left behind in

Kaabong."

"With the medical emergency taking precedence for the plane, we have a Land Rover for you and your family to take to Nairobi," Frank explains to Byron. "Tim is working on lining up some crisis debriefing and would like the Wittes all to be in Nairobi by Sunday."

With alarm in her voice, Linda asks, "Why? Is there a crisis? What happened? Just tell me."

She is concerned something may have happened to the missionaries Byron supervises in southern Sudan. It never crosses her mind that she and her family are the crisis. Linda has moved through the day's calamities, one step in front of the other, with the same do-what-you-have-to-do, calm, practical, non-emotional way modeled by our parents. That and maybe a little spice of denial are at play.

"Just call Tim," is Frank's short response to Linda's torrent of questions as he shows the way to the Land Rover for our trip to Kampala.

"What an amazing love Jim has for fellow missionaries," Byron shakes his head as we clamber in. "When he said it was getting ugly and he was going to have to clean the plane, he was trying to joke and lift our spirits," he chuckles. "He meant the mud splashed on the outside. He knew how apprehensive we all were."

"The takeoff was pretty scary, Dad!" Jordan exclaims.

"He said after the test with Aunt Cinda and Uncle Stanley he knew we'd be fine, as long as the engines kept up and no animals or people ran onto the runway."

"Why did it bounce?" Ben is returning to his usual, curious self.

"The runway's full of holes and puddles," Byron tells him. "He had to keep pulling the nose up so they didn't slow the plane. If too much water splashes, it can shut down the engines. If the nose is up too long, then the plane is too slow and he'd run out of airstrip."

"It was like being catapulted," Ben grins, not grasping the implications of any error of pilot judgment.

Jim's perspective brings a greater understanding of the event, but it also brings me face to face with the stark reality — Linda was right. Ouch!

44 The Dust Settles *Vumbi Kutulia*
Uganda 2004

Driving through the gates of Chipper's home, I find refuge in an oasis surrounded by tropical greenery as I immerse in the love, comfort, and familiarity of family. It seems weeks since we spent that brief night between our jet arrival from America and our single-engine flight to Kaabong four days ago. Chipper and Rose's beautiful girls almost fall over each other as they tug open the heavy wooden Zanzibar front door and gaggle down the steps to jump into our arms.

Chipper and his wife, who is of the Baganda tribe, have girls with dark hair and dark brown eyes from their mother, sharp angular facial features from their father, and silky smooth skin like milk chocolate. Darker in color, these girls have the inner and outer beauty matching that of my Witte nieces. Maya, age nine, tall and graceful, is the big sister in every way. Seven-year-old Cinda Ann, named after me, is nicknamed "Cinda Two" or "Little Cinda." She is beautiful, spunky, and has a tendency to test boundaries.

When Maya visited me in America, I asked her if Little Cinda looked like me. Studying me, she said in her cute British accent, "Yes, she looks like you but her eyes are a little darker." They live in a wonderful world where one converses about skin color without mentally treading on landmines, just like talking about the color of eyes or hair. Four-year-old Roseanna is full of smiles, giggles, and warmth.

The day's tumultuous events leave me conflicted, yearning to connect with my loved ones, but also wanting to eat and disengage for a while. Cookies on the plane were the only calories since the cup of chai at dawn, which seems like two lifetimes ago. With wonderful smells of dinner coming from the kitchen, I slip out to Steve's small guesthouse in the back.

I am unable to connect, feeling disjointed and stumbling as I try to express my thoughts, but soon I begin to relax, and enjoy just being with my big brother. His physical presence is really all I need from him right now. He has been big brother and fierce defender through many journeys in my life.

Although the five of us — Steve, Jim, Linda, Chipper, and I — grew up together in East Africa, our lives have gone in different directions but our hearts stay connected. Jim and I made our homes in America. Jim plies his passion for fishing as a fly-fishing guide and an artisan, building fly-fishing store fixtures. I combine my profession as a registered nurse with the passion of teaching fitness and survival for a career in game warden training. Linda, Steve, and Chipper returned to their roots in Africa. Linda came back with Byron for missions, Steve and Chipper made Africa their home, marrying Ugandan women and raising daughters while riding the challenging journey of business endeavors in a third world country. Together they started businesses in auto mechanics, sign production, security, bookstores, and an ice cream store.

Steve named his daughter after Linda. Linda and I each having a niece with our name is a hint of the bond between us. I haven't met "Mini Linda," as she was nicknamed.

Returning to the main house to sniff out supper's progress, I find that Linda has finished talking on the phone to Mother. She knew we were flying out of Kaabong early but didn't know the extent of our duress. Chipper purposely held back the details as they unfolded, promising one of us would call her when we got to Kampala.

I am eager to call and connect with my friend, Georgia. Early this morning I wrote her an email telling of the impending conflict and the developing plans to evacuate but I couldn't send it while Byron was on the radio. Of course, the radio took precedence. It's hard to believe that was just this morning. It seems days ago.

Georgia awoke during the night, sensing I was in trouble. She prayed and emailed me the message I now read before I dial her number:

> Bud, this is one of those times I can't express my heart. The Holy Spirit will have to help me with the translation. I feel there is something wrong. Are you in trouble? I need you beside me on our rocking chairs in our old age. Do I need to get our friend Kathy to charter a plane to go get you? Bud, our hearts are knit together and half of mine is across the world. Larry thinks half my brain is too. I know God has you. I can just picture Him holding you in the palm of His hand, protecting you like a little sparrow. Guess I will just send this and get back to praying.

Georgia had no idea how much we needed prayer. With the time difference of nine hours, she would have written this email as we headed out of the house on foot this morning.

My heart leaps as I hear her familiar southern accent. As I sit on a rock under the banana tree, we begin to reconnect.

"Your Mother called and said you all got out and are safe," she exclaims after our warm greetings. "So… what happened?"

As I begin to talk through some of the day's events, I become aware that

Georgia doesn't understand the intensity of the conflict.

"Bud, did Mother tell you about the bullets or about running to the airstrip?"

Georgia is confused and so am I. I push the thought to the back of my mind that maybe Linda left out details to protect Mother from the realities of the truth. It is so good to feel safe as I update Georgia with today's journey.

In the excitement of connecting with her, I have forgotten my hunger. Seeing my family crowded around the dining table, I feel a twinge of guilt for coming late to supper. When Mother called mealtimes, getting to the table was a priority because no one could start eating until everyone had sat down, shirts on, and prayer was said. Well, shirts were on, I don't know about the prayer. This I do know, they sure hadn't waited.

"Were you protecting Mother from something?" I ask my twin between bites.

"What d'you mean?" Linda looks at me in puzzlement.

"After you talked to Mother, she called Georgia who says there was no mention of bullets, artillery, or a run to the air strip."

"What bullets?"

I stop in midbite and stare with disbelief. Linda looks confused and stumbles, "What d'you mean? I know we had to run to the airstrip. What bullets?"

We all watch and wait for Linda to laugh and admit she was kidding, but she doesn't.

Seve speaks first. "Mom, weren't you scared when you heard the bullets overhead when we sat under the tree at Sakatan?"

"Yeah, Mom, when all the people ran to the rocks," Ben chimes in.

"I'm just confused," Linda mumbles. "I'm not sure if I remember bullets or not. Maybe I heard them and it wasn't significant to me. I had so many decisions to make… "

*****

After two nights at Chipper's, the Wittes load up for an early morning departure for the two-day drive to Nairobi to be in place for critical incident debriefing on Monday. I'm sad to see Linda leave. She and the kids don't want to go for counseling and debriefing but Byron convinces them.

Linda learns a lot about our evacuation day from stories her children tell the psychiatrist. She discovers the scariest time for Seve was when we were waiting under the tree and she heard the shots overhead. Linda had still been oblivious during this time.

The kids' responses to the psychiatrist's questions fascinate their mom:

"What do you grieve? What was the hardest to leave behind? Where do you see God in this?"

During the session, Ben hooks Linda's shoes together with a carabiner and drags them around the floor like a car and trailer, but he is listening. "Dad, is it OK if I tell him about what I left?" he whispers.

"Yes, you can trust him."

"But it's not registered."

Ben tells the psychiatrist that the hardest thing to leave behind was the BB gun his granddaddy brought for him. Ben knew that bringing the BB gun into Uganda wasn't legal and he wasn't to talk about it.

The psychiatrist focuses on Jordan since she saw her father come under fire. He asks her how she is going to handle that image when it comes back to her in the night. She says she will pray and recite scripture she had been learning.

I think God had been preparing Jordan for this time. Just the week before, she had overheard Linda tell about a dream that was obvious spiritual warfare. It was a scary dream. That night she went to her parents' room to tell them she couldn't sleep because of Linda's dream. Byron prayed with her and shared some scripture she could memorize.

Jessica says she is just going to add this to her childhood memories. She thought it was exciting.

The psychiatrist asks each of the kids to write about the experience. Jessica's poem reflects her attitude toward the debriefing:

Counseling

I don't like going to counseling
It makes me feel like yelling.
It's supposed to help
But it makes me feel like
Grinding him into kelp.
I'm supposed to cry,
But I think I'm gonna die.
He wants to hear my feelings,
But I just care about my earrings.
He wants to hear about my strife
But he's ruining my life!
He thinks I have grief,
But this is ridiculous beyond belief!

When the psychiatrist asks Seve a question, she just smiles. Linda has read Seve's journal of the evacuation and is puzzled because she kept referring to the enemy with tanks:

> A while later we looked outside and saw tanks lined up on the hill and our warriors running down the hill toward our house. Well, now it's tanks against AK-47 rifles. Our warriors are better fighters but the enemy has better equipment.

Seve always said "enemy," not military. Linda started correcting it, and then it hit her. That is her perception. To her, there were our people — "our warriors" — and "the enemy" — the Ugandan army. She sees the same thing in Jordan and Ben's journals.

"You know, Roger, I'm so proud of how my kids did, how my family worked through this together," Byron sums up as the meeting ends. "We've raised the kids in the way we think best, but never knew how they would do when a crisis comes."

"In all of this, I never thought a tank could fire on us," Linda admits to Byron afterwards. "It never occurred to me that I could lose a kid. I didn't even pray, I was so busy packing."

"Maybe it was just as well."

"I think some of it was that Cinda was there. Growing up, it was her job to handle problems. I knew I could turn the kids over to her and she would take care of them. I knew you, Stanley, and Cinda had things covered so I could focus on packing. We were a calm, cool team."

"Well, someone had to do the packing," Byron laughs with her.

"There are a few things that really puzzle me. I was so confused over the talk of bullets — I wasn't sure I heard any. But I get it now. Cinda told me tunnel vision and blocked sounds are classic symptoms of critical incident stress. Did you experience any of that?"

"No, I don't think so. I do remember time really slowing down. I remember seeing the sand blast close to me and it seemed an eternity before I heard the blast. I remember thinking if I can hear the boom, I'm still alive."

"Cinda also said I would have trouble sleeping for a couple of nights as I re-lived our evacuation. She was right! Each time I re-lived it in my dreams... no, wait... I was awake... anyway... the picture became clearer with the sights, sounds, and amazing details."

"And the counseling?"

"I think it was really good for the kids. It made them all grieve what was lost but also look at the positive. I loved the way the counselor helped the kids, well, and me too, take a look at where we saw God in this. What I really got out of it was the kids' perspective. Fascinating!"

"I'm so proud of my family. We all just did what we had to do."

"You know, that first night we got to Chipper's, I woke in the middle of the night with the realization — *we* were the crisis. Everything came back to me in living sound and color. It wasn't scary; just like watching a movie in slow motion. I could see, hear, and feel the details — I was there and reliving it. I heard the pop of rifle fire interspersed with the explosions of artillery. I didn't just hear the artillery; I felt it in my chest. I didn't sleep at all after that."

"Well, you should have woken me, told me," Byron hugs her. "And now, how do you feel?"

"The second night I awoke again. This time it struck me the mighty act God had done. The awareness of His protection and preparation was overwhelming. I prayed the rest of the night, my first time to pray since the incident began. As I re-lived the day, I began to see the expressions on my kids' faces and I heard the shots. I saw Cinda's white, tight-lipped expression when I asked her if you were OK. The expression I saw this time said everything she was unable to put into words."

The Witte family recover well, they are resilient, family ties are tight, and their faith is strong. Linda suggests the crisis may have traumatized the rest of the missionary family they work with more than her own because they felt helpless to help. Working inside the crisis, we just moved on, one step at a time. The Wittes are now in a time of transition, staying at a mission guesthouse in Nairobi as they search for a place to live.

45 Heartprints and Puzzle Pieces *Alama za Afrika Moyoni*
Uganda 2004

Stanley and I have an unexplainable longing to return home. Since changing tickets is an expensive option, we decide to plug into Chipper's family life in Uganda for a few days longer. I go for long runs through the countryside. As my eyes take in the sights of villages, fishing boats, cows, and people, my mind rolls back through events. My heart overflows with gratefulness for being alive and for the survival of my family. I begin to put the puzzle pieces together of how God orchestrated so many events for our survival.

The Witte family share two rooms at the guest house, before moving to Limuru in the highlands, about an hour away, where Stanley and I now join them. This home seems right; I can imagine them staying here for a long time. I remember spending time with missionary friends in this large colonial two-story house when we attended mission meeting when I was my nieces' age.

With a heavy annual rainfall and an altitude of 7,000 feet, the spacious yard is a lush, tropical paradise. I enjoy watching Linda's kids delight in the things I loved to do as a kid years ago in the same area. They catch chameleons in the hedges and watch Colobus monkeys shriek in the towering trees above. Linda and I savor long runs, revisit our childhood memories, relive the evacuation, visit old girlhood friends, and just relax and enjoy family. All is well.

In their new home, the kids are at play in each of their individual rooms. Each room is already in the process of transformation into the character of its new resident. They have hung curtains, made beds from plywood, and displayed their few essential treasures in their rooms. The kids are busy making their space their own.

The day before Stanley and I begin our trip home to Texas, Linda and I settle under the shade of the cashew tree. We had had only three days of our original one-week plan to sip chai, watch for the hen to leave her nest, and soak up family. A plan that started a rollercoaster ride we never saw coming, which would yank Linda's family to two more houses and a move to another country. It is time to relax, reconnect and, of course, have a cup of tea.

The pieces that prepared us for this time began decades ago with parents that left a known and prosperous life behind to board the Queen Mary with their family of seven to launch to Africa. We formed strong family bonds that are unshakable, enduring through the ups, downs, and strains of life. Some of the puzzle pieces I carry from early life experiences to fit into my own life journey become like heartprints. They are a part of who I am, of the value of connecting with people on a real level, savoring diversity, loving adventure, keeping going through adversity, finding joy in every moment, and never backing down from a challenge. Mother and Daddy taught us resiliency and about faith through their handling of hurt, disappointment, and obstacles.

Mother was our anchor, her gentle, quiet spirit was nurturing and encouraging, but turned to fiery defense if values were crossed or family safety breached. She made our home safe, warm, fun, and peaceful. Daddy set the horizon for the family, keeping our life full of challenge, adventure, laughter, and play. He made each of us feel that we could tackle anything. Mother, on the other hand, taught us we didn't have to tackle everything and we didn't have to do everything just because we could.

They spoke life into us; loving, teaching, and guiding. We learned from their modeling, more than their words, to keep it together in crisis, never show emotions, hang onto your faith, keep thinking, and do what you have to do.

The intricate puzzle pieces of preparation, protection, and provision have interlocked into an amazing picture of God's work. Puzzle pieces that may have seemed insignificant or coincidental, as we just stepped one foot in front of the other, have now come together and we relish God's orchestration.

Hearing the kids' laughter as they chase each other up and down the stairs in their new home, I think how fitness and outdoor activities have always been a part of our lives and have been passed on to the next generation. Daddy always included us in his projects and problem solving as he worked on the Land Rover, fixed mechanical problems, or set up camp. He taught us to problem solve through difficulties and keep thinking if something failed.

Mother and Daddy modeled how to live out faith, not just talk about it. Their lives showed us how to invest in what matters, to make a difference in the world, but also how to find a balance for family, fun, adventure, and laughter. They prepared each of us for our life's path, wherever it may lead, instead of preparing the path for us.

"When I saw the girls pull off their shoes and give them to the boys before we boarded the plane, it hit me," Linda confides. "They get it. Their tears were not for their own safety but for their friends left behind in chaos and danger. As young as they are, they understand that life is not all about them and their things."

We relish the fact that growing up with brothers also gave us valuable skills we would need for life's journey. We learned to get along, negotiate, and maneuver among conflict without looking to others to fix it. In my career as a Texas game warden in a predominantly male environment, these lessons have served me well. My twenty years teaching cadets fitness, health, defensive tactics, critical thinking, and survival are vital pieces too.

"A few weeks ago, I had almost let the daunting price of air tickets keep me from accepting your invitation."

"You never told me that!" Linda chides. "What made you change your mind?"

"Your friend, Shannon, the doctor you connected with while doing medical missions in Kenya. She told me I needed to come, not just to see this amazing country but because you wanted me to see it. She said it was part of who you are." I hug my twin. "She was right." My voice cracks as we embrace, both now fully aware of the dangers we have just come through.

The phone conversation with Shannon was pivotal in motivating me to spend the money and go. It put us in a place to be in the way or to be a help when the crisis unfolded. I would like to think it was the latter.

As kids, Linda and I parallel played; we focused on different activities but we were there, immersed in each other's presence. In the crisis, it wasn't play, but we found comfort and confidence in our togetherness. Stanley's military experience and decades of law enforcement leadership brought a cool, clear problem solver to the crisis. He was able to see the big picture and communicate calmly and humbly. He worked well with Byron, also a cool problem solver, who knew the people, the country, and the resources.

"Remember running along the dry riverbed, pretending to be warthogs," Linda giggles and leans into my shoulder as she has done for decades. "The same riverbed we would take refuge in hours later from the sun and the bullets."

"How our day's plan changed from building sandcastles at the bridge to fleeing from tanks parked on that same bridge! I'm so grateful to Stanley. It was his insistence we stay together and not go traipsing off to do surgery that kept our family from being separated."

"With no way to communicate," Linda shudders, "and, at worst... well... lives could've been on the line." It is a sobering thought. "It's amazing to look back. D'you know, Jonathan Parsons was on a temporary assignment from America to fill in for one of our missionaries in Kampala?" she continues. "He's a young, tech savvy, and superb problem solver who pulled on resources to coordinate our evacuation."

Pilot Jim had to make a hard decision whether to risk life and his job to save this missionary family. I don't know the experiences in Jim's life journey that prepared him to make such a decision, but we believe we may be here to tell this story because he did. I do know that faith is a cornerstone in why he chose to leave corporate aviation to support missionaries and mission efforts in rural Kenya and war-torn areas of Uganda and Sudan.

Even the annoying detail of my training in Galveston, during packing time for the trip, proved to be a valuable puzzle piece in our story. Training in critical incident stress gave me some wisdom to help as we journeyed through the emotional aftermath.

I cherish the realization that never once did I walk alone. I see God's hand, and those of family and friends, all along the way.

"Have you noticed we're already saying 'adventure' instead of 'crisis?'" I grin in the midst of our chatting, hearing the kids moving in and out of earshot as they play. Linda is relaxed; everything about her says, "All is well."

"The president has been to Kaabong," she updates me. "The military sent a helicopter gunship in a show of power and they've extended the deadline for the return of weapons to December 1."

"Then what?"

"Military force."

"Oh, my, I feel for your people. So, Sis, how long will it take for this place to feel like home?"

"You know, Cinda, this is feeling like home. I hated leaving Kaabong. I'll miss the bush experience and riding flat-out across the country on my motorcycle though."

"You loved that place." I squeeze her arm.

"Yep, but we lived out of suitcases. In eleven months, we've never even opened our crates from America. They were in storage in Kampala. We had to move in and out so much that it just wasn't practical to take much there."

"And now you even have curtains in your windows." We chuckle.

"Byron says we're not going to move until the kids are out of school."

"Hmmm... I'll believe that when I see it!"

She nudges me with sisterly affection, knowing it's probably true. Byron has a restless spirit. It seems as soon as Linda gets curtains hung, rooms decorated, and the family settled into a routine, he is ready to move to a new place and a new endeavor. He is a visionary who loves to start new things, bringing along his family in tow.

"So, it's time to set up household with my things and pick fresh vegetables from my garden. We'll be starting homeschool in a few weeks. All is good. You know, I think I might just get a setting hen."

We laugh, bellyaching laughter that brings tears to our eyes as we remember Linda's email beckoning me to visit. "Just come, the only stress in Kaabong is waiting, with chai in hand, for our hen to leave her nest so we can seize her eggs."

A Tarzan yell interrupts our thoughts and laughter. Ben swings along a homemade zip line out of his second-story bedroom window to a tree limb. The rope stretches and his yell stops with a thud as he hits the ground. He jumps up in a victorious whoop. The kids are back to play, laughter, and life. The crisis is just another adventure in their life journey.

It is hard saying goodbye to my brothers and their family in Uganda. Our family, divided across two continents and a world apart, is firmly connected. Mother and Daddy instilled in us tight family bonds as they opened up the whole world to us by immersing us into the world of travel and diverse cultures. Along with that blessing came the curse of constant painful goodbyes.

Once again, we are laced with the unknown answer to the unspoken question "when will we meet again?"

Acknowledgements

I fumble to find the words to express my heartfelt gratitude to all who have been a part of my life story and those who have journeyed with me through the challenges of writing and producing this book. Thank you to all including:

My husband, Stanley, for his enduring patience and support, and for helping me chase my dreams and adventures, even though he thinks I'm "trying to get him killed."

John Byron Witte for his investment in the lives of the people God puts in his path, including his family.

My friends and family who have trusted me with our story, encouraged, read the countless versions, provided ideas, and heard me out.

My mentors, "Pup" Price, Ben Henson, Bob Chancellor, Lynn Walker, Marque Mooney, Lynn Goodwin, and Amber Starfire who reviewed, edited, guided, taught, and encouraged.

My missionary aunts and uncles who were there for me, with special thanks to Peggy Oliphint and Eucled Moore for my Swahili translation.

My "real" aunt, Mabelle Adams-Mayne, who, for twenty years, collected, retyped, and distributed my parents' letters so friends and family could be a part of our lives. They give the book my parents' voice and serve to fill in gaps in my girlhood memories.

Aaron Campbell for bringing life to a treasured old photo and **Graham D. Lock** for creating a cover design that pops.

My publisher, Victoria Twead of Ant Press, for taking a chance with a new author and my editor, **Jacky Donovan**, who walked the publishing marathon with a newbie author who thought the book was finished when the last word was typed. A woman who can somehow instill the confidence to entrust her with my family's story as she cuts, slashes, questions, and cracks her whip. Her professionalism, attention to detail, and experience as a writer are priceless.

As I reflect on my life and the five year journey to write *Heartprints of Africa*, I am amazed at the diversity of people — their personalities, life journeys, and stories spread over two continents. Yet there is a common thread that runs through them all. I see God's hand at work as He weaves our lives together. There are too many of you to list, but I thank all of you. I thank all of you and God for bringing each one of you into my life.

Message from the author

I sincerely thank you for reading this book and hope you enjoyed it. I would be extremely grateful if you could leave a review on Amazon.

I'd also love to hear your comments and am happy to answer any questions you may have, so do please get in touch with me by:

- Email: Cindabrooks28@gmail.com
- Facebook: www.facebook.com/cinda.adams.brooks
- LinkedIn: Cinda Brooks

To enjoy the photos that accompany this book, please join my mailing list. http://eepurl.com/bthcOD. You will also be amongst the first to be notified when my next book is published.

Further information can be found on my website www.HeartprintsOfAfrica.com

If you enjoy reading memoirs, I recommend you pop over to Facebook group We Love Memoirs to chat with me and other authors there. www.facebook.com/groups/welovememoirs

Ant Press books

If you enjoyed this book, you may also enjoy these titles:

Chickens, Mules and Two Old Fools by Victoria Twead
(Wall Street Journal Top 10 bestseller)

Two Old Fools ~ Olé! by Victoria Twead

Two Old Fools on a Camel by Victoria Twead
(New York Times bestseller x 3)

Two Old Fools in Spain Again by Victoria Twead

One Young Fool in Dorset by Victoria Twead

Simon Ships Out: How one brave, stray cat became a worldwide war hero by Jacky Donovan

Fat Dogs and French Estates ~ Part I by Beth Haslam

Fat Dogs and French Estates ~ Part II by Beth Haslam

How not to be a Soldier: My Antics in the British Army by Lorna McCann

Into Africa with 3 Kids, 13 Crates and a Husband by Ann Patras

Paw Prints in Oman: Dogs, Mogs and Me by Charlotte Smith
(New York Times bestseller)

Joan's Descent into Alzheimer's by Jill Stoking

The Girl Behind the Painted Smile: My battle with the bottle
by Catherine Lockwood

The Coconut Chronicles: Two Guys, One Caribbean Dream House by
Patrick Youngblood

Midwife: A Calling (Memoirs of an Urban Midwife Book 1) by Peggy
Vincent